Carol Klein

HORTOBIOGRAPHY

A gritty woman's tale of people,
places and plants

WITNESS BOOKS

UK | USA | Canada | Ireland | Australia
India | New Zealand | South Africa

Witness Books is part of the Penguin Random House group of companies
whose addresses can be found at global.penguinrandomhouse.com

Penguin Random House UK
One Embassy Gardens, 8 Viaduct Gardens, London SW11 7BW

penguin.co.uk
global.penguinrandomhouse.com

First published by Witness Books in 2024
This edition published by Witness Books in 2025
1

Typeset by Jouve (UK), Milton Keynes

Printed and bound in Great Britain by Clays Ltd, Elcograf S.p.A.

The authorised representative in the EEA is Penguin Random House Ireland,
Morrison Chambers, 32 Nassau Street, Dublin D02 YH68

A CIP catalogue record for this book is available from the British Library

ISBN 9781529144345

Penguin Random House is committed to a sustainable future
for our business, our readers and our planet. This book is made
from Forest Stewardship Council® certified paper.

To my family, past, present and future, with all my love.

Introduction

I hope you're going to enjoy this book. Despite the skill of my editor in honing down the excessive word count, it has ended up becoming longer than intended and yet there is still so much more to say. This is partly due to my having already lived a long life but more to do with the fact that I always want to tell everybody about everything.

One story reminds me of another and I often feel compelled to share them. There is almost certainly a word for this condition, and it is probably well recognised. Well, at least it means you are getting more for your money!

A wonderful woman who became a true friend, Erica Hunningher, edited my first book, *Plant Personalities*. She was brilliant and an excellent guide in what was for me uncharted territory. She was also very gracious; when I handed over a list of twenty-seven chapter titles when nine was the limit, she politely named me 'the mistress of digression'.

But the world is interesting; the people, plants and places within it are so fascinating, and frankly my life *has* digressed. I have never had a life plan – in fact until a few years ago I hadn't appreciated that people do. Fortunately for me – and for you, come to that – my life has zigzagged rather than run in a straight line. That is not to say there have not been recognisable themes throughout it: family and friends, work and education in one form or another, and of course plants. These strands have woven themselves together to form the fabric of my life. It has been a bit tatty round the edges sometimes, a little threadbare in places, but enduring and, most importantly for me and those I love, it continues to weave. I do love living.

Over the next far too many pages I hope you can share in my experiences, get to know some of the people I have been lucky enough to know. I hope I can take you to some of the places I have visited, from playing 'murps', or marbles, in the backstreets of Manchester to wading up to my waist in a vast South Korean lake full of prehistoric water lilies.

There are many wanderings back and forth in these pages (yet another headache for my editors), but its order is fairly chrono-logical. I presume that the great majority of all those who read this have bought or borrowed it because you are interested in plants and gardening and you know that I share this passion. Plants have been an intrinsic part of my life ever since I can remember – from when I was a toddler pouring soil onto the lino on the kitchen floor to create a garden, to planting nasturtium seeds with my mum, through to making our own garden at Glebe Cottage, running a nursery and exhibiting at flower shows, including recently making another garden at the RHS Hampton Court Flower Show in the capacity of 'RHS Iconic Horticultural Hero' (their designation).

In 2018 the Royal Horticultural Society honoured me by bestowing on me their highest accolade, the Victoria Medal of Honour. Established in 1897, it is awarded to British horti-culturists who are considered worthy of recognition for their work, and the rules state that at any given time only sixty-three people can hold the award, this number corresponding to the length of Queen Victoria's reign.

It is worth noting that in 1897 when it was first awarded en bloc, only two of the sixty-three recipients were women! As in all other areas apart from as wives and mothers, women have had to fight for acknowledgement of their talents and achievements in horticulture. It is ironic when there are more women who garden than men. When humankind stopped roaming, depending on hunting and gathering, and started to cultivate, it was women who sowed, planted, nurtured.

I have always loved plants and nature and was lucky enough to be encouraged in this interest by people close to me, my mum and one of my teachers in particular. Although I am a city girl, born and bred in Manchester, I have always felt close to nature, curious to learn more about it but much more than that – under its spell, full of wonder for it, almost over-awed by it yet always feeling part of it.

Although I have never thought of an account of my life as a social history archive, there are elements of this book that are just that, albeit on a very prosaic level. Some of you will identify with its timeline, having lived a parallel existence; you will remember white boots and black eyeliner, and recognise the time before tights, when nylons were held up with suspenders. Hopefully there will be plenty of young readers too, already developing an interest in gardening, for whom this book has insights into the latter half of the twentieth century, when your parents, and in some cases your grandparents, were young.

There is lots here about gardening and styles of gardening, about changes I have seen and lived through and occasionally influenced to a slight degree, and as such the book also includes extracts from some of the many articles I have published over the years. I have done my best to contribute to the debate surrounding topics such as organic gardening, gardening with nature, gardening for wildlife and climate change. My opinions on such topics are not academic but based on my experience and my practice.

I am immensely lucky that, due to my television work and my published writing, my voice has been heard, albeit quietly! (I mean that metaphorically; everyone knows my voice is not quiet. My mum once told me I had a penetrating voice, to which I rudely replied that it was hereditary.)

For the last forty years my life has been mainly concerned with my family and with plants. My family might feel the emphasis has been on plants; on the other hand, since I ran a nursery for thirty years, plants, or at least their sale, provided our livelihood. Would that it had been more lucrative, but it has given us a living, food and shelter and much happiness. People who can declare that they always enjoy their work, that they are doing something for which they have a true passion, are in the minority. I am lucky to be one of them. I love growing plants and gardening, I love exhibiting at shows and putting plants together, even if it is for just a week or so, and I adore presenting.

Because I feel passionately about what I do and get excited about it, I want to pass on that passion. When I'm on the box, it isn't a question of do as I do and accept it just because I said so. When I am passing on information about what I have learned through my experience and what works, and most importantly why and how it works, it is a privilege to feel I'm enabling people to share and to learn through their own experience, to do it themselves.

Gardening is a wonderful combination of art, science and craft. Different people's priorities vary. Where there are questions (I hope this isn't sounding like Margaret Thatcher), there is often more than one solution, providing we respect and follow nature's laws.

I have witnessed and been part of enormous changes in gardening. By gardening, I mean the gardening that the great majority of people practise. There is no doubt that money dictates tastes and trends in gardening. For some with money it is an expression of that wealth, and they may well not be involved with the nitty gritty of it, preferring to delegate to designers and gardeners. This relationship has barely changed over centuries, though there may be more people in that position than there were a few centuries ago and their money is more likely to have been made with IT and hedge funds than the slave trade.

For many others, gardening has taken on a different significance in the twenty-first century. People's gardens or allotments or even the containers on their balconies have become as much a part of their reality as their homes. For these people, gardening has become a delight rather than a chore. Where else in modern life do you get the opportunity to create, to express yourself and simultaneously to be at one with nature, nurturing plants and being part of the true cycle of life? I consider myself privileged to be part of this ever-expanding group and to have the opportunity to enlarge it further.

Chapter One

I owe my successful entry into the world primarily to my mum's effort and determination but also to two plants. I was born at midday on 24 June 1945, between VE Day and VJ Day. I was due on 31 May. Even in those days I was late. There were no drugs around to induce birth at that time, so when my mum was taken into St Mary's Maternity Hospital, Oxford Road, Manchester, she was given castor oil and Guinness to help her to give birth, produced respectively from *Ricinus communis* and barley. It helped. I was a big baby.

I've never grown barley myself, except accidentally from spilled bird food, but have often cultivated the castor-oil plant. For me producing plants from seed is never dull or mundane, but to grow something exotic that in a few short months will excel on a grand scale, grabbing the limelight wherever it is used, is something to get especially excited about. *Ricinus communis*, the castor-oil plant, is just such a showstopper and gratifyingly easy to start from seed. Seed is not expensive; sometimes it is even free. For years here at Glebe Cottage we successfully germinated some of its beautifully marked though deadly poisonous seeds, collected by me and my youngest daughter from a particularly dark-leaved plant on a piece of waste ground in Greece. (I collected the seed, she sat on a wall pretending she wasn't with me.)

If you think taking a Greek holiday is an expensive way to come by seeds, buy some. Go for cultivars or selections such as 'Carmencita' or 'New Zealand Purple'. Sow the big, striated beans from March onwards into modules or cell trays. They should germinate within a fortnight and make chunky little plants to pot on a month later. Their big, crimson hand-shaped leaves are an outstanding feature of the late summer border.

A packet of seed will give you enough plants to play around with. Used liberally their crimson palmate leaves instantly create a sultry atmosphere. We use them in hot schemes with oranges, reds and bronze but they are equally effective providing dark accents in my daughter Alice's garden with sanguisorbas, meadowsweets, geraniums and roses. Sometimes later in the season plants are embellished with strange red prickly flowers, but despite global warming, so far, the weather is never hot enough here to change those flowers into seed.

Despite the Guinness and castor oil, my mum's labour was not easy, but at midday on Midsummer's Day, I was born. I can't remember much about it, but I know I was there. The moon was full on the next day. It was in Sagittarius. Everyone likes to romanticise their birth.

Although I don't know for sure, as we never discussed it, I presume we went back to Holly Avenue, which was where my dad's family lived. My dad, though, wasn't there: even though the war was over, he hadn't yet been demobbed. On the one hand it must have been a very unsettled, uncertain time, but on the other there must have been a surge of relief and optimism. The war was over at last. Not so, of course, in many other parts of the world. Six weeks later, atomic bombs were dropped on Hiroshima and Nagasaki. Early in August, Japan surrendered and the war was ended officially on 2 September 1945.

When my father was demobbed not long after, one of the first things he did with me after he had returned home and seen me for the first time was to sit me on the tank of his Rudge Ulster motorbike and take a photograph. I'm not saying he'd wanted a boy, but apparently both he and my grandad called me Bill for the first year or so of my life. My eldest brother, who *was* called Bill, was eighteen months my junior, but I believe we shared his name for a few months after he was born. I like the name, although might have felt differently about it had he been christened William. He wasn't – the name was always Bill. My mum wasn't very well towards the end of that pregnancy, and gave birth to him in a nursing home. After he was born, the registrar came round to register new births and asked my mum what the baby's name would be.

'Bill,' she said.

'You mean William?' asked the registrar.

'No,' replied my mum, 'I mean Bill.'

'But you can't call him Bill, that's not a proper name.'

My mum was incensed. Looking round the room, her eyes alighted on a chair. 'I'll call him chair if I want to.' And so Bill it was.

During those last years of the war, after she and my dad had been married, my mum lived with his parents. She worked in the post office in Walkden and it was quite a bicycle ride to get back to her mum's house in Pendleton, some six miles away, near Salford. It was here, in my dad's home, that much was passed on. First, cookery skills – my mum became a first-rate cook – and then gardening.

My grandad had an allotment and both that and the small back garden behind 10 Holly Avenue must have been turned over to food production during the war. Though my mum had never before had the opportunity to garden, she was a natural. Hasn't everyone got green fingers though, given the opportunity? When we would have starved had we not produced our own food, it was imperative to grow it.

Since human beings first settled in one place, coming to rely less and less on hunting (never a reliable source of food) and foraging, we have been growing our own food. Women would always have been at the heart of this process. They were the ones who would have foraged and who knew about plants. If you are feeding and caring for children, going hunting for days would be out of the question; hungry children couldn't wait on the off chance that their dad might bring down a deer. Even today, 25 per cent of the world's population rely on subsistence farming, and 70 per cent of the world's food is produced on family farms.

When my dad came back from the war he bought a house in Tynesbank in Walkden and my mum, my dad and I moved in. He was moving between Germany and France at the end of the war and he and several mates, recognising that in France there was a lot of champagne but nothing to bottle it in, whereas there were lots of empty champagne bottles in Germany, helped the situation by selling the bottles where they were needed. I have no idea whether or not there were other schemes.

The house had a proper garden which I loved, with a bird bath and a bit of a lawn. Apparently though this wasn't enough for me. I would bring toy buckets full of soil into the kitchen and empty them on the kitchen lino, decorating the piles of soil with leaves or flowers. (I feel as though I should add a footnote here for those of you who don't know what lino is. It was the most popular flooring, especially for kitchens and bathrooms, made almost entirely from natural materials including linseed oil, pine resin and sawdust.) Before I learned to walk my mum would sometimes put me in my pram and push it outside, but I learned to climb out of it, and she would find me sitting on the grass or crawling around amongst the flowers.

My brother Bill was born in February 1947 so not long between us. It was soon afterwards the family left Walkden for Bispham.

I would have loved to have met my mum's father. He was called Isaac Parkes, and he died when my mum was only eight. Although his life was short, it was interesting. He was of Scottish heritage, and as I understand he was one of several brothers; his family came to Manchester seeking employment and prosperity. Many men in the north-west worked as coal miners (they had at least stopped sending women and children down the pits by then). But Isaac was determined not to be one of them and immediately after he had married my grandma Sarah Jane, they went to Liverpool, boarded a ship and left for Canada, where he hoped to make their fortune. En route, he was offered a job – in a copper mine in British Columbia. Ironic, except it was at least a copper mine, so no underground tunnels would be involved and, as far as we can work out, the work was on the management side.

He took the job, and during the next few years my grandmother gave birth to two daughters, my aunties Cath and Grace, and conceived another – my mum. It cannot have been an easy life, especially for Sarah Jane. There is a photograph of her sitting beside a local First Nation woman driving a covered wagon.

By this time, the Great War had started in Europe, and so the family moved back home to Lancashire so that Isaac could enlist. As far as we can make out, however, he did not have a strong constitution and he also had flat feet, so was not allowed to join up.

Instead he joined the Red Cross. We are not sure exactly where he was sent, but he was in France for the rest of the war, based at field hospitals, probably working as a stretcher bearer. There are a few postcards, and we have some photos of him at the front. On his return, he got a job with the YMCA, who had been working alongside the Red Cross and the army. His new job involved fairly frequent travel to Europe, especially Turkey. Meanwhile, the family moved to a new house in Folkestone with hollyhocks that reached the bedroom windows.

All members of the Malva family, including hollyhocks, thrive on chalky or alkaline soils. I can see them in the few photos I have of my mum, who looked a bit of a wild child at that age. Some of the photos are taken in the garden, and a few are in the surrounding countryside. Even though they are black and white you can imagine the colours. There is green and corn yellow, but above all you can see the red, red poppies, a latter-day Manet or Monet.

You can feel the sun's warmth and the pale, chalky soil reflecting it back. These poppies were the same poppies that Isaac must have seen in France, or would have seen had he returned there a few years later.

Poppies

What is so unique about poppies? Long before the poppies of the twentieth-century battlefields, they have fascinated humankind. John Ruskin wrote:

> We usually think of the poppy as a coarse flower; but it is the most transparent and delicate of all the blossoms of the field. The rest – nearly all of them – depend on the texture of their surfaces for colour. But the poppy is painted glass; it never glows so brightly as when the sun shines through it. Wherever it is seen – against the light or with the light – always, it is a flame and warms the wind like a blown ruby … Gather a green poppy bud, just when it shows the scarlet line at its side; break it open and unpack the poppy. The whole flower is there complete in size and colour – the stamens full-grown, but all packed so closely that the fine silk of the petals is crushed into millions of shapeless wrinkles. When the flower opens, it seems a deliverance from torture.

But today it is the scene of poppies surging up on the old battlefields that captures our imagination the most:

In Flanders fields the poppies grow
Between the crosses, row on row,
That mark our place: and in the sky
The larks, still bravely singing, fly
Scarce heard amid the guns below.

We are the Dead. Short days ago
We lived, felt dawn, saw sunset glow,
Loved and were loved, and now we lie
In Flanders fields.

John McCrae

* * *

There are some plants that, whilst we may grow and adore them in our gardens, have huge significance in our lives whether we know it or not. Such a plant is the poppy. It has come to signify life and death – the annual renaissance of the blood-red flowers of the corn poppy, *Papaver rhoeas*, in fields and road verges is one of the most exciting sights of early summer, yet those same flowers have come to signify remembrance, painting red the Flanders fields where so many fell, each time the land is ploughed. Though poppies must be amongst the most ephemeral of blooms, they imprint their image on our minds more strongly than almost any other flower. From Flanders fields turned blood red with the massed blooms of *Papaver rhoeas* to the equally red and even more demonstrative flowers of *Papaver orientale* 'Goliath Group' on their four-foot stems – poppies get noticed.

There are numerous species of poppy, but one of them, *Papaver somniferum*, is almost wholly responsible for the fact that none of us need suffer undue pain. The opium poppy is the source of morphine and many other painkillers as well as, on its downside, heroin.

It was *Papaver somniferum* that the British introduced to China from Afghanistan, and through this introduction came to control important aspects of Chinese power and trade and eventually succeeded in extracting the secrets of growing tea, thence introduced to their 'protectorate' India.

At the Chelsea Flower Show each year, there will be opium poppies galore on many of the stands in the floral marquee and, if they've opened in time, in many of the gardens too.

They are annuals and crop up in a host of different colours, some with single flowers, many with very striking double flowers. Some are pink and frilly, a sort of floral version of the blouses Barbara Cartland used to wear. Others are single; the simple, single white is the one from which opium is derived and is probably the most beautiful of all. You sometimes see huge fields full of it in Wiltshire, grown as a crop for chemical companies. In common with all poppies, it is a transient flower, the single varieties sometimes lasting for just one day. Equally, like all poppies it is spectacular, a true shooting star.

Sometimes I'm walking down one of the paths at Glebe Cottage only to come across the fallen petals from some voluptuous oriental poppy strewn on the ground. It's gone. When they are putting on their show, no flower could be more alluring – but it is fleeting. Perhaps in some ways, it is the fact that they are so ephemeral that makes them so attractive.

The wild ancestors of our cultivated oriental poppies are plants of the hot hillsides in Turkey and the Middle East. *Papaver bracteatum* is tall with huge red papery flowers. *Papaver orientale* 'Goliath Group', which used to be known as 'Beauty of Livermere', must be very closely related. They advertise their wares to pollinating insects by waving their great frilled petals.

It isn't nectar that attracts the insects, poppies don't produce it, but they make copious amounts of pollen – and it's purple. You'll often see a fat bumble bee coated in purple pollen leaving a flower where it has just gorged itself. The poppy mason bee obviously appreciates poppies, using the petals of *Papaver rhoeas* to line the tunnel to its nest.

In its natural habitat, having been pollinated, the plant will die down until the next year. In our beds and borders, oriental poppies can look messy after they've flowered. The great English gardener Gertrude Jekyll made several suggestions about how to camouflage their demise, including growing perennial sweet peas behind them so in summer they would flop forwards over the tatty poppies. At Glebe Cottage we shear them back to the ground and within weeks they've made fresh clumps of neat leaves. As a bonus there are occasionally a few extra flowers. When you're planting anything, it's a good idea to recognise where that plant's wild antecedents come from and give them the same sort of conditions. These poppies need sun and good drainage.

If you prefer your poppies pale, pretty and pink, perhaps Shirley poppies would be the best choice. It is an annual developed by a vicar, Reverend William Wilks, in the last couple of decades of the nineteenth century. There are lots of mixes from which to choose and as with all annual poppies, direct sowing is best; poppies hate root disturbance. They can be sown either in early spring to flower the same year or in the autumn to flower the next year, or both to create a longer flowering season.

Though it is exciting to see these annual poppies appearing magically, nothing beats seeing the first blooms of *Papaver orientale* as they break free of their bud cases and spread their petals. There are so many exciting oriental poppies which bloom in early summer, but none are more glamorous and showy than *Papaver orientale* 'Patty's Plum'. She has to be the true femme fatale of the group. Her darkness and mystery are further dramatised when surrounded by the jagged icy foliage of artichokes or cardoons or the silver lace of artemisias. Some complain about the way in which the colour fades from her deliciously damsony petals and becomes tinged with brown, just before they fall. Who cares how disgracefully she dies when she lives so exuberantly?

The petals of all their flowers may share the same tissue paper quality, yet the plants themselves range from venerable perennials to flash-in-the-pan annuals, from tiny, ground-hugging alpines like *Papaver miyeabanum* to the tall spires of *Papaver spicatum*, dressed in fat buds and covered in silvery fur, or the even more statuesque stems of *Macleaya cordata*, the plume poppy. The emerging leaves of Macleaya, in their colour, form and the way in which they emerge from the soil in pairs, clasped together, closely resemble bloodroot, *Sanguinaria canadensis*, a woodland wonder from eastern North America. It is a one-off, the only sanguinaria within the family Papaveraceae. The whole plant, including the thick, spreading rootstock which bleeds red sap when damaged, is succulent and fleshy. Each emerging flower bud is wrapped tightly in one scalloped leaf which unfurls as the flower stem pushes up its fragile flower. The simple, pure white flowers are fleeting, almost ghostly in their transparency, seldom lasting more than a day or two – a mere nuance of a flower.

Less graceful but much longer-lasting, the double form, *Sanguinaria canadensis f. multiplex*, is more often cultivated and probably more garden-worthy. Its chunky, globose flowers are laden generously with pristine petals, in telling contrast to the puckered grey of its protecting leaf. Once seen, never forgotten. This is an ooh-aah, can't live without it, absolutely must-have plant. Its preference is for leafy, acid soil but even when conditions seem perfect it sometimes disappears, much to its owner's chagrin. But addicts never give up. There are gardeners who have tried as many as seven or eight times to establish this temperamental beauty despite increasingly large holes in their bank balances as well as their shady borders.

In the main, poppies are sun-lovers but there are several amongst the meconopsis arm of the family that are more at home in the dappled shade beneath deciduous trees. Our own Welsh poppy, *Meconopsis cambrica*, frequents stretches of woodland, throwing seeds around and colonising ground between bluebells and wood anemones. Usually yellow-flowered, occasionally they are orange and rarely red, and although the wilding is single with papery petals and a boss of quivering golden anthers, there are double-flowered cultivars too, more showy but lacking the grace of the simple single.

Blue flowers are always a draw but none have such magnetism as those whose colour reminds us of the sea and the sky. The blue Himalayan poppy, *Meconopsis betonicifolia*, is another ooh-aah plant. Looking into an individual flower is a revelation. Each deep cerulean blue, slightly crumpled petal is elegantly poised. As the flower opens fully the petals are stretched smooth like wet silk drying on a hot day. At the centre of their shallow cups, a boss of fine stamens, their anthers dusted in gold, surround the central stigma which thrusts itself forward intent on pollination.

The elegant foliage, the stems and the drooping, dimpled buds are all covered in a fine bronze fuzz designed to catch every drop of dew on the high eastern slopes of its homeland. Meconopsis do best where the climate is closest to their natural environment, cool and moist. High humidity and rich soil are what they need.

M. betonicifolia is short-lived, often monocarpic, whereas *M. grandis* is a perennial but loath to set seed.

There are poppies for every taste. No one had better taste than the artist-gardener who gave his name to *Papaver orientale* 'Cedric Morris'. Its opulent, dusty pink flowers with slightly ruffled petals each with a huge bluish-black splodge at its base are worth camping out to see in their first emerging glory. Plant breeders are busy creating varieties with stronger stems, unusual petal shapes and distinctive colours. Each year there are new ones for us to inspect or try. 'John III' is a good example, with upright flowers of a clear translucent red held erect on 60cm/2ft stems. 'Aglaja', despite its commendable habit – only 60cm/2ft tall and strong stemmed – is completely over the top with large, luscious, wavy-edged flowers in soft coral pink. The artist, the pope and the belly dancer have all won the Royal Horticultural Society (RHS) Award of Garden Merit.

Poppies are very persistent. Poppy seed can live for hundreds of years. Germination often follows the ground being disturbed. *Papaver rhoeas*, the corn poppy, is a nice illustration, a new generation germinating each year as the land was ploughed and the grain scattered. *P. somniferum*, the opium poppy, is a crop itself in some parts of the world. In our gardens it is appreciated for its ornamental value. At a rapid (some would say alarming) pace its stout stems shoot up, wrapped with wavy-edged glaucous leaves and lateral shoots all terminating in plump, dimpled buds. At this stage there are waves of excitement to see what colour and form the flowers will have when the buds finally burst. Even when there is only one poppy in the garden, its progeny can be completely different from one another and from their mother. There are reds, pinks and purples, black and white. Some are single and elegant, some as fussy and frilly as a Barbara Cartland blouse. They are all followed by round pepper-pot seed pods, immensely decorative in their own right.

Sometimes we sow poppies deliberately if we are hankering after a particular colour to wash through a border. Seed firms often sell selected varieties, though inevitably there are plenty of rogues! I love this riotous invasion whether it is planned or spontaneous. In fact, we would always welcome poppies of all descriptions into every part of our garden.

Chapter Two

Who knows how many post-war trips my granddad Isaac made. There were several documented in photos showing him picnicking with ladies in Istanbul. Clearly he was good at his job, as he was promoted and once again the family upped sticks, this time moving to Uxbridge. By now, my mum Jeannie had a baby brother Maurice. It seemed all was set fair for a comfortable middle-class existence but just a few years later tragedy struck, and Isaac died after a short illness. Sarah Jane and her four children moved north again.

They had no money, and presumably the little house in Kersal Avenue where they lived, and where my grandma continued to live until her death, was afforded from some sort of pension. Although extended family rallied round, times were hard. My grandma knitted and sold what she made, but this was her only saleable skill and there was no way she could go out to work, being as she was solely responsible for four young children.

Grandma Jane was a Christian Scientist, so when anyone was ill they had to rely on God for their recovery. My mum later told me the tale of her mother's advice on an occasion when the household all had flu or a very bad cold at the same time. From the top of the stairs, Jeannie called her mum: 'Mama, I'm hot!' 'Well,' replied her exasperated mum, 'blow on yourself then.'

All three sisters and eventually their little brother too did well at school. My mum always had a great thirst for knowledge and secretly read book after book by candlelight in bed. She always blamed her poor eyesight on this practice.

In the front room of Kersal Avenue, some of the spoils of Isaac's trips had been retained. There were Turkish carpets six or seven deep, very difficult to walk on but then despite its being a small house with five people living in it, it had become a sanctuary and the children seldom went into the room.

* * *

My other grandparents, my father's parents, lived in a small semi-detached Edwardian house in Holly Avenue, just five minutes' walk from where my parents would later settle. The road took its name from two variegated holly trees that stood outside a much grander detached house further down the road. When I was a child, I found them fascinating, exotic and socially superior to the familiar plants of my grandad's garden. His front garden was small with a round flower bed edged in rope-twist tiles. In the front porch were a bucket and a shovel often involved in a fierce competition for free manure when the milkman's horse deposited its droppings on the avenue. The roses did alright, though the dung must have been quite fierce.

I would often go to visit my grandparents in Holly Avenue, and would cut across from Blantyre Avenue via the backings opposite one side of the National Insurance building. The reason I went that way was because on the other side was Mrs Moreton's garden. It was her back garden, but because hers was the first house in the road, people could see right into the garden from the backings. There was a low fence, but even I could see over the top of it. Mrs Moreton was a keen gardener and grew all sorts of interesting plants. Occasionally she would be out there gardening as I walked past and we got to talking. Later on I would actually go into her garden and she would show me different plants. On one particular day, the most magnificent rose was in full bloom just at my eye level and facing me as though it wanted me to appreciate its beauty. Mrs Moreton introduced us and told me all about her.

It was a Peace rose, which has become very successful in our gardens. She told me that it used to be known as the *Rosa* 'Madame A. Meilland', developed by a French horticulturist name Francis Meilland in the years before the Second World War. In 1939, before France was invaded by Germany, he is said to have sent some cuttings to the United States to protect the new cultivar, and there it was successfully propagated by the Conard Pyle Company. I loved the creamy, light yellow flowers, which were warmed pink at their edges.

She must have been quite 'up with the times' to have had such a well-established specimen growing so well in her garden by then – there were no garden centres at that time so she must have bought it bare root by post.

I remember my grandad unpacking mysterious parcels with strange roots in the winter, some wrapped in hessian, some in newspaper. This was really the only way to come by new plants apart from the time-honoured method of swapping or donating plants to friends, family and neighbours or growing them from seeds or cuttings.

There were flower shows, but until the advent of the plastic pot and the garden centre access to new plants was limited. Far more gardeners would grow their own new plants from seed, a practice that is becoming much more prevalent again and one that I would whole-heartedly endorse. My grandma took me to Southport Flower Show several times. What a treat, even more exciting than going shopping in Manchester. It was a real day out: she had made sandwiches, of course, and there was cake, but the real thrill was to see all these exciting plants I had never seen before in any of the back gardens of Walkden, my favourite of which were the towering delphiniums.

Every detail of the house at Holly Avenue remains vivid: the oval stained-glass window in the front door, the panels that separated the hall from the staircase, the cold white-tiled bathroom where, on the few occasions we stayed overnight, we had to clean our teeth with salt. This bathroom was a fairly recent installation but I still made use of the outside toilet, especially in March and April, because alongside it were planted two of the most lovely and most fragrant of early flowering plants, *Daphne mezereum* and auriculas.

These days, when I smell a snowdrop, I am instantly transported back to one of our most memorable family rituals in that house. There we are, my brothers, cousins and me, pressed close to our grandma in the glass lean-to through from her little kitchen. She breaks the sealing wax and unties the string on a small brown paper parcel which has arrived from Cornwall, from one of her sisters. Inside is a cardboard box and as she lifts the lid the twin perfumes of damp moss and honeyed snowdrop flowers assail the nostrils of the company clustered round her knee. There are the pristine white flowers, single snowdrops, their stems wrapped in lush moss, soft and brilliant green. Before we looked and marvelled our noses took in the honeyed perfume mingled with the smell of the ancient earth. Have you noticed how people always close their eyes when they are smelling something?

And who doesn't love a snowdrop? 'A snowdrop is a snowdrop is a snowdrop,' some would say. As I know now, to the increasing number of galanthophiles this is heresy. There are more than 150 snowdrops listed and new varieties are being discovered all the time. Each is an individual.

The first and the best is *Galanthus nivalis*. Its simplicity and perfection of form are unsurpassed. There are bigger snowdrops. There are snowdrops with quirky markings or unusual forms, but none can outdo *G. nivalis*. At first, one or two shoots peer outwards, inspecting the wintry scene, like animals emerging gingerly from hibernation, sniffing the air. Each shoot lengthens gradually. The 'eye' of the stem eventually expands until the twin leaves that have held and protected the nascent bud agree it is time to part company and allow it to emerge. As the flower swells and the stem lengthens, the papery sheath opens and the big white drop is free to dangle and expand at the end of the hair-fine pedicel that joins it to its stem. No matter how fierce the weather, the flowers survive unscathed. The overhanging petals and their green-tipped underskirts bob and dance through gale and tempest, effortlessly protecting the inner workings. It is truly a feat of botanical engineering. Once the flower is pollinated, the ovary to which the pedicel is joined swells, and the flower stem lengthens. This is the only stage in the snowdrop's career when it looks messy, but such untidiness is short-lived and essentially fruitful. The weight of the ovary brings it down to ground level where its casing eventually bursts or rots, exposing the seeds. When they germinate and make new bulbs, they do so far enough away from the parent plant to enable independent existence.

Snowdrops are seldom seen as isolated specimens. We always talk about them 'carpeting' a woodland floor, and the gradual whitening of a piece of dank earth that their emergence produces is magical. Even now, the sight of snowdrop shoots pushing through the sleeping earth is, for me, all it takes to banish dejection.

But the snowdrop ritual could only have gone on for a few years – my grandma died when I was eight. It was my first experience of death. She had had an attack of angina in the newsagent's shop at the bottom of Church Road where we lived. She was taken back to Holly Avenue, but died that same day. When I was told the news, I hid behind the couch and could not be persuaded to come out. I loved her and she loved me. I was her only granddaughter and she made a fuss of me – not with toys or sweets or holidays, as these were the years immediately after the end of the Second World War, but instead, and so much more meaningfully, she used her skill and enterprise to make me clothes. She was a brilliant seamstress and she knitted too. I can still remember the subdued but rapid clunk and click of knitting needles, sometimes a solo, sometimes a duet with my mum and occasionally as part of a trio with my grandad, who also knitted. No television, but the warmth from the oven in the wall beside the coal fire whose flickering flames lit up the knitters' faces. There was a side light too but no one needed it to knit.

There is a photo of my grandma and me standing and smiling together on the short path outside our front door at 12 Church Road, she in a dark coat and hat, best shoes and handbag, me in the long dress she had made me to accompany the Rose Queen on a float for the Whit Walks.

Although the photo is in black and white I can remember the dress exactly, white with tiny red dots and a slender red velvet ribbon to both tie up the matching dolly bag and tie round my unruly hair which she had made a brave attempt to curl. I was thrilled about the whole affair, being made an attendant, even though I may have been the most lowly one, and having such attention lavished on me by my grandma. Most of all I remember her kind smile – that was the most precious thing about knowing her.

*   *   *

My mum and dad were married on the last day of May 1943 (her bouquet was delphiniums), and for the rest of the war my mum lived with my dad's parents.

When he returned from the war, he took up his old job in the civil service. At first that must have been in Manchester but later, when my brother Bill was still a baby, he was moved to Bispham just along the coast from Blackpool. My mum related the story of her, me and Bill walking along the sea front, Bill in his pram just a few months old, when I took off and ran straight across the beach and into the sea. It was the first time I had seen it; I still love the sea. She must have been in a quandary, but by the time she put the brake on the pram and ran after me I had started to come back to her, laughing loudly and soaking wet.

With my mum, my baby brother Bill and me in tow, we moved to Newcastle upon Tyne. Our new home, in Harnham Gardens, was a brand-new prefab with a small bare patch of land. There was a coal shed too and apparently my friend Diana and I used to try eating the coal. Although electricity was installed it was not connected. My father achieved local hero status by shimmying up a telegraph pole and connecting the street to the mains supply. Gradually a garden started to emerge, though my mum can't have had much time for it. I attended school there for just a few weeks. My youngest brother Pip was born on 9 June 1949 and shortly afterwards my family moved back to Manchester.

Filming at Belsay Castle once, years later, there was a spare hour before my train back from Newcastle and I asked my assistant producer who was taking me to the station if we could just see if Harnham Gardens still existed. The prefabs were still there, and we found Diana's grandma still living in the same house. The gardens were a treat, unrecognisable from the mud patches we initially inherited. They had been tended and loved all those years. Though houses can be done up and changed, it is their gardens that make the place what it is: a dump or a des res.

Back in Manchester, my dad was installed in the National Insurance building where eventually I was to meet my first coltsfoot, and where I was to stand on the brick wall at its entrance singing a duet with Fergy Bailey – 'Some Enchanted Evening'. The same wall that injured me when I was practising hurdling, missed my step and cut open the back of my head. The bricks were shiny and had sharp edges. My mum went pale and almost passed out when I reached home. Needless to say I was fine.

A member of the daisy family that flowers earlier in the year was to be found in the vicinity of 'the croft', which was the name we gave to a square of waste ground complete with bomb shelter (in its midst) and a wide street, Blantyre Avenue, to one side, an ideal venue for a game of football since there were the fenced-off grounds of the National Insurance building to the other side. This particular flower, though, was in forbidden territory, beyond the fence of the National Insurance compound, though that didn't stop me from welcoming it when at long last it made its first appearance in February.

Until quite recently I was good at climbing fences; I have never been good at sitting on them though! One of the regrets about getting older is that I am not so agile when it comes to scaling walls and climbing fences. Once I had discovered the coltsfoot, especially with the added frisson of its appearing on forbidden territory, I awaited its arrival with bated breath. Peering through the chain link fence to try to detect the first glint of brilliant yellow on a sunny day, I would feel disappointment and frustration at its no-show. But when one day there was a flash of yellow then it was over the fence to engage with the plant, to feast my eyes on those sun-like daisies and to feel the strange furry stems. Its common name of coltsfoot is supposed to be a reference to the similarity of its emerging leaves to the foot of a young horse, but it flowers long before the leaves push through, presumably an evolutionary policy to ensure its flowers can make full use of light and warmth without having to compete with its leaves, which eventually become huge.

Come to think of it, I must have had to wait for the weekend when work had closed down to visit the plant – it was February and it would have been too dark at the end of the day when everyone had gone home.

Coltsfoot has a wide distribution throughout Europe, Asia and even North Africa and is common now in Canada and the United States, probably introduced by European settlers who valued it for its medicinal properties. Its Latin name, *Tussilago farfara*, is derived from *tussis*, a cough, and its flowers were used and maybe still are to make a tea to treat coughs. Ironically its leaves, which come after the flowers, were used as a tobacco substitute.

Richard Mabey, in his botanical and cultural compendium *Flora Britannica* (1996), includes oral testimony by an informant with a sweet tooth who resorted to eating Coltsfoot Rock, because this could be obtained from a chemist as a remedy for coughs rather than a confection, and so it was not rationed in wartime.

Sweet supplies were very limited when we were little. They were rationed through and for some time after the Second World War. I can remember being in charge of the ration book. The only sweets available most weeks were sherbet in a conical paper bag (later I was to buy my five Park Drive cigarettes in the same kind of bag) and a liquorice stick we called 'Spanish' which was liquorice root. A bit limited but perhaps our teeth stood a better chance.

I am not sure how we were related but later on, when we were living at 87a Manchester Road, two aunties would visit sometimes on a Sunday afternoon. They were called Aunty Bertha (same as my grandma) and Aunty Florence. Bertha was small and busy, a canny little woman. She had a sweetshop in Boothstown close to Ellenbrook where my grandad's family came from; perhaps they were cousins. Aunty Florence was tall with sloping shoulders and glasses and always very quiet and benign. Sometimes Henry would come with them. I am not sure how he fitted in; perhaps he was Bertha's son, and perhaps she was widowed, as both aunties always wore black and they wore hats that they kept on indoors. Henry seldom spoke, but he smiled a lot. I think he had a disability. He had a shiny red face as if it had been scrubbed that reminded me of a rosy apple. Just before they left, Aunty Bertha would distribute three bags of sweets, one each, for which we would say thank you and give her a peck on the cheek. We would kiss Florence too, as they left.

Our sweet consumption always followed the same pattern: Pip would usually get through his by bedtime on Sunday night, Bill would stagger his consumption so that even when it got to the following Sunday he would have a couple of pear drops left, and I would be somewhere in the middle. It was the same scenario too when we turned up at the big shed with the pot-bellied stove on Grandad's yard on Saturday morning for our weekly pocket money drill. Pip would spend his silver sixpence, I might keep mine for a bit then spend it, and Bill would save his. Bill and Grandad

Higham were very much like each other, acquisitive without any of that word's negative connotations – they would collect anything and everything, just in case.

* * *

When we moved back to Manchester, we lived first at 10 Church Road. There was a back yard and a little front garden with pinks running alongside the path. The soil in the area was thin and black. Later on when my mum visited us in Devon, she was astonished at the difference in rates of growth here compared to her home. On heavy fertile clay, our plants would have literally double the vigour of hers. Nothing to do with gardening skill, everything to do with the soil. The garden at Church Road was very tidy and well kept but there was not much room for expansion and development.

There were only houses on one side of the road; opposite was a big fence made from railway sleepers on their end, and beyond that was a graveyard and a wooded area with a broad pathway which did a sharp left down a short hill, ending up at the schoolyard of the primary school. This was my friend Alex's and my way to school, and we found ghost moths living on the boards that we loved to study and adopted as pets. We never found it gloomy there, the opposite in fact, stopping to admire fresh flowers that had been brought. We certainly didn't associate the place with death or dying.

* * *

When I was little, my dad used to take the family out on excursions on Sundays, partly to treat us but also to indulge in his favourite occupation, going as fast as possible in whatever fancy speedmobile he happened to have at that time (there were lots and he constantly changed them). One of the favourites, it was certainly mine, was a tomato-soup red Austin Atlantic convertible, a car built secondarily for export to the USA but primarily for speed. Whenever there was open road, we would all shout 'Faster, faster, faster!' and scream when we took off going over a particular hump-back bridge.

My mum and I, though we enjoyed the excitement just as much as the male contingent, had another agenda.

A favourite destination for these trips – reachable from Manchester – was North Wales, and as we hurtled along country roads the scenery changed until we were immersed in steep banks under the canopy of trees. In April the branches were bare but the ground beneath them was already bustling with spring's cinderellas. 'Please can we stop, Dad, we need to spend a penny.' Out we'd tumble, crashing up the slope through old hazel coppice until we were out of sight and then collapsing in fits of giggles and squeals of delight into cushions of violets and carpets of primroses. We forgot all about having a wee, and once we stopped giggling, the quiet magic of the place took us under its spell.

When we visited North Wales, we saw our relatives in Colwyn Bay. Brian, who was a second cousin twice removed, had an enormous collection of birds' eggs. I was horrified that they had all been stolen from nests and could all have become new birds. I was fascinated though to see them up close, to marvel at their pure colours or the perfect dappled camouflage of oystercatcher eggs.

Decades later, when filming *Wild About the Garden*, I came across an oystercatcher's nest – not so much a nest as a scrape in the ground in a shingly, pebbly hollow on a Norfolk beach. The two eggs were so well camouflaged, speckled and mottled cream and brown, I almost trod on them, but one of the parents came quickly on the scene and warned me. Many ground-nesting birds adopt this subterfuge, leaving their eggs and distracting intruders away from them, but if this doesn't work and they feel their eggs are imperilled, they will return and sit on them. Birds who live by the seaside are different from those of other habitats, especially fascinating because they are not part of the everyday for those who don't live by the sea. You have to go to their wild and wonderful domain to meet up with them.

The year after my dad died, my husband Neil and I took my mum up to Morecambe Bay in April, to watch the wading birds. This has to be one of the most spectacular sights ever; it's estimated that a quarter of a million waders pass through here every year swishing through the wide sky in huge, twirling ribbons. We saw literally hundreds of thousands of waders, knots, redshanks, sandpipers and oystercatchers cavorting themselves in great ribbons in the CinemaScope sky above the wide sea.

Later we explored the limestone pavement at Silverdale, up behind Morecambe Bay, and saw *Helleborus foetidus*, the stinking hellebore, and Daphne laureola, both with green flowers.

When we were on that particular visit, we went up into the hinterland of the bay on a voyage of exploration and accidentally found the great gardener Reginald Kaye's wonderful nursery. Over the years, we were honoured to be taken on several guided tours of his own private garden, which, despite the limestone pavement just below the surface, contained magnificent magnolias.

Reginald Kaye was a world authority on ferns. When we met him on that trip he was already in his eighties but had just returned from a trip to Crete where he had been abseiling down cliffs searching for erodiums. He was a lovely man, and very tolerant. I was a total novice at that time and had wandered into a slightly ramshackle greenhouse and picked up a precious hundred-year-old alpine to ask how much it would be. He and his two sons carefully removed it and followed us around closely until we left the premises. We were allowed to buy a wisteria, however, which my mum looked after for a couple of years until we had somewhere to plant it. At one time, that same wisteria covered the front of the cottage. Nowadays a layer from the original threatens a repeat performance.

My relatives in Colwyn Bay sometimes took us just along the coast to Llandudno. The view is dominated by a great limestone headland, the Great Orme. Leaving everyone below on the beach, on my own I clambered up its steep paths and through the coarse pebbly soil with its sparse grass. It was unlike anywhere I had been before. It was a warm, breezy day and I could smell the sea; ozone filled my nostrils. Then I was brought to a sudden halt, not knowing where to put my foot next, because the ground was so densely covered by a mind-blowing mix of common spotted and pyramidal orchids. Aptly named, the latter is a lovely purple-flowered orchid with dumpy almost conical heads. This was my first experience of orchids apart from meeting them in my copy of *The Observer's Book of Wild Flowers*.

Back home, we lived amongst coal mines and cotton mills, but there were snatches of nature here and there. There were little gardens and allotments, railway embankments and waste ground, and they all yielded flowers and leaves, fruit and seedheads. I wondered at the big white trumpets of bindweed that abounded on every fence. How could such an exotic plant feel so at home amongst those dark, satanic mills?

That said, I knew that parts of the man-made world could be wonderful. Grandad's yard was one of the best places in the world to play. It was a big cobbled yard with a miscellany of sheds around it packed full of exciting things. There was timber of every shape and size, building materials, veneer and, in the main shed, where he held court warming his backside on a fat pot-bellied stove, there were shelves from floor to ceiling, groaning with boxes full of nails – oval, flat, lost head, wire, serrated, horseshoe, twist, panel pins, brads – and screws – wood screws, set screws, machine screws, hex-head screws, countersunk, flat head, raised head – of all different diameters and dimensions. Whatever your hardware needs were, they could be found in the boxes on these shelves, and what is more, my grandad had the entire stock list in his head and could fetch down the required items within minutes even if it meant employing a ladder. Smells pervaded the air, coal and wood burning, machine oil and resin, fresh sawdust, pine resin, particularly intense in the winter when the heavy, industrial sliding doors of the shed were rolled shut.

There were exciting smells and sensuous textures in another shed too. It was a small shed, very dark, with a couple of big plan chests. Each drawer contained sheets of veneer of different woods from different trees from different countries and continents. Each was unique, with its own colour, texture, character. I loved to creep in there on my own and open, peruse, then close every drawer. These thin sheets of wood took on special significance, treasure hidden away waiting to be rediscovered each time I entered the shed.

My grandad had bought the yard and started a small business selling timber, building materials and ironmongery with the insurance payout he got when he had removed the tops of his fingers on a circular saw. His father Yebby sold insurance initially, probably to supplement his main job as a corn-cutter, which both my great grandads on that side of the family appear as on birth certificates.

To go to work on the yard, he would always wear a yellow ochre duffle coat. He invariably had a cigarette on the go and his white hair had a slight yellow tinge at the front from nicotine. After working as a garden boy at Worsley New Hall (which is now RHS Bridgewater, of which I am an ambassador), he apprenticed as a cabinet maker and eventually became chief carpenter at the big cotton mill, Burgess Ledward. It was one of the biggest mills around and had one of the tallest chimneys. It was from the top of this chimney he shouted a proposal of marriage to Ethel, the mill nurse with whom he had been in love for ages. She turned him down and he married my grandma Bertha Morte, but many years later, after my grandma died, he proposed to Ethel again. This time she accepted. We always called her Aunty Ethel.

At the top end of the yard behind the collection of miscellaneous sheds, one of which was an old horse tram, was a big, old black fence which we used to climb up and down. One day I slipped and impaled my knee on a chunk of wood protruding from the fence. When I stood up my knee was black with scores, possibly hundreds, of splinters. When I got home my mum got out the tweezers and started to try and extract them. Her task was made doubly difficult because the wood was soft; it hadn't hurt when I did it. We tried to get them all out but some had gone so deep they were impossible to remove. For the next twenty or thirty years splinters would occasionally appear just under my skin, but not necessarily in my knees.

Despite the dangers, the yard was an exciting place to play. At the Sandwich Street end, to one side stood a small greenhouse which my grandad let 'Dirty Jimmy' use to grow coleus. The 'Dirty' was an allusion to his general appearance. I was intrigued by his ability to produce hundreds of plants – he simply couldn't stop – and this was the first time I had seen anybody taking cuttings. He plunged them into milk bottles full of water. He explained what he was doing but his accent was so broad I couldn't understand him. His dialect was so strong he wouldn't even have made it to a viewer's slot on a present-day *Gardeners' World*.

Sandwich Street had a long row of terraced houses, each with its own step up from the pavement and into the living room. Most of these steps were whited by the woman of the house using a Wigan 'donkey stone'. It was quite a competition to see who could get the edge of their steps whitest, women down on their hands and knees with a headscarf, sometimes even a shawl, a wrap-round pinny and often wearing clogs.

Two doors down from the yard was the bread shop (appropriately enough in Sandwich Street) where my mum would send me to buy our bread. Church Road, where we lived then, was just across the main road, Manchester Road, from Sandwich Street. Sometimes I would take my brother Bill with me on this important errand, but one day as we approached the main road, he shook off my hand and ran into the road in the path of a huge lorry. The lorry came to a screeching halt with him underneath it.

I still shudder at the memory and shall never stop feeling guilty. I can't remember exactly what happened next. I ran around the lorry and the lorry driver, and with help from passers-by got Bill onto the pavement. Mercifully he only had one simple fracture in one leg; because he was so young it was a greenstick fracture and healed relatively quickly. He had a plaster cast for a couple of months, a constant reminder of my negligence.

There were lesser incidents around the same time which nonetheless made an impact on my child's psyche, some good, some bad. On an errand once, I dropped half a crown and watched it roll across the pavement and down a grid. I didn't know what to do; I couldn't reach it.

On a happier occasion, I remember striding down the same pavement dressed as Robin Hood on my way to school en route to the Whit Walk. I was determined not to be cast as Maid Marian, so my mum had come to the rescue with green tights, a tunic she made, wellington boots and an old hat, steamed to shape with a pheasant's feather for extra panache. I even had a bow made from an aircraft rib, of which there were a stack on my grandad's yard. His woodworking skills were in demand during the First World War building wooden aeroplanes.

I loved the idea of being the hero. I don't think I had cross-dressing tendencies, although there were a couple of occasions when I so strongly wanted to be a boy, I tried to borrow Bill's clothes. They were too small, so I took them off and had to go along with being a girl. It was hard sometimes; I wanted to explore the Amazon and could imagine myself in a canoe paddling furiously, only stopping from time to time to discover a plant or animal new to science, but whoever heard of a girl doing that?

Meanwhile I contented myself with the limited local flora and fauna. I think back to the bindweed that lined the fences. I can still feel the soft and silken stems of the coltsfoot, standing unclothed alongside the gravel path that ran around the National Insurance building. It was my secret. I remember seeing a lone foxglove at the edge of Farmer Johnson's field, probably the last ever field in Walkden, where he kept Dobbin, who pulled his milk cart (and incidentally occasionally supplied my grandad with manure for his roses). It was the first I had ever seen and I've loved foxgloves ever since.

Foxgloves

Our hedgerows are punctuated by the tall spires of foxgloves, an annual performance to be enjoyed, exclamation marks in nature's calendar to sign the beginning of summer.

Even earlier, as winter gives way to spring, there is excitement to be had as each woolly rosette advertises a preview of what is to come. In spring the hedges are crowded, and there are lots of them presaging a bumper year for foxgloves. They are never in exactly the same spot two years running because they are biennial.

Once they have flowered, they set seed, and lots of it too. A single foxglove can produce more than a million, possibly 2 million seeds, an insurance policy that guarantees the continuous production of plants. Although for the gardener, foxglove seed should be sown as fresh as possible (the fresher the seed is the more viable it will be), there's no doubt that in the wild, seed can remain viable for a long time.

There are several tracts of forestry land close to where we live. A few years ago, after several acres of spruce had been clear-felled in the river valley a couple of miles from here, the hillside looked bare, ravaged. In the first year there was nothing much to see; the ground looked bleak apart from encroaching bracken and a few other ferns. But in the following year it was illuminated with spires of foxgloves, most of them purple (I'd describe it as a very bluish pink) but with patches of pure white. The whole hillside underwent a breathtaking transformation. The seed bank must have persisted for years, lying dormant beneath the soil until conditions were right for germination – more light, more water, more warmth – hey presto – up they come. There is something magical about the way these tall spires appear from nowhere.

Soil disturbance seems to help with germination too. On my walks with Fifi and Fleur, our sometime Lakeland Terriers, we notice (it's probably just me who notices, I think their only interest is the rabbits) that around the entrance to the burrows and often around the badger sets we encounter, foxgloves are a feature. Their success in these busy places is testament to foxgloves' robustness.

Not only are they rugged plants able to endure animal traffic, but they are impressively versatile too. One of the most awkward situations in any garden is its edges, whether its boundaries are hedges, walls or fences and whatever their size and scale. The plants that grow with them or in front of them need to be extra accommodating, able to contend with uneven light, sometimes bright and baking, at other times plunged into shade and with erratic amounts of water. Foxgloves are more than up to the job simply because they thrive in the wild in exactly the same conditions – they are archetypal hedgerow plants.

Hedges aren't a natural phenomenon, they are man-made, but along with such plants as *Euphorbia amygdaloides*, the wood spurge, and our wild primrose, foxgloves have successfully made the transition from their natural habitat, the woodland edge, to the hedgerow.

This is a wildflower that no one can ignore, sometimes growing as tall as a tall man and much, much taller than me. Sometimes it's good being short – in this case those of us who are vertically challenged can look up into the foxglove bells and view the secrets inside with ease. We can watch the transit of bumble bees as they visit in search of nectar and emerge covered in pollen.

There are close encounters with foxgloves to be enjoyed long before you head for the hedgerow, before ever you leave the boundaries of our plot. Foxgloves have always been in the garden here because we love them so. We grow our straight native species, *Digitalis purpurea*, as well as *Digitalis purpurea* 'Alba', the pure white form, and *D.p.* 'Sutton's Apricot', whose warm though subtle colour always looks in keeping with the pure form of the classic species. Choosing your foxgloves is a matter of personal taste but for me nothing can improve on the native, with pendulous bells perfectly spaced and all on one side of the stem.

Whilst our native foxglove is a biennial, there is a whole clan of perennial, albeit short-lived, foxgloves from the European mainland. Most are perfectly hardy though they are liable to need more sun than in their native habitats to compensate for lower temperatures. Though many would grow in partial shade 'at home' most are happy out in the open garden here. They have been much used in recent years by innovative designers alongside grasses and umbels.

Pale flowered foxgloves are particularly easy to incorporate in any colour scheme. *Digitalis grandiflora*, which used to be known as *Digitalis ambigua*, is a lovely plant with large cream bells. It makes a real clump and produces stem after stem of flower. It can live for many years. Try it close to the glossy leaves of *Acanthus mollis* or associate it with *Baptisia australis*, agapanthus or blue aconites. It is also perfect set against Bowles's golden grass, *Milium effusum* 'Aureum'.

Even more unusual, *Digitalis parviflora* has tiny rich brown flowers held tightly side by side. Both the inflorescence and the stem are covered in fine soft fluff. This foxglove creates a small stage at the entrance to each flower on which small bees and other pollinating insects can land. Immediately inside the bell of the flower are two bright yellow anthers, bristling with pollen with which any prospective pollinator is anointed. The seedheads that follow are remarkable. Firstly they are thick and full, crowding the stems. Each seedpod is barbed at one end, presumably to put off grazing animals in their native Spain and Portugal; they are tough, too, and almost impossible to penetrate. When saving seed even though seedpods are fully developed and seed is ripe you sometimes have to crush the pods slightly to extract the seed. Secondly, the stems are straight as a dye. These bronze ramrods which last all winter through make the perfect punctuation to a narrow herbaceous bed where there is no room for a fastigiate shrub. Its colouring and deportment make this a very beautiful plant, rather odd but very desirable.

Isoplexis canariensis merits a place on its own as a specimen plant and some gardeners grow it in a pot in loam-based compost, taking it outside for the summer season and returning it to a cold greenhouse when temperatures drop.

The rest of the bunch probably look at their best growing together with others of their ilk in a mixed planting with other woodland subjects or, for the Southern European species, flowering alongside *Scabiosa ochroleuca* or the dramatic *Scabiosa atropurpurea* in a sunny site.

Close your eyes and you can almost hear the bees buzzing.

These are my favourite kinds of foxglove:

1) The shrubby evergreen foxglove, *Digitalis isoplexis canariensis*, is unique. Although it is tender, most of us would be prepared

to go to great trouble to protect it each winter just to get an annual view of its rich amber-chestnut bell flowers.

2) The rusty foxglove, *Digitalis ferruginea*, a short-lived perennial from Iberia, goes with everything. Its flowers, small and hooded, are a bizarre mixture of browns, creams and yellows and they thickly clothe the stout stems.

3) *Digitalis mertonensis* is another one-off. Bred at the John Innes Centre, it had artificial colouring introduced into its genes, giving it a most unusual shade: its broad squashed bells have a delightful strawberry, raspberry smoothie kind of colour.

4) *Digitalis purpurea* 'Alba'. Possibly my all-time favourite. Its purity of form and immaculate bells, and its elegant deportment make it an outstanding plant. Unimpeachable. Looks its perfect best in shade which is where it wants to live.

5) *Digitalis heywoodii*. Surely the softest and most silvery of foxgloves. You just want to stroke it. Its woolly coat is composed of down that covers the leaves to protect them from hot sun. which gives you the clue to where it wants to be. Being from Portugal, it loves sunshine.

6) *Digitalis lutea* has small fine creamy-coloured bells on stems between 45cm and 60cm tall. It may keep going for a few years.

7) *Digitalis* 'John Innes Tetra'. A result of a deliberate cross between *D. lanata* and *D. grandiflora* and purportedly a fairly

vigorous perennial. Enchantingly coloured bells of raspberry and cream (sounds good enough to eat but don't – all foxgloves are highly poisonous).

8) *Digitalis purpurea* 'Pam's Choice'. Very dramatic plant up to 5ft high with distinctive maroon spots within joining up to form blodges. Biennial and just as easy to grow from seed as any of the others.

Whether you're growing perennial or biennial foxgloves from seed, the procedure is much the same. I sow all my foxglove seeds in half-trays in open compost, loam-based with plenty of grit added. Firm the surface of the compost so it's perfectly level. The perfect tool is a little presser board made to measure; Neil, my husband, made me one thirty years ago from a bit of marine ply and a piece of split broom handle and it's still going strong.

Thinly sprinkle seed onto the surface of the compost (never sow seed too thickly since this creates the conditions for damping off, a fungal disease that causes seedlings to collapse). Cover with grit and water by standing your tray or pot in shallow water until the grit looks damp. Take it out, drain, then place in a warm, bright situation – the greenhouse staging or a windowsill.

As soon as the seedlings develop true leaves and are big enough to handle, prick them out individually into modules and eventually transfer them into separate pots. Overwinter your plants in a cold frame – they can stand frost but will benefit from extra protection. The alternative to sowing in trays for the biennial species is to sow directly into the ground in little rows in the vegetable garden or a nursery bed. When seedlings are big enough, separate them and either transplant them so they're more widely spaced in the same bed or lift them carefully and pot individually.

When planting, prepare the site with lots of leaf mould or home-made compost. Don't leave it too long, foxgloves swiftly make masses of fibrous roots (that's how they can cope with such inhospitable conditions). If the root ball is congested, dive in with your thumbs or a dinner fork and loosen it, even if that means breaking roots – this will prompt the plant to produce even more feeding roots.

And where to plant them? Try to imagine where they would grow themselves if they wandered over to the perfect place. *Digitalis purpurea* in all its many forms prefers a slightly shady site, though given fertile, moisture retentive soil is happy in some sun. If you're trying some of the Iberian species, they appreciate good drainage and can take full sun – if we ever get any!

Chapter Three

Other than brief detours to Bispham and Newcastle, following Dad's work, my whole childhood was spent around Manchester. When I was four, we settled in Walkden, in a house on Church Road. Now we had a new addition, my youngest brother Pip. (His name is Phillip, but no one has ever called him anything but Pip.) He was born in Newcastle so he is officially a Geordie.

Now, it was decided, I would go to school at St Paul's Infant School. From my house it was just a short walk through the graveyard, and a turn left past the trees to enter the playground on the right. I was probably the only child to go in that way, through the back; everybody else went in the main road entrance. Sometimes, later on, I would come home that way, though I didn't like it much in case I stood on the cracks in the pavement. If I came that way I would always run, and if I came the back way I would invariably walk past the trees and the graves taking note of the leaves and observing any new flowers laid by the headstones. I don't want a grave. I found those flowers fascinating when I was little, but nowadays I find them sad. Much better to plant up a grave. Not only will there be life, plants that will grow, but they will need nurturing and tending, which implies participation and remembering.

We moved back from Newcastle in the autumn and I started school a little later than the other children, so by the time I arrived, they were used to it, whilst I was very much the 'new girl'. I was put into one class to try me out, to see what I could do. I was always a sociable child, never shy, and though it was slightly daunting to be amongst so many children who all seemed to be bigger than me and who all seemed to know the ropes, I soon felt at home. And I quickly discovered I had a penchant for art. At one stage I was sent round by the headteacher to all the other classes with a picture I had painted, which was shown to them by their class teachers with my standing by. After this they moved me up, into a different class.

I was quick to learn to read and write and this, together with the drawing event, obviously caused resentment with one child in my new classroom, the biggest boy. His name was Dennis Hardman, not a very apt surname, because when he made a beeline for me in the playground and, accompanied by some derogatory words, gave me a thump, I clouted him back and made him cry. As I say, I was never shy.

There were two other memorable incidents at infant school. I was made to wash my mouth out with carbolic soap and then confined to the cloakroom by one horrid teacher, who was not my class teacher. I was supposed to have uttered a bad word and though I cannot remember what it was, it seems unlikely that it was a swear word, since my parents didn't swear and we didn't yet possess a telly, not that anyone on the BBC would have used bad language then anyway.

This whole episode upset me hugely, and I can still remember the taste, though the worst part was sitting in the cloakroom on my own until it was home time. I was shunned, not allowed to rejoin my class, and ashamed, dreading telling my mum when I went home especially since I had no idea what crime I had committed. She was furious and hugely upset.

On another occasion though, I was only too pleased to speak up. Because I lived so close to school, I always went home at dinner-time. On Wednesday 6 February 1952, when I reached our house, my mum told me that the King had died that morning. Wolfing down my food, I raced back to school intent on sharing the news with my teacher and then making sure that I told all my friends and classmates that it was I who had brought the news.

Things must have moved fast in the Higham household over the next year and a half. By the time of the Queen's coronation on 2 June 1953, I had moved up to junior school, our family had moved house, my dad had opened a television shop (on the same premises) and on that memorable day, friends and neighbours had crammed into the front room, aka the television shop, to watch the coronation. I think some of them brought their own chairs.

* * *

One sunny mild day in late spring in the back garden at Holly Avenue, our grandma was pegging out washing. My brothers and I were milling about – it must have been a weekend or school holidays. Our grandma was asking me how I would like to go on a trip with her to Manchester. This would have been a very special treat since visits to Manchester were normally confined to visiting Father Christmas.

'What about us?' was my brothers' reaction.

'Oh, your dad will be taking you to lots of football matches later on and Carol will stay at home.'

'What?' I piped up indignantly. 'I want to go and watch the football!'

As far back as I can remember I loved football. When we lived on Church Road I was always kicking a ball about and when we moved to my dad's newly opened television shop on Manchester Road, to my delight there was 'the croft' behind. In those days there were few cars about. My dad was keen on my playing football. I don't know that he had ever played himself, but he was always intent on encouraging any sort of sportiness amongst his children. Perhaps ironic that, as the only girl, I was the 'sportiest' of the three of us. In the kitchen-cum-sitting room behind the shop he would have us all practising sit ups, sometimes cheating slightly with our feet lodged beneath the couch and armchairs.

In September 1952 my infant school class had moved down the road to the local junior school. In my class four photograph – I am on the front row seated on the ground next to Susan Mayall, who is clutching the board proclaiming 'CORONATION YEAR 1953' with a picture of the Queen – I have my usual broad grin minus my front teeth. I am wearing my pinafore and short-sleeved shirt, with long thick grey socks knitted by Grandma Parkes who knitted all her socks long, thick and grey regardless of the feet they would encase. My white shoes are shabby but I'd probably been playing football, and my hair is au naturel. Almost every girl in the class has neat hair with hair slides and ribbon bows. Later on at grammar school, my first maths teacher, Hilda Robinson, would screech at me, 'Carol Higham, go and comb your hair, you look as though you've been dragged through a hedge backwards!'

There are twenty-seven girls and twenty-one boys all in one class.

On the left of this class picture is our teacher, Mrs Thompson. This is one of the few times she smiled in our presence. She disliked me from the word go and my memories of her include her smacking my knuckles with a ruler on several occasions, her face gradually turning beetroot red, and making me stand in the dunce's corner with my back to the class and a conical paper hat with a big D on it. I still do not know how I sinned or what I got wrong, though for Mrs Thomson there was only ever one answer to every question. She did not encourage independent enquiry or imagination. It was not my best school year.

My favourite teacher at junior school was Miss Westhead. She was kind, warm hearted and tried to encourage all of us, no matter where we came from or what talents or lack of them we had. Her classroom was bright and sunny and busy; lots of the posters and pictures that adorned the walls were illustrating royal Commonwealth tours. But there were maps and charts with trees and flowers and in one corner of the room there was the nature table. Everyone could bring in anything natural they could find and we would consult books to identify it, write labels and chat to each other and our teacher about all their whys and wherefores. To my huge joy, when Miss Westhead realised how mad about nature I was, she put me in charge of it. I was not given any exclusive executive powers, rather it was my responsibility to ensure that everything was kept bright and current, labelled correctly and was as interesting as possible.

During our year with Miss Westhead each of us wrote a book, for all of us probably our first. It was entitled 'My Book', with white paper inside and a grey sugar paper cover decorated in my case with various geometric patterns forming a border and a self-portrait, walking in profile in the manner of an Ancient Egyptian tomb mural, all arms and legs visible, long hair tied up with a blue ribbon (which was imagined) and a sideways smile.

The most important page for me was the one about my hobbies, where I drew and wrote about the nature table. In pride of place was a picture of a milk bottle with a horse chestnut twig, its sticky buds just opening to its big, palmate leaves. Feeling those fat buds sticking to your fingers and watching the leaves expand day after day was so exciting.

We were all given a jam jar labelled with our name, a piece of blotting paper and a runner bean, a simple but genius way for children to learn about seeds, germination and plant growth. The first thing we would do when we came in each morning was to rush and inspect our bean's progress, seeing first the two halves of the seed gently part company and the radicle, the root, emerge and travel downwards, followed shortly afterwards by the shoot, its two seed or cotyledon leaves spreading out overtaken by the stem with true leaves. To see that for yourself, to have helped it happen by providing water to keep the blotting paper damp, was as exciting as watching the best slo-mo photography on TV nature programmes. I was utterly enthralled.

Each week we would write the next chapter of our book. Titles included 'My house', 'My way to school', 'My pets', 'My friends'. Each chapter was read and marked by Miss Westhead. I was so proud to get big ticks and an E for excellent for some of my work. I wrote about 'My house' – 'My house has many draughts', and was thrilled to have learned how to spell draughts correctly.

'My way to school' listed in detail not only descriptions of the houses I passed and the roads I had to cross but every detail of any plants in the few tiny front gardens en route – in particular one patch of ground after you'd crossed Sandwich Street, passed the off licence and Mrs Rowlands' haberdashery shop and two houses in the same terrace and before you got to the doctor's house which was detached and, I thought, rather grand. A privet hedge ran between the two and if you squeezed between it and the wall there was an expanse of waste ground. At its back was a big brick factory wall.

I don't know whether or not this was a bomb site, there was rubble here and there amongst the weeds, but at one end was a magical plant, a perennial sweet pea. It had pale lavender-pink banner or standard petals and darker magenta wings and keel. I have never been able to identify it exactly; the closest species is *Lathyrus grandiflorus*, a Mediterranean plant that, on occasions, has escaped from gardens into the wild. But this is said to have little scent, and my sweet pea was fragrant as can be. The first time I discovered it I was about eight, and it was better than any hidden treasure. It filled me with joy and continued to do so every year until I left home for art college ten years later. When we returned sixty years later whilst making a *Gardeners' World* special called 'Plant Heroes', I went apprehensively to investigate and refamiliarise myself with the experience, doubting I would be able to recapture that magic. It was still there.

It was always a secret, and one shared only with my mum. Whether or not anyone else knew of its existence was unclear, but selfishly I like to think not. My mum thought she did not know much about wildflowers, and her own mother was not particularly interested, but although Mum's knowledge was general, it was wide-ranging, and it must have been she who passed on this knowledge – and, much more importantly, this need to enquire and observe.

Whilst the sweet pea was in flower I would pick a bunch of its flowers every few days and take them home to my mum. At first this would be on my way back from junior school, but later from secondary school, work and art college. It was a vital flower ritual. Both my mum and I, along with millions of gardeners, have always loved sweet peas. The annual sweet pea, forms of *Lathyrus odoratus*, is one of the most straightforward and rewarding plants any of us can grow. Picking the first bunch of sweet peas is one of the highlights of the gardening year, an affirmation that we have all made it, summer has arrived.

My other love was the nasturtium. Around the same time, my mum put a few wrinkled nasturtium seeds into my hand and encouraged me to push them into the soil in our back yard. A couple of weeks later we stepped out of the kitchen door together to marvel at the twin round leaves, newly emerged. At the end of the summer we collected seed from the plants and squirrelled it away in brown paper bags. I could hardly wait for the next year. We all remember the first seeds we sowed and the thrill we got when the first tiny green shoots began to appear. Who didn't run back to have another look to check there was no mistake? Who didn't smile?

* * *

This square – 'the croft' – was just a piece of waste ground with an old air-raid shelter. It was delineated by Blantyre Avenue and Chilham Road with two dirt roads forming the other two sides of the square. Although we adventured further on occasions, this square was the hub of all our games, all our 'playing out'. Alongside school and home life, playing out was central to our existence and just as formative, arguably more so. This was where we chose to be, where we decided what we would do. Numerous activities took place there. Sometimes it was running races, and the square became a track. On one of the dirt roads, the backings between a row of wooden garages and sheds and the back walls of the terrace along Manchester Road, marbles was the main activity. 'Murps', we called it. I was no good at it – all too considered and skilful for me. My brothers on the other hand were excellent and Bill was supreme champion, winning game after game in his quiet way. When you beat someone, you won marbles from the other player.

Both Bill and Pip had quite a collection. I was far more interested in the marbles themselves, small spheres of glass in glorious colours, amethyst and the colour of the sea, transparent or milkily opaque with twirls and swirls, every one unique.

On the croft, whose land was rough and undulating, the vegetation was mixed weeds, but in one spot close to the air raid shelter was a stand of helianthus, taller than me when it produced its bright yellow daisies with a darkness about them as though someone had decided that the perfect tool to ornament them was a fine black or dark green ink pen. The journeys plants make around the world are fascinating. How did this sunflower, a dweller of North American prairies, end up decorating a bomb site in Walkden?

It was always important to me to be as good as any of the boys at everything. I had to win any running race around the croft, I had to score more goals than anyone else. Come to think of it, I was the only girl, so it was doubly important to be the best – or be at least as good as anyone else. At the bottom of Blantyre Avenue, Chilham Road and Holly Avenue (they were all parallel) ran another dirt road and beyond that was the railway. Separating the two was 'the boards', the fence made of old upended railway sleepers. There was a row of young ash trees on the road side of 'the boards' which were ideal to climb up. From the croft we would race down Blantyre Avenue then climb the tree. I usually won, but one day as I was crowing from the top of the tree, the others, fed up with my showing off, conspired to shake me down from my perch. Their united effort resulted in my falling to the ground and, even though my progress was slowed down slightly by my bumping into branches on the way down, I landed with a thump, winded but otherwise unhurt. I couldn't get up for a few minutes and when I did, everyone had scattered.

There were very few scraps between us, although I remember one lad, Kenny Bent, resorting to throwing stones at me and, when my brothers told my dad, his charging down the road to take Kenny's dad to task. I was upset, preferring to fight my own battles.

There are only a couple of significant clashes I can remember, both of them involving saving or at least protecting my brothers. The first was not so much a question of fisticuffs, more an undercover raid to rescue hostages. At the back of Church Road was wasteland and across the way was a track running parallel to our road with a corral of scrubby hawthorn trees. Under these trees a boy called Graham Caffrey kept his pet ferrets in wooden hutches. He also ran a gang of younger boys and terrorised other children whenever he got chance. One day, both my brothers were nowhere to be seen until eventually, hearing their shouts, I discovered them tied up to stakes beside the ferret cages. I untied them and we went back across the waste ground and into our back yard via the gate. There was lots of wrist rubbing and tale-telling about what had happened but the basic story was that Graham Caffrey and his gang had grabbed them and tied them up, accusing Bill and Pip of trespassing on their patch. They were about six and four at the time. I was furious and vowed to take vengeance.

A few days later – it must have been summer holidays because we were all off school, and a Monday because my mum was doing the washing – I asked my mum to fill a couple of jam jars with water. Graham Caffrey's gang had lit a fire and I was determined to put it out.

I was with Alex Kirby, who had recently moved in next door but one from us. We were all set to embark on our mission when I realised my mum had given us hot water from her washing. My understanding of basic physics was not very good (it's not much better now), and I equated warm water with heat and was concerned it wouldn't do the job of extinguishing a fire. I couldn't ask my mum for cold water because I would have had to tell her about our secret mission. We threw the water onto the fire but it failed to put it out completely. The day afterwards, to complete my revenge, I opened the ferrets' cages and let them out.

My other defence of my brothers was more pugilistic. Bill and I were both attending St Paul's Junior School, though we were in different years. A big boy in the year above me, Ian Foster, had been bullying younger boys including our Bill. There were two playgrounds, one for boys, one for girls, though I frequently made forays into the boys' playground to play football. I had witnessed Foster's bullying and told him to lay off, but he ignored me and carried on so I challenged him to a fight. We arranged to meet after school outside Bell's cake shop. Norman Bell was in my class and it was his mum's shop, one of four or five shops on Hodge Road adjacent to the school with a broad flat area in front of them. If I'm truthful it was all a bit shambolic, like real fights usually are. Have you ever seen the fight scene in Jean-Luc Godard's *Weekend* when neither combatant lands a single punch? Ian was a lot taller than me too. At least he stopped bullying my brother and a small circle of schoolchildren were entertained for quarter of an hour.

Alex Kirby, who came with me on the ferret foray, became a good friend, perhaps my best. He and his mum and dad had recently moved from Lincolnshire. They spoke with an intriguingly different accent from the broad Lancashire I was used to, much more sing-song and with different words I had never heard before. Mrs Kirby was kindness itself. She had big warm hazel eyes and a weather-beaten face. Mr Kirby was tall and skinny with glasses, like a Quentin Blake drawing, and both he and Alex wore similar

Fairisle cardigans with collars and zips up the front, all beautifully crafted by Mrs Kirby. Alex was their only child and was very precious to them. He had had polio as a small child and wore calipers as a consequence. Though he was a year older than me, we were in the same class – he had spent a lot of time in and out of hospital.

They had brought with them from Lincolnshire a bird, Jack the jackdaw. He was Alex's pet but I was allowed to have part shares in him. I have always been mad keen on birds. My best present ever was a magnificent bird book that my parents bought for me in London on their first trip to the Radio and TV Show at Earl's Court. It made me feel very special. Although my mum knew how important birds were to me and shared my love of them, for my father to give me a book in whose subject matter he was totally uninterested and for which presumably he had paid was remarkable.

Jack the jackdaw came everywhere with us when we were 'playing out'. He would travel around on Alex's shoulder, occasionally on mine. He became a bit of a status symbol and increased our social credentials no end amongst other children. I love birds and have always been deeply interested in them but this was the first time I had been in such close proximity with one. My mum, though she liked them, did not share my total obsession. On another occasion, another Monday, Jack, Alex and I walked into the kitchen whilst she was doing the washing. Jack was on my shoulder, and I was so proud and wanted to show my mum. The second we crossed the threshold, he took off and headed for my mum, who screamed and made a break for it, soggy socks flying in different directions.

I think this was just before my father had a terrible road accident. Late one night he had been driving back from a snooker match in Bolton in his black Austin Atlantic with a young man from his team. Going very fast, he hit a lamp standard. His passenger was killed outright and he sustained terrible injuries. There were no seat belts in those days. He was comatose in Bolton Royal Infirmary for several weeks and remained in hospital for a long time. He had cracked most of his ribs, had six simple fractures in one leg, two compound fractures in the other and countless other injuries.

He would have been a short-tempered patient. We made cards; most of mine had flowers which he wouldn't have appreciated, though the sentiment was probably welcome. He felt no affinity with the natural world whilst I searched for even the smallest relationship with it. When finally he came home, my grandad had made him a bed in our living room-cum-kitchen-cum-dining room. He was in plaster all over and had a set of improvised back scratchers. He didn't cope well with being immobile.

One of the ways he transferred his angst was to get us to move about for him. I don't know that he had ever exercised or played games himself, but he was always intent on encouraging any sort of sportiness amongst his children. He encouraged a sense of competition between us. At that stage, I trusted him implicitly. One of the ways he joined in was to get us to throw ourselves backwards, eyes closed, and he would catch us under our arms – except one time he didn't and I hit the floor with a crash. My brother made me laugh recently when he reminded me of something from our youth that sums Dad up so well: 'My old man was firmly of the persuasion that what doesn't kill you must make you stronger, from the age of about nine or ten we'd had bows and arrows, air guns, knives with unfeasibly long and sharp blades but had never stabbed, shot or injured anything or anybody.'

There was even a sense of who could do best when it came to pleasing our mum. Our bikes were a great way to escape into a different reality and in early June – it probably happens even earlier now – Bill and I would make an important trip, a quest for flowers for our mum. We would collect armfuls of bluebells from Oak Wood, the one little patch of woodland left where we lived, with the tracks of the trains that carried coal from Sandhole Colliery on its outskirts. The stream that ran through it was almost orange with rust and iron from the excavations for coal. There was massive excitement as Bill and I flung down our bikes at the top of the wood and dashed down as though this carpet of blue might disappear at any moment. The bluebells were always at their best when the youngest beech leaves first unfurled and both were gathered greedily (although it was called Oak Wood, there were far more beech trees than oaks), the only problem being how to carry them safely home to my mum when we had to grasp the handlebars of our bikes. Bill must have engineered some way of transporting them – he always had a scientific solution to every problem. I was good at riding with one hand anyway or with no hands come to that so one way or another we got them home to my mum unscathed.

One year at about bluebell time a national event took place: the coronation of Queen Elizabeth II. On the day of the coronation, having overdosed on pageantry, Alex and I snuck out through the kitchen and stood on the back step. There was no garden but a couple of sheds with flat roofs which would eventually become workshops. Perched in the middle of them was a big bird, not quite as big as a pigeon but bigger than a blackbird or a thrush, with a grey back and a white breast striped in grey almost like a matelot's top. I recognised it instantly from pictures in my *Observer's Book of British Birds*. It was a cuckoo. No coronation could compare with the excitement I felt. Initially I wanted to run in and tell everyone, but I soon realised it was better for Alex and me to just share and keep it a secret. It felt as though it was there just for us. There are occasions, and they are magical, when you see or hear something in nature and it seems as if there are no boundaries: nothing between you and the down on a red admiral's body when it is freshly hatched and warming itself in the sun, or the heartbeat of a swallow, rescued from the house, held in your hands and then – away.

Sweet Peas

Sweet peas are a universal favourite. Not only are they the most pickable of cottagey flowers, making the most beautiful of bouquets or kitchen table bunches, but they have the best fragrance. Few things in the world smell as good as sweet peas. One sniff can send you into paroxysms of delight.

Sweet peas combine an elegance of form, a range of colours, from the pale and delicate to the dark and dramatic, and a scent unmatched in any other flower.

There are literally hundreds of sweet pea varieties but all are descended from a sweet pea first introduced from Sicily by Franciscus Cupani in the very last year of the eighteenth century and still grown and treasured to the present day. Its name is *Lathyrus odoratus* 'Cupani'. It has flowers of an engaging colour mix, crimson and deep purple, and the best scent of any sweet pea. It is my favourite and I grow it every year. I grow it up a frame of rusty quarter-inch steel rods made specially for them in two big metal pots either side of the front door. They also clamber up dangling string and bamboo bean poles in the vegetable beds. In other words you can grow them up any structure, from trellis to obelisks, hiding eyesores or lending height to any planting. And of course the more you pick the flowers, the more replacements they make.

You can start your cultivation in the autumn because the seeds are robust enough if you give them protection from extremes, or you can sow the seed in spring and they will catch up. Sow into individual pots, not together, because they don't like competing with each other and they will get all tangled up. They also don't transplant well so you don't pot them but plant the whole potful or sow direct.

I use the cardboard cores of toilet rolls filled with compost to start each pea in, then when they are established and the weather has warmed up, I plant them deeply in the place I want them to grow. The cardboard dissolves in the ground and the roots are undisturbed.

Sweet peas climb up by sending out tendrils which hook onto any support they can find and draw the plant upwards. A lot of the pea's energy is spent on these adventurous tendrils so leaving them on the plant results in small flowers. Once your plant has reached the size you want, you can take off all new tendrils and you will get bigger flowers. For showing sweet peas, growers train them up 'cordons', almost in a straight line, and take off the tendrils at the earliest opportunity to channel all the plant's energy into the flowers. They tie the pea onto the support using 'sweet pea rings', which are just a loose ring of stiff wire about the diameter of a fat finger. I use rings to guide the sweet peas onto the slanting bamboo bean poles and then again as and when they're needed to encourage the plant to climb up and straight.

Cupani's cultivated cousins, a vast array of beautiful flowers, some with frilled petals, some with rich colour, others with delicate picotee edges, are a hybridist's dream, and every year countless new varieties are introduced, often named after celebs or royals and launched with a fanfare at the Chelsea Flower Show. An old variety, 'Painted Lady', white with a red blush at the edge, still holds up, as reliable and beautifully scented as any new one. At the end of the

Victorian era, a breeder called Henry Eckford developed a range of bigger-flowered varieties called the grandifloras. At the turn of the twentieth century, these were selected and reselected to give even bigger and frillier flowers by Silas Cole, head gardener at Althorp House. These became known as the Spencer varieties, launched first as 'Countess Spencer' (as in Princess Di's dynasty).

How you choose a sweet pea to grow is down to personal taste for looks and scent. Summer flower shows are a great way to get introduced. Trawling through seed catalogues (like Suttons or Thompson & Morgan) and sweet pea nursery catalogues is another way.

I am nearly always drawn by scent and restrained charm, for example the mauvy-blue 'Heathcliff', but year after year it is seeds of 'Cupani' that I say I MUST sow.

Wherever you live, even with the tiniest growing space, flowers can transport you to other places, different realities. And big seeds, like peas and nasturtiums, are tailor-made for introducing children to propagation and helping them feel at one with the cycle of growth. The interest that every child has in growing plants should be kindled from the start.

In 1972 I planted both nasturtiums and sweet peas in the window boxes I had installed in our first-floor flat in Kensal Rise in west London. Our sweet peas grew up (so much so that we could hardly see out, the whole white-painted room took on a greenish underwater look) and our nasturtiums grew down. They grew so heartily that they began to obscure the view from the downstairs windows. Our landlady Mrs Forbes, who lived there, was not amused, though the Jamaican family who lived opposite once applauded our floral efforts from the pavement across the road. For sure the sight would have cheered up anyone as they rushed to catch the bus at the end of the road.

Chapter Four

One day at junior school, I was taken out of class to complete an entrance exam for Bolton School. I think I was nine at the time. Later there was an interview too. My dad was particularly keen for me to go to a public school, as he had been a scholarship boy at Manchester Grammar, but since I had the thoughtlessness to be a girl and Manchester was boys only, the next best thing was to try for Bolton School which had a boys' half and a girls' half. His younger sister Barbara had been a scholarship girl there and had received a good education.

I was successful and my family qualified for a full bursary. Historically Bolton School too had been boys only but in 1915, Lord Leverhulme, the big benefactor of the school, made a condition of his endowment that there would henceforth be a girls' school alongside the boys' school. Before that happened a local movement had opened a girls' school in Bolton supported by Millicent Fawcett, which probably became the first intake of the new school. Ironic then that in 1913 another suffragette, Edith Rigby, burned down one of Lord Leverhulme's residences on Rivington Pike in protest that he was dining with the king and not concentrating on bringing the plight and position of women in society to public attention.

On the Sunday night before my first day at Bolton School, my mum sat me down in a chair, put a pudding basin on my head, with her sharpest scissors, cut off any hair protruding from it. What a start. A true basin cut.

I was ten years old, a bit bewildered by the place, tall windows, parquet floors, long corridors and walking along them a teacher who took her Bedlington Terrier to every lesson. On my first day I could hardly wait for school to finish, because ever since I had found out that I would be going to the school I had been hatching a plan. There were two bus journeys involved in travel to and from my new school, from Walkden into Bolton and a short ride from Bolton to the school on Chorley New Road. I had heard that a place called Doffcocker Lodge was not far from the school and that great crested grebes could be seen there. This was a bird I was longing to see. It carried its chicks on its back, and it could dive under-water for as long as thirty seconds. Even though it was the wrong time of year for chicks I was determined to see these birds, and this was my big chance. I walked there, but when I arrived there were iron railings between me and the edge of the water. I climbed up, chucking my new school satchel over first, and as I jumped down there was a loud ripping noise. I had torn the back of my blazer on the sharp spikes. I saw the great crested grebes, managed to climb back, caught a bus back to Bolton and another one to Walkden.

Slowly, on the journey, the euphoria of seeing these precious birds was replaced with the dread of telling my parents what had happened. As I walked round the back of the house past the living room window, my mum rushed to meet me at the back door. She was worried by my crestfallen expression, and I turned to show her what I had done. She whipped off my blazer and smartly sewed it up. My dad, thankfully, never knew.

My uniform had been pricey and the blazer was by far the most expensive item of all. I little realised at the time that it was also a status symbol, with the school crest emblazoned on the pocket.

It was a shame, rips or no rips, I would only wear it for a year.

* * *

Bolton School, one of the oldest schools in Lancashire, stands within a large acreage of fields and woods. One of the joys of going there was this landscape: we could see wildflowers for ourselves, we could feel the bark of trees, see how their branches grew, watch their buds burst, pick up their leaves. We could take what we found indoors to examine, to draw and write about.

Even in my teenage years, when perhaps it wasn't cool to be interested in flora and fauna, I maintained a quiet passion for nature that would only become stronger and deeper. Miss Westhead at junior school had encouraged me, letting me run the nature table that made me as proud as can be. When I went to Bolton School, nature study was actually on the timetable. I could hardly believe it. Our teacher was Miss Growser – I thought rude girls in my class were making it up. They weren't, but Miss Growser was one of the kindest and most sensitive teachers ever. Most of our lessons were conducted outside.

But I didn't stay long at Bolton School. In his attempt to amass adequate capital for the television shop that he had always dreamed of owning, my father fell foul of a scam at his workplace, the Ministry of Pensions and National Insurance. In those days employers were required to buy a stamp each week for all those working for them. The stamps had to be bought from the post office or my dad's ministry, but one of my dad's colleagues had been cutting out the middleman and selling stamps at a reduced rate to local businesses, pocketing the proceeds. My father, having been refused a loan from his own father, could not resist the temptation and when propositioned, joined the scheme. When he had enough money to buy his little shop he left and after a couple of years of hard work and enterprise it had begun to take off. Right time, right place, wrong money. The authorities caught up with him and he was taken to court, found guilty and sentenced to a year in prison.

We were too young to understand any of the finer points. All we knew was that, out of the blue, we all travelled together with my dad to Butlin's in Pwllheli. One of his friends, Uncle Lyn, came too in his own car. Dad left after the weekend and we didn't see him again until we visited him in Preston Prison.

I can recall meeting marram grass in Pwllheli for the first time and discovering a kestrel's 'nest' perched on scrubby undergrowth on a precipitous escarpment on the sand dunes. I visited it secretly and told no one else. It helped. Although I knew that something was going on when he didn't return and that my mum seemed preoccupied, which was most unlike her, I mostly sensed a feeling of doom that my visits to these beautiful birds, here in front of me, getting on with their lives for real, not on the pages of a book, seemed to allay.

There was no realisation then of the bleak and difficult year ahead, especially for my mum, nor of the repercussions for my education later when, after a year at Bolton School, my father was summoned to the headmistress Miss Higginson's office to be told that I was no longer eligible for my scholarship place at the school since the catchment area had changed. He was furious, realising as the conversation progressed that this decision was linked to his prison term, although this was denied. He was also told that I could continue there if he paid the full fees. I was standing outside her study door but although I could hear raised voices, I had little idea of what was being said. Our exit with slamming of doors was rapid. So too was the drive home.

* * *

'My pa's car is a Jaguar and Pa drives rather fast.'

This sentence was one of those we were supposed to repeat out loud in unison during our assemblies at the next school I went to, Worsley Wardley Grammar School. There were others too but this is the one that sticks in my mind. My dad was probably one of the few dads of pupils in those assemblies who did drive a Jag, but the one that he drove was a Jag with an a as in apple and it didn't just go rather *farst* it went bloody *fast*, a as in apple again.

There were several attempts during the first couple of years the school was open to replace our mainly broad Lancashire accents with a BBC RP form of speech. All to no avail, thank goodness, although my mum wanted me to have elocution lessons, which I roundly refused. Once I was reprimanded by a teacher for pronouncing chair as churr and book as booook, being told it was 'common'.

I had heard posh accents. Long before I went to secondary school and before my dad's dreams of having a television shop came true, we had a television in our living room. Here were people who spoke the Queen's English, whether it was *What's My Line?* or the news. I realised that people spoke differently but wasn't quite aware then what those differences denoted. Nevertheless, I had an emerging sense of class consciousness.

It was probably during a French exchange that realisations about class differences really began to sink in. My exchange partner was the daughter of a doctor. The family were well-to-do, bourgeois to a T. I did my best to fit in but Madame did not approve of me nor did Catherine, my exchange partner, although I got on fine with her sister and her father. We had dinner, a proper sit-down, three-course dinner, and there was even a servant. When we were taken to the circus one evening, it felt like freedom at last just going outside and meeting a few of the other folk participating in the exchange. I wore my best clothes, a new dress, turquoise gingham with broad straps and a little semi-circular insert at the front which was white and pleated. It had a full skirt and a tight waist. Over it I wore a fluffy apricot mohair cardigan which, it being a hot summer's evening in a stuffy big top, I attempted to take off but was prevented from doing by admonishments from Madame.

I got into much more trouble when in the second week of my stay we were taken to the family's seaside home at La Baule in Brittany which was run by Madame's mother. Everything was fine until on the second day, whilst swimming and sunbathing on the beach, we were approached by a couple of lads. It turned out they were sailors and one of them wanted to take me out that evening. It was a festival day, *une fête*, and there would be lots happening. Mr Moulton's French lessons had not prepared me for such a scenario. I of course declined but at the end of the afternoon Yves and his friend walked us back and that evening he climbed up to the balcony of my room – good job it wasn't Grandma's – and we both climbed down to the street below. We had a lovely evening, but on my return, Grandma was waiting on the doorstep. I was persona non grata, confined to quarters for the rest of the trip. My French was much improved though.

Catherine had visited my home prior to this. She was somewhat shy but also, I immediately felt, disapproving. It was not until I returned *chez elle* that I understood why.

I was also made to do Latin at school, do being the operative word – it would be a lie to say I *studied* Latin. When I came to take it as an O level subject, I failed but only just, so I retook it, getting five marks less than the first time. I retook it and got five marks less again. Lizzie Lowe, my Latin teacher, suggested I give up. Perhaps I couldn't see the relevance of translating stories about Trojan travellers or conjugating verbs that were no longer spoken.

She was a very special woman, Lizzie Lowe, tiny, with six-inch heels to make up for it, tottering up and down the parquet corridors of Worsley Wardley Grammar. She always wore a black gown, as did her friend and colleague Mr Cowgill. They reminded me of a couple of bats, their gowns flapping gently as they glided towards the staff room. They once saved me from getting expelled, my sentence being transmuted to a fortnight's suspension. Being in Lizzie's class also introduced me to twin brothers, John and Paul Jackson, who later became my best friends.

Virgil's *Aeneid* never managed to hold my attention, but I use Latin every day now in plant names and find it fascinating; it's intriguing, for example, to learn that *mollis* means soft, as in *Alchemilla mollis*. I can feel the velvety texture of those round leaves with their gently scalloped edges and see raindrops collected in their centres, glistening and glimmering.

* * *

To get to Worsley Wardley Grammar School, we travelled on the trolleybus, what we'd now call a tram. Just down the road from our new school was a pit, a coal mine, and many of the miners from Walkden travelled to and from work on the same trolleybus as us. Though they had changed clothes and had baths after their shift at the pit, they invariably had a residue of coal dust around their eyes like kohl or mascara. This made their eyes, especially when they were blue eyes, look bright, almost brilliantly coloured. Most would laugh and joke on their way to and from work and they would all call each other love.

Many years later, when I went to Bolton College of Art, one of our teachers, Tony Roberts, arranged a visit to a coal mine. It was eye-opening, to travel deep down through the earth in a lift, journey through broad tunnels and talk to men on their knees and up to their knees in water, picking away at the coal face for a whole shift. It was hot and airless. All this was happening underneath our feet every day and I had never had a clue about the journey that the coal that the coalman carried on his back in big, dirty sacks, that fed our fires and kept us warm, had made, how it had got to our coal shed.

You could never forget the mines and the heavy industry that surrounded us. When we'd travel into Manchester, sometimes the smog was so dense you could only see a few yards in front of you.

I was keen to get out in the world, and having done a term in the sixth form I gave up and went straight to work, much to the disappointment of my dad, who had already plotted my future academic career, probably studying languages and fulfilling his own envisaged career course, curtailed when he left Manchester Grammar School at the age of sixteen, after his father cut off the ends of the fingers of one hand with a circular saw. However he felt about school, when his father had this dreadful accident, he left and got a job. He also bought himself a motorbike. As I understand it, his first job was in Leeds and he would have travelled back to Manchester every weekend. Reading between the lines, I think he might have been a bit of a tearaway. My grandma told all sorts of tales about his escapades including the story of her going into his room on a Saturday morning and not recognising him.

He had come off his bike and gone flying through a hawthorn hedge, scratching his face very badly. It was one of several accidents: he had some terrible luck.

* * *

On the whole I enjoyed grammar school for the first four years. I loved English, French and art best. I was lucky and had brilliant teachers who encouraged me and made their subjects seem relevant to me. I was not so hot at history or geography or science, nor maths or Latin. I might have done reasonably well at biology but was never allowed to study it. Because it was a new school, still with a limited intake, options were limited and art and biology could not be combined.

I was hopeless at learning facts for their own sake. I have never been able to learn lines and would have been stumped if my television 'career' had depended on learning lines and scripts. If I understand something and find it interesting and worth passing on and there is the possibility of inspiring others with my enthusiasm, that is what I love.

Although it might be difficult to imagine now, I was good at sport. I was on the school hockey team (left wing, of course) and captain of the rounders team, but it was athletics I was really keen on. I was a fast sprinter, a good hurdler and did well at high jump and long jump. Hilda Clough was my teacher; she was young, pleasant and pretty and encouraged me to train and take sport seriously. Over quite a long period you would have found me doing circuit training in the gym every lunchtime.

My dad was thrilled I could run fast. For my eleventh birthday he had bought me a pair of football boots. As a recognition of my prowess in athletics, the next year he bought me some spikes. The few kids who were lucky enough to own spikes had red and white, blue and white or white with stripes. My dad knew a bloke who had a small factory that produced spikes, amongst other types of footwear. I was presented with the box and opened it agog – the spikes he had bought me were black all over. I tried to hide my disappointment, convinced that 'proper' spikes would have made me run faster. There was a similar storyline when it came to tracksuits. Again, only a few kids had tracksuits – probably the same kids who had spikes. They would be all one colour, blue or red. For example, John Craggs, the only boy I ever fancied at school, who looked as though he would become an airline pilot and did, was a good athlete. He had a blue tracksuit and spikes to match. My parents had found a second-hand tracksuit, my size, maroon with a white piece on the front. My mum washed it and you guessed it, it ended up as a two-tone maroon tracksuit. Although I always took it to school I never wore it. Nowadays it would have been the source of all sorts of bullying posts on social media. How ungrateful I was – we didn't have loads of money, they did their best, they just wanted to support and encourage me.

It didn't slow me down, though. When I won the Victrix Ludorum at school sports day for the third consecutive year, the rules stated that I was allowed to keep the cup. But this was a new school that couldn't afford to buy new trophies. My dad was furious and made an enormous fuss about it. I was happy to keep the cup for another year then give it back. For me it was the taking part that was important – but the winning that really mattered!

I, meanwhile, had passed 5 O levels. It was a new school, we were only the second year of intake, and it was decreed that, to establish the school's academic credentials as quickly as possible, one class would be entered for O levels after just four years.

My birthday is at the end of June, so I was fourteen when I took most of my exams. I can remember doodling down the edge of my geography paper and answering a question about why the Yangtze River flooded from time to time by saying perhaps it was because it rained a lot. I wrote poems in the margin of my physics with chemistry and was once again flummoxed by Latin.

But in the subjects that I loved, namely English lang and lit, French and art, I did quite well, even getting a decent grade in maths. Later, when results were out, my maths teacher Mr Jones, who was also my form teacher, observed that perhaps they had got me mixed up and had marked the wrong paper.

After one maths exam we were allowed out onto the playing field, where I studied wildflowers around the perimeter and lit a cigarette. All too promptly we were summoned back to school to tidy up, grab our things and go home. Thinking Mr Jones had already left I went into our classroom, cigarette in hand, but no sooner had I reached my desk, which was at the back of the class, naturally, than I heard his footsteps approaching – he must have forgotten something. Without a moment's hesitation I opened the lid of my desk and dropped in the cigarette, trying to disperse the smoke with my other hand. I might have got away with it; Mr Jones was halfway out of the door again when Carol Siddall, whose desk was at the front of the class, shouted loudly, 'What's on fire?' Mr Jones turned back, the cigarette and a few smouldering papers were extinguished and you can imagine the rest.

One way or another I had often been in trouble at school. It wasn't that I was rude or unruly, more that I often deviated from the straight and narrow. First thing in the morning we had to walk right round the building to the playgrounds and though the school was co-educational there was a girls' playground and a boys'. I would usually end up, weather permitting, on the boys' side playing three card brag until the bell went. I have always tended to be on the late side though and had honed to a fine art the skill of sneaking in the front way. One Monday morning I was doing just that and sidling in past the aquarium in the entrance hall when I came face to face, through the glass and angel fish, with my head-master, Mr Smith. Sinking feeling. He ordered me to his study where I joined a small group of girls already assembled. Together we were then ushered into his office and lined up in front of his desk. He had decided that I was the ringleader; however, we would all share the same punishment. He pronounced the sentence for the crime we had committed two days previously. We were being suspended from school for a fortnight. We should not get the idea that this was an excuse for a holiday – it was an opportunity to repent and to think carefully about the seriousness of what we had done. Whilst we were doing so, we had all been set work in each of our academic subjects which it was thought by our various teachers would take us a fortnight to complete. We should think ourselves lucky since this was a remission of the original judgement which had been expulsion.

Our crime had been reported by the head girl, Doreen Cardus, and had been committed on the previous Saturday night.

Several of us had volunteered to take part in a school produc-tion of *H.M.S. Pinafore*. It was being organised by Wilf Mannion, the music teacher, and though after my hymn singing I wouldn't have been allowed anywhere near the music room, my friend Chris Knowles was there frequently, partly to flirt with Mr Mannion. As a favour to him and her we had agreed to form part of the chorus. During the weeks leading up to the performance we were fitted out with costumes, probably designed and sewn by the domestic science department, which was another area where I was persona non grata. We had long dresses with puffed sleeves and bonnets. Since we were doing this as a favour, we were determined to have a laugh. On the way up to school that Saturday evening (we were all in civvies), we called in at the Morning Star, a pub just down the road from our school, with empty flagon bottles and got them filled. Our organisation and planning was faultless. We had all clubbed together for the beer but the two buying it were the ones who looked oldest, whilst the rest waited outside. Between us we had acquired several packets of cigarettes and matches. Whilst getting changed we stashed our beer in the loos close to the gym and furthest from the hall where the audience and cast would gather. We secreted cigarettes and matches in our puff sleeves, where the matches added an extra percussive element to our rendition of 'Over the Bright Blue Sea'.

During the interval we dashed up the corridor in the opposite direction to everyone else, dived into the toilets and, comfortably seated on the floor, passed round the bottles and lit up. A few minutes later, the door onto the corridor opened, and in walked our head girl, who incidentally had one of the leading roles in the production and come to think of it was the captain of the school hockey team, with her older sister. At first speechless, she soon found her voice, insisting we stop what we were doing immediately. With a sinking feeling I took a last drag of my fag and asked her if she would be reporting us, emphasising that this was really our own time and that after all we weren't in school uniform.

All in vain. The next Monday after our sentencing, we left the premises straight away, but by the time we reached the bus stop we had come up with a comprehensive plan for the next fortnight. We all came back to my house where my mum, hoovering and doing the washing at the same time – it was Monday – was surprised to see us filing past the living room window There were no reprimands, just an 'Oh Carol'. When my dad returned at dinner (lunch) time he had much more to say. We girls held a summit in the front room, which was never used. We would divide the work between us, each concentrating on the subjects we were best at. By Thursday everything was finished and reallocated. Some essays and notes would need to be copied in the correct writing but basically we were free. For the rest of our suspended sentence we organised trips to Manchester, having a high old time wandering around the shops and drinking coffees that had to last all morning.

If I wasn't playing brag with some of my mates, I would often sit down leaning against a wall in the girls' playground and read a book. Sometimes it was a library book, sometimes a set book from our English syllabus – I loved English and Harry Liptrot, our English teacher. It might even have been poetry; Keats was my favourite. One day, several shadows loomed towards me and I looked up to see that I had been surrounded by all the girls in my class. 'What do you want?' I enquired. There was no reply but in unison they all began to tickle me. Completely taken aback at first, I soon regained my bearings and started to punch and kick, quite difficult and ungainly when you are seated. Gradually I staggered to my feet and continued with the counter-attack until they all fled. Who knows why they felt the need to attack me, if you can call a sustained mass tickling an attack. I was probably unbearable.

One of them, Elaine Potter-Smith, lived at Roe Green where the twins John and Paul Jackson and several of my other friends lived. I confess to using Elaine shamelessly, going off on my bike purportedly to do homework at her house and instead riding across the green to Glen Avenue to meet up and go to Charlie's. Charlie's was a very important part of my life at that time and off and on for a few years afterwards. It was a shed in Charlie McPhee's back garden, but he had converted it gradually into a hideaway for local kids, mainly boys. I was probably the only person who wasn't quite local – I had to ride my bike from Manchester Road a mile away. But my credentials were guaranteed by John and Paul.

As you entered the shed, on your right was a cupboard where Charlie's stock of records, playing cards and cigarettes was kept. The records were mainly EPs and on top of the cupboard was a deck where he would play them and a kettle where he would make tea and coffee. Everything was a penny: a tea, a coffee, a matchstick or a cigarette. There was always a plentiful supply of pennies which came in useful for the main activity – gambling.

Around the rest of the shed were low benches flush to the wall and in the centre an upturned bucket with a square of plywood with its corners cut off. Presumably that was to make it slightly easier to get in and out of what was a very cramped space. In the main we played three card brag though occasionally we would play a few games of pontoon. Several of the boys would play rummy and poker but I was no good at either of them. We played with matchsticks, which we had to purchase from Charlie. To avoid confusion and prevent cheating nobody was allowed to bring their own matches into the shed. If you bought a cigarette, Park Drive or Woodbine, Charlie had to light it unless Jimmy Deakin was there. He was already working and had a lighter.

Music was played constantly, Buddy Holly, The Big Bopper, Little Richard, Chuck Berry, Jerry Lee Lewis and Elvis, of course.

We were a motley crew but enjoyed each other's company. Although Charlie's shed was our headquarters, in the summer months we moved operations outside. At the end of Glen Avenue was a big piece of open ground and at the end of it a railway embankment. To the left was a big chunk of woodland and beyond that more open ground. Beyond that was the East Lancs Road, at that time the main thoroughfare between Manchester and Liverpool.

As far as we were concerned this was our land, our meeting place, our playground. Hide and seek is usually associated with young children but we had our own version of it. Having congregated on the field in dribs and drabs, sitting together on a collection of logs and abandoned furniture, we would divide ourselves into two groups. There were never any leaders, no one person in charge – it was a kind of organic democracy. One group would go off and hide, they would be given ten minutes to do so, then the other group would seek. When you were caught you would join the seeking group. This gave added frisson to the chase in that it meant not only did you have to hide from the seekers, but also from fellow hiders in case they were caught. Including the woods, there must have been five or six acres in which to hide. Sometimes it would take an hour until everyone was found. On a couple of occasions the last person was not found and a truce was declared, but if you were the yet to be discovered one, you would only emerge if everyone in the seeking group called – otherwise it might be a cunning trick.

One of the best aspects of this game was that there were not really any winners or, more importantly, any losers. It was thrilling, especially trying to find somewhere to hide that nobody else would think of. I can remember my heart thumping as voices approached, or hiding under old grass or branches and watching shoes and ankles inches from my face. Sometimes I would be looking down through the branches of a tree, trying to hold my breath and keep absolutely still.

These trees were ours. Towards the field side of the wood was 'the canyon', a deep gulley with a stream running through it. On the lowest branch of the biggest tree spanning the canyon was a rope swing. It was just a thick rope securely tied to the branch above and had a huge knot on which you sat when you had taken off after a rapid run across the bank. The object was to go so fast and so strongly that you reached the other side where you would leap off. This was the only game I have ever played that scared me so much that sometimes I could not bring myself to participate and became an onlooker. I fell off once and it hurt. What was more painful though was when I broke my arm just a few yards further on from the tree with the swing.

John and Paul Jackson were twins, fraternal, not identical. They were both handsome, with dark hair and tawny skin and dark brown eyes, but they looked quite different from one another. Their temperaments were different too. Paul was academically gifted but not very worldly. He was an ambling, shambling sort of boy, partly due to his poor eyesight. He often wore a mucky, light-coloured mack like a latter-day Columbo, or perhaps it was the other way round. He wore glasses but later tried contact lenses – we spent an hour and a half one Christmas Eve searching for one of his contact lenses through fallen snow by the no. 12 bus stop outside Green's chip shop. John was an affable lad, always friendly, always smiling. He always looked after Paul.

On this occasion I was leading them both into the woods. I think I was supposed to be taking them to meet some of the others and I was the only one who knew just where they were. I dashed ahead, keen to show I knew where we were going, when I stumbled over a tree root, crashing to the ground with my left arm under-neath me. Stunned, I got to my feet, assisted by my two friends, intent on continuing, then coming to a halt. We all knew I had done something serious. They took me back through the field, me clutching my left arm with my right hand trying to support it, to the house of a neighbour who it was believed locally was the font of all medical knowledge. We all went in. He insisted that I take my right hand away which I did only under extreme duress. It was as though my arm had developed an extra elbow. Very rapidly I replaced the support and turned so pale they felt it imperative to phone home. Fortunately my dad was in and drove straight down and took me to Salford Royal Infirmary where I was X-rayed and plastered up. Both bones, the radius and the ulna, were broken, but the good news was that they were 'nice clean breaks'. Unfortunately I had an 'idle ulna' which meant that weeks later, after another X-ray, they broke my arm again and reset it. I have no idea of whether or not it healed, though the radius did – I just have a big bump on my arm. I wonder if it would be classed as a distinguishing feature.

Sadly this unforeseen event put paid for the time being to the Roe Green part of my life. I couldn't ride my bike and I wouldn't have been able to hold my cards or chuck in the matchsticks if I had a winning hand. Despite tripping over a root and temporarily calling a halt to my social life, I have always loved trees.

The Roe Green experience was a way to escape and find freedom, to do what I wanted to do even though, or perhaps because, it was frowned upon. Like so much teenage behaviour and so many teenage activities, it was a rebellion and yet a necessity to conform to the mores of my peers. It was innocent enough, and despite having identical hormonal issues, being a teenager then presented few of the challenges that are faced today by our counterparts.

We were lucky too in some ways that the whole concept of 'the teenager' was gradually becoming recognised, though not necessarily with approval from adult society.

Sometimes there were specific acts of defiance. Although I had got on well with my dad whilst I had been fulfilling his ideals of what I should be, being a good footballer, an athlete, a keen and attentive student, our relationship changed for the worse once I entered my teenage years. I must have been difficult to live with. There was little give and take and never any discussion about how I felt or of any of the problems I was encountering. It is easy to feel lost in those circumstances.

Perhaps as a cry for help, but also because of a feeling of rejection by my peers, on one occasion at a friend's house where we had gathered as an alternative to Charlie's because the parents were away, I went into the bathroom and helped myself to a large quantity of codeine tablets. Although this is a prescription-only medication now, it was the go-to painkiller for headaches and even hangovers in the fifties and sixties. I didn't tell anyone, and half an hour later rode my bike home and went to bed. I didn't sleep and as the night wore on the thumping in my head grew louder, I began to see more and more flashing lights, and I became more and more intent on not dying. It was not a question of wanting to live – I just knew I didn't want to die.

I was so relieved to feel the day getting lighter, to hear the first blast of the mill hooter to tell everyone to get up, the second to tell them to get a move on. I could hear clogs on the pavement as people hurried to work.

My mum came in to wake me up and I told her what I had done. She dashed to tell my dad, who was always the last to get up. He had grabbed his trousers and appeared at the door.

'Get up,' he said. 'Get up and go to school.'

He must have been shocked, confused, terrified. There was no way I could have got up. My mum phoned our lovely Irish doctor Sean Gill, who appeared soon afterwards, looked me over and declared that if I had got through the night, there was nothing much to be done. He stayed talking with me in his soft and soothing Irish brogue whilst my mum got the boys off to school. She joined us, bringing him a cup of tea, and we carried on talking. Dr Gill did most of the talking, as he usually did. Not only did he have the kindest voice but also the kindest face. He was handsome too, though it is with hindsight that I remember that. He suggested I stay in bed and maybe have a few days off school. I read a bit and eventually my mum acceded to my request to let me paint a picture. She didn't criticise or cross-examine me though she must have been full of questions.

I remember the painting: it was all exercised in a sort of cubist fashion, heavily stylised with a central figure, a man, falling through the picture with stalactite forms pressing in from the edges.

After a few days I was deemed well enough to go back to school. There was a terrible sense of shame hanging around, even though it is not certain that anyone at school knew what had gone on. It was probably just in my head, but that didn't make it any easier.

Trees

Everyone has a favourite sort of wild place. For my mum it was a mountain top. She loved feeling the wind in her hair and the sun on her face. She was connected to the openness, in tune with the freedom of it. We were very different people; for me it is the magic, the mystery of woodland to which I feel akin, that silence that is only broken when the twigs snap underneath your feet, the smell of moss and the very earth itself. Sometimes you can smell deer and see where they have broken through the tangle of fallen branches and the tangled honeysuckle that festoons them, to feast on the lichen or the bark of trees.

Woods are secret places where anything is imaginable. Every wood has its own presence.

Very few of us go out to the garden centre or nursery specifically to choose a tree or shrub for its bark. We tend to be more interested in its foliage, its flowers and its fruit. Perhaps we are looking for a particular shape, something columnar that won't take up too much room, or the opposite, something that will spread its branches overhead so we can sit in its shade on hot summer days. It is strange that we give little thought to what lies underneath leaves and flowers, the bark, branches and stems, even though in the case of deciduous plants, for at least half the year, that is what we see.

Visit a garden that is open during the winter and for sure parts of it will major on stems, trunks and bark. Not only can they be breathtakingly beautiful in their own right, but they also act as a foil for the first flowers of the year, carpets of snowdrops, twinkling winter aconites and hellebores.

They mix well with the first flowering shrubs, daphnes, witch hazels, winter jasmine and viburnums. Woody plants give structure and interest and in many cases vivid colour and rich texture.

Highly coloured twigs are at a premium during the winter. If you can offer it a sheltered spot (it doesn't mind cold but it hates dry winds and scorching sun, as do all *Acer palmatum* varieties), *Acer palmatum* 'Senkaki' is a glorious example of these delightful Japanese trees. Its common name, coral-bark maple, describes it perfectly; its young twigs and branches are bright eye-catching pink. In autumn its leaves take on lovely amber yellow hues. *Acer capillipes*, the snakebark maple, and *Acer pensylvanicum* both have exciting bark. The bark of *Acer griseum* is quite different. This is the paperbark maple, beloved for its shaggy trunk, the tissue-thin top layer of its bark constantly peeling.

White stems are particularly noticeable during winter in contrast against dark dreary soil. Many of the ornamental brambles are superb during winter. Both *Rubus cockburnianus* and *Rubus thibetanus* have handsome purple-red stems white-washed to give an almost ghostly appearance. For a dramatic planting in a dark, inauspicious corner, their white stems complement the huge, sharp, silver arching leaves of *Astelia nervosa*. You need plenty of room for the rubus though.

Stems form light frameworks and structures through the winter garden but trunks make more substantial statements.

Our own silver birch, *Betula pendula*, is hard to beat. Its pale trunks are a striking feature in the winter landscape. For those who want something even more dramatic, some forms of *Betula jacquemontii* have such white bark that gardeners have been known to give it a regular scrub down to maintain its sparkling stems.

Forms of *Cornus alba* are renowned for their crimson winter stems. Plant them where they will catch the winter sunshine. There are numerous selections of this straightforward Asiatic shrub, some with variegated leaves which give them great summer interest too. The foliage of *Cornus alba* 'Elegantissima' is broadly splashed with white, sometimes tinged with pink. *Cornus alba* 'Spaethii' is an outstanding form with strong yellow variegation.

Any of these cultivars make a first-rate background for snow-drops or winter aconites. *Cornus alba* will tolerate wet or dry conditions, but if you've got really wet ground the North American species *Cornus stolonifera* revels in damp conditions. It too has dark red stems except in one version. The new stems of *Cornus stolonifera* 'Flaviramea' and 'White Gold' are bright yellow-green. These cornus form the backbone of many a winter garden. They are reliable and easy and look good planted together.

Our own common dogwood, *Cornus sanguinea*, has coloured stems. Though they are not so remarkably red as those of the American and Chinese species, *Cornus sanguinea* does very well on thin, dry, chalky soil and its autumn colour is second to none. You see it planted on motorway embankments in Wiltshire, Hampshire and other counties where chalky soil predominates and it creates a spectacular autumn scene.

There is a very beautiful version of this which comes into its own now, called *Cornus sanguinea* 'Midwinter Fire'. It is a twiggy, dense small shrub with brilliant orange stems. Planted with chion-odoxa or any of the early bright blue bulbs around its base the colour is emphasised even more.

Arbutus unedo, the strawberry tree, has rich, chestnut-coloured bark which also peels away. This lovely tree is finding the climate more to its liking. It produces delightful urn-shaped flowers and fruit reminiscent of strawberries amongst its dark, glossy green leaves. Its ability to withstand coastal gales makes it a perfect maritime tree.

Stewartias are seldom seen in the UK yet they are some of the most beautiful of trees. As well as flaking bark, an elegant profile and rich autumn colour, they have the asset of sumptuous white flowers during high summer. Related to camellias, they thrive on good loamy soil and dislike lime.

If you only have room for one trunk in your garden then perhaps *Prunus serrula* has the most outstanding bark of all. Its high polish and rich chestnut colour make it a focal point wherever it is, especially in midwinter.

Gardeners with small plots sometimes feel there isn't enough room for a tree. Although planting a small tree in your garden won't do much to offset carbon emissions, every little helps and it will have several benefits both for gardeners and wildlife. If it is well chosen and properly planted it should last a long time, becoming a central character, a focal point – especially in a small garden.

Deciduous trees are calendars: one glimpse and its branches will indicate just where the year has reached, full of spring promise with new buds and impending blossom, celebrating the autumn cavalcade clothed in rich reds and oranges or in stark silhouette against a caerulean winter sky.

As it grows and burgeons it will set the tone for the rest of the garden, probably becoming the most dominant feature – so it has to be the right tree.

As with any plant it must fit happily into the site you have chosen, so it must feel at home in both soil and situation; at the same time, aesthetically it must be just what you want. Most trees offered for sale are going to be ornamental, but before you decide it pays to do some detective work. Visit gardens where small trees are a feature, RHS gardens or National Garden Scheme gardens, National Trust properties or even your local park, to get a feel for trees you like, and if possible look at them at different times of year to see them in their seasonal garb. Identify what type of soil you have. Is it acid or alkaline? Is it heavy wet clay or thin and free-draining? It's not as fraught as it might first appear. The majority of trees are reasonably accommodating and will thrive in most gardens. If you have extreme conditions – boggy soil, or an exposed coastal site – it is worth consulting a good book with lists of trees for special conditions. The one to which I constantly refer is *The Hillier Manual of Trees and Shrubs*, with major input from my favourite tree guru, the best there is, Roy Lancaster.

Make sure your tree is versatile. Look for a species or cultivar that will afford more than one season of interest – perhaps spring blossom and autumn colour. Think about when it will feature most prominently in your garden. If you are out there during the winter or have a good view from the kitchen window, textured or highly coloured bark could play an important role.

Crab apples are the most often recommended of small-garden trees. All are laden with apple-blossom in April and May followed in the autumn by arresting edible fruit. It needs cooking but is high in pectin, just the job combined with blackberries in jam or jelly. *Malus* 'John Downie' has been around more than a hundred years but is still arguably the best, with typical coral and cream shiny crab apples. There are cultivars with cherry red fruit too – *Malus* 'Red Jade' is exceptional and its weeping habit makes it ideal in a small garden.

The mountain ash or rowan is a big family of trees and includes several species suitable for small spaces. Quite unique is *Sorbus cashmiriana*, with a pretty, even habit, pale pink frothy flowers in May and pendulous bunches of white fruit which last deep into the winter. *Sorbus* 'Joseph Rock' is renowned for its rich autumn colour and pale yellow fruit which becomes deep amber yellow and lasts far longer than the foliage.

From North America, *Amelanchier lamarckii* is a bushy shrub or small tree, easy to grow and a delight in early spring with cascades of white flower. In autumn, leaves turn to pinks, oranges and reds. Bone hardy and easy to cultivate, amelanchiers will grow in part shade or out in the open. They prefer neutral or acid soil.

Trees that blossom in late summer are few and far between. *Eucryphia glutinosa* has delightful pure white flowers, unexpectedly showy at 6cm across with a fuzz of stamens and anthers. Most of the genus are evergreen but this one is deciduous with glorious autumn tints.

Japanese acers are hugely popular but sometimes difficult to incorporate into informal planting schemes. There are other small acers that might fit in more naturally, including several with highly textured bark. It's difficult to keep your hands off the peeling cinnamon bark of *Acer griseum*, the paperbark maple. The snake-bark maple, *Acer davidii*, is equally tactile, with its green and white striated trunk.

Cercidiphyllum japonicum or katsura is one of the most enchanting of all trees, and one of the most ancient. Pink-bronze in the spring, its simple round leaves take on a kaleidoscope of colour in a good autumn, from creamy yellow to pinks and oranges, and on cold mornings emit a delicious toffee-apple aroma. After hundreds of years it can become a big tree but there are numerous cultivars and selections suitable for a smaller garden. *Cercidiphyllum japonicum* 'Rotfuchs' is a narrow fastigiate cultivar with dark crimson leaves. A new selection *C. j.* 'Heronswood Globe' makes a spherical shape and is slow growing.

Cercidiphyllum takes its name from *Cercis siliquastrum*, or 'Judas tree'. At Glebe Cottage we have one that my mum grew from seed. It's getting old now but when it finally gives up the ghost it will be replaced by one of the baby *Cercis* we grew from seed given to me by kind friends.

Chapter Five

When I first left school, I wanted to go to Manchester College of Art and Design. I was only fifteen, a year too young, and anyway my dad was all against such an idea. I worked at Kendal Milne, Manchester's answer to Harrods, hoping to get into window-dressing which I thought might have something to do with art. Instead I sold first buttons and then hosiery – which consisted of 'nylons', this being before the revolutionary introduction of tights. What a liberating product they were, no more suspender belts. This was 1960, it wouldn't be until five years later that mini-skirts burst on the scene and tights became an essential, especially if your legs weren't as good as Twiggy's, or the weather was cold.

On Saturday nights, I loved to go into Manchester. On one such evening, it was so smoggy that the bus conductor had to get off the bus and walk alongside the cab on the edge of the pavement so the driver could tell where to steer. It was senseless to leave the house on a night like that but there was no way I was going to miss going out on a Saturday night. I was probably headed for Amigos Coffee Bar where I would meet up with friends, especially boyfriends, and drink coffee from Arcoroc glass cups.

I would sometimes help out drying up in the kitchen there mainly to earn the bus fare home. Mrs Bridges, a small Salford woman wrapped in a printed cotton pinny, with steely permed hair and a dearth of teeth, was in charge of washing up and showed me the ropes. I never saw her without a huge stack of glass saucers and a tea towel. She would wipe the top one then move it to the bottom of the pile in one fluid movement. It seemed eternal, as though she would never get to the end of it.

The wage at Kendal Milne was £3 per week, paid in a brown envelope at the end of the week. By the time I had paid my bus fares and bought a few cigarettes and some lunch there wasn't much left. I supplemented my income occasionally by choosing horses for my friend Azzy, a graphic designer with a penchant for gambling and the blues. Occasionally I'd go for a drink with him at the Shambles, just up the road from Kendal Milne. Azzy was always studying form. One day he asked me to choose four horses. I did, he put them on an accumulator and they won. Instead of passing on some of the winnings he gave me some of his treasured LPs, including records by Little Richard, Muddy Waters and Bessie Smith, which I kept until we came here to Glebe Cottage. They were ruined by damp when we left them in the extension our predecessor built tagged on to the end of our cottage, presumably to increase the value of the property. Perhaps built is not the word. If the floor was swept vigorously, it would lift and you would be left with a pile of sand.

On account of my low wages, I was still dependent on my dad financially, but now I sought my independence. There had been several occasions in my early teenage years when he took a strap to my legs to punish me for wrongdoings. He kept the 'straps', a couple of leather belts, in a drawer in 'the cocktail cabinet'. Since there were two of them he must have chosen his weapon. It can't have been easy; since his road accident, his mobility was much reduced. He managed. On one occasion when I was fifteen, I must have answered back in a particularly rebellious way. He angrily went to the drawer, took out a strap and headed for me. I grabbed the belt, there was a tussle but I managed to take it from him and throw it on the fire. Before anyone could move, I dashed to the drawer, took out the other belt and threw that on too. They didn't burn in a dramatic Hollywood way, but this act symbolised my rejection of his power over me, and more importantly established my independence.

I particularly recall one New Year's Eve, when there was a dance at Roe Green. I love dancing, and one of my few regrets is that I haven't done more of it. My gang from Charlie's were determined to get in on the celebrations. We went down the road first to the Cock, the closest pub, and managed to get served, all dolled up for our night out. John and Paul always looked older than they were. We returned to the dance and stayed until we had seen the new year in. I was supposed to be home by 10.30 p.m.! In gallant style, John and Paul walked me home. We laughed and joked and told silly stories, but as we got to the top of Cow Lane we could see headlights. It was my mum and dad all dressed up from their New Year's Eve night out, who had come home to discover I wasn't there and had come out to try and find me. My dad gave my companions short shrift and ordered me into the car. When we reached home I was told to go to bed, but my father could not contain his fury – he had been disobeyed again. He followed me up the stairs with my mum in swift pursuit and smacked me hard on the face and then tried to hit me some more. He was drunk, my mum was less so. She got in between us and tried to stop him. It was like a scene from another Jean-Luc Godard movie. No further blows hit their target and everyone went to bed.

It was rare that my dad resorted to violence but it did happen, and I don't think he ever felt any remorse. When we were young, I was perhaps seven and my brother Bill five or six, we were woken on several occasions by shouting downstairs and hearing my father hit my mother. We sat together on the top of the stairs wondering what to do, and whether or not to do anything. Here were the people who told you what was right and wrong and yet one of them was hitting the other.

On one occasion on holiday in Betws-y-Coed our family group was walking down the lane, straddling it from side to side. I was eight or nine, never a quiet child, and perhaps, being very excited by the prospect of the day ahead, I was gabbling even more than usual. I was walking on the outside of the group next to my dad, who suddenly turned and dealt me an adult-sized smack on my head, knocking me into the ditch. When violence is done to you, the violence becomes yours.

I got out of the house as often as I could. As often as possible I would stay on in Manchester at Amigos. Sometimes we got invited to a party and I would extend the evening by saying yes. On one night, arriving at such a party I noticed that quite a few of the girls seemed excited. It was whispered that some lads from a group were there. I had heard of the Beatles but didn't know much about them. They had been playing at the Oasis Club just down the road from Amigos, I think. I would never have had enough money to go to a club. I got talking to one of them but the place was so crowded and the music was so loud that we repaired to the bathroom and sat in the bath to have the conversation. We talked about all sorts of things but mainly art. He was several years my senior but our chat was very much as equals. He had to go back to Liverpool; I had to go home. I didn't realise until later that year when their first 45

'Love Me Do' and 'P.S. I Love You' was released that I had shared a bath, albeit fully clothed, with someone so famous – John Lennon.

I became a big Beatles fan. On the day of the first moon landing I remember Bob Quick, who had been in my class when I studied at Brighton, bringing a Beatles LP (I think it was *Abbey Road*) round to the flat at the Angel I shared with my friend Joannie, and playing it continuously.

In the years after leaving school I had a series of jobs, each poorly paid, though Kendal Milne's was the lowest. One weekend, when I had just left one of these miserable jobs, still visiting Charlie's on occasions, a few of us were talking about getting away. By that time several of the boys had motorbikes. My dad loved cars, and speed, even having had a terrible motorcycle accident himself in addition to his car crash, and I must have inherited my love of bikes from him. On a few occasions previously my gang had gone up to the Lake District and camped not far from Ambleside, having the best time, paddling in streams pretending we might catch a fish or two, building fires, cooking on them (sausages rather than fresh trout), telling stories and drinking beer. They were lovely, innocent times.

This excursion was different, though: it was more about the motorbikes and heading for a destination, Kielder Castle. One of our gang, who shall remain nameless, had gone to the same school as me where he had gained a certain notoriety for allegedly blowing up the chemistry lab. His parents spoiled him but he was never anything but rude to them. He was not a pleasant person. He had a cruel mouth and was always putting other people down. There were three motorbikes when we set off. Nobody had any money and when his bike ran out of fuel halfway through the Lake District, he insisted that all the bikes be parked up and we continue to our destination by hitchhiking. I can't remember how we all kept track of one another, as there were no mobile phones, but somehow we all met up. Kielder Forest is the largest man-made forest in England, going on for more than 200 square miles. Once we were there, we realised there wasn't really a there, it was just endless forest. Our last lift had dropped us off at a Forestry Commission settlement. It was dark and late and all we wanted to do was go home. He hit on the idea of stealing one of the Land Rovers, the only vehicles around.

I don't have a criminal disposition and was against the idea but when they started up one of the Land Rovers and lights began to go on in the buildings nearby, I quickly got in the back and held tight. The idea was to 'borrow' it until we got close to a main road from where we could hitchhike. On approaching a main road, after driving pell-mell through forest lanes, we dumped the vehicle at the side of the road, scrambling out as fast as we could. We had got away with it, we thought.

When I returned home, my father decided since I had no job I could work for him. It was incredibly boring, taking payments from people for hire-purchase and rental for their television sets, occasionally selling a television, radio or electrical appliance, double entry book-keeping on a Saturday afternoon. My father was there as seldom as possible. The only alleviation to the crushing boredom was occasional interruptions by Johnny Wall, our engineer. He would travel around in a little grey mini-van repairing sets we had supplied or bringing them back to work on them in the garage-workshop behind our shop. Johnny was from Salford. He was short, though his bandy legs, a result of rickets in his childhood, made him even shorter than he would otherwise have been. He would regale me with Salford tales in his lovely Salford accent, subtly different from a Mancunian accent – rats running rampant round the River Irwell, going to bed hungry, bunking off school, making extra money lighting fires and fetching in fuel for Jewish families on Shabbat.

One Thursday afternoon, months after our Lake District adventure when my dad was in the shop for once, the bell went and I stepped out from the 'office' to serve. There stood a policeman. I told my dad and he invited him into the office. 'Are you Carol Higham?' he asked. 'What were you doing on the such and such of such and such?' 'I have no idea,' said I. He then told us that one of the lads on our trip had dropped his wallet with name, address and full personal details in the back of our escape vehicle. This despite my having been told off in no uncertain terms at the time for not thoroughly wiping my fingerprints off the tailgate of the Land Rover. Obviously he had spilled the beans and given a full list of everyone involved.

* * *

For two years I did a variety of jobs, from being a shop assistant to becoming a statistician at the British Insulated Callender's Cables near Wigan (Mr Jones, my ex-maths teacher, would have laughed – figures were never my strong suit). There were also many adventures, some of them repeatable – but those would be the boring ones. Throughout this time though I kept up with my artwork. I would draw and paint regularly, with help and encouragement from a friend, Richard Squires, who would check up on my progress from time to time. He encouraged me to try to get an interview at my local college of art in Bolton and take my work to show them.

This had to be undertaken surreptitiously. One day I smuggled out my art folder containing drawings and paintings I had completed during the two years since I had left school. It's difficult to hide a full-size portfolio but I managed it, jumped on the bus to Bolton, arrived at the college in Hilden Street unannounced but eventually was ushered into the principal's office and duly showed him my work. Even though their term had started two weeks previously, he gave me a place.

All I had to do then was break the news to my dad (my mum was informed straight away and was delighted). It was not until a month later that he discovered what was happening and though he never made it easy or encouraged me in any way, he accepted that at least I had had the initiative to go for it. Eventually the small grant they had decided I was entitled to arrived – but since I was living at home it went not to me but to my dad. He gave me five to ten shillings a day that was supposed to pay my bus fare and buy my lunch. By this time I was a seasoned smoker so lunch meant cigarettes. When I managed to save a few pence for a few days, a lunchtime trip to Yates's Wine Lodge with fellow students ensued. No doubt this resulted in more spontaneous expression during the afternoon.

More than anything, I loved to draw, and during this year I drew a lot. For our drawing class we had to go up the road to Bolton Technical College, as there wasn't enough room in the art college. This was the in-between year when art was about to be recognised as a degree subject and presumably the college had found itself having to provide a foundation year for the new degree course in addition to running the NDD – National Diploma in Design. Bolton Art College was the last in the country to maintain a junior school for thirteen- to sixteen-year-olds who showed a propensity for art. What a different mindset from so many modern governments, particularly Conservative governments where creative subjects not only play second fiddle to academia but are sometimes thought of as totally dispensable and banished.

Personalities play such a huge role in teacher–student relationships, and I will never forget the woman who taught us drawing. I may have forgotten her name but not her, nor what she taught me or got me to teach myself. Her teaching boosted my self-confidence and helped me believe in the validity of what I was doing. Not only was I thrilled that she liked my work, but I was pleased and happy that I liked it too. Isn't that what a teacher should give their pupils – a sense of self-worth, the feeling that they can contribute, and that whatever their contribution is, it is valid and welcomed?

There were new opportunities every day to learn and experiment, with paint and colour, with drawing and observing, and with lithography, grinding great stones in huge sinks to make flat surfaces and apply designs in tusche and print them.

Not only was there the opportunity to learn, to experiment, to express but there was also the chance to get to know other people. I made a lot of friends at college and invited a few of them home. My mum was keen to meet them, not so my dad. Most of my fellow students had come straight from school. In some ways I felt I had more street cred than them – after all I had been out to work for the previous two years. On the other hand they had stuck it at school and passed exams. We were a mixed bunch. Rick was a member of The Magic Circle and entertained us at our Christmas party, attired in top hat and tails and producing white doves from who knows where.

There were posh kids and working-class kids but almost without exception they lived at home. Two of my classmates, Ian and Rita, did not. They seemed older than the rest of us. Although they weren't romantically attached, they shared a flat which I was invited to a few times. It was dirty, the flat itself was furnished in a meagre way, nobody did the washing up and there was food in cupboards and ashtrays full of rollie dog-ends. These two were worldly wise. Ian was always ill. Later in the year they were both diagnosed with TB and sadly Ian later died of it.

There were two girls in my class I got on with very well, Loretta and Sylvia, and later on in the academic year we started to put a plan together for an adventure that would take us far away from Bolton.

Meanwhile, I got to know the place.

Directly behind the college the ground slopes down steeply to the Croal Valley. At the foot of the slope ran the Manchester Bolton & Bury Canal – though it didn't *run* because it was already derelict. You weren't aware of it from the road above but could get down to it quite easily. Although I love other people's company, especially if they are people I like, it is also good to be on your own. (That is one of the joys of gardening. It can be described as a solitary pursuit but sometimes that is its benefit.) In early summer I had scrambled down there one dinnertime and the whole place had turned blue. Thousands upon thousands of blue lupins were in full bloom. Who knows how they got there but their effect in the midst of Bolton's grime- and soot-stained buildings was a miracle of almost biblical extent.

Lupinus polyphyllus, the large-leaved lupine, is a North American plant with blue flowers that has become naturalised in numerous places in both hemispheres and classed as 'invasive' in some places. I do not know whether this is my Bolton lupin, but whatever its name, it was unforgettable. The power of plants in immeasurable numbers in the landscape is a reminder of whose planet this was and still is. I have been lucky enough to see it happening all over the world, from the grassy slopes above the Greek temples of Agrigento thick with *Anemone pavonina*, to the South African veldt in September, to home-grown oxe-eye daisies on road verges and motorway embankments and the blaze of red from the indefatigable corn poppy. Nature paints us such perfect pictures – how do we dare ignore them, or worse still destroy them? There is an element of poetic justice when a plant or a colony of plants take over a place. This is particularly true when they move in to industrial and man-made developments – lupins by the canal, primroses and cowslips on the embankments of motorways, verges and roundabouts smothered in wild carrot and oxe-eye daisies.

Lupins

The Romans introduced lupins to this country. They used them as food, both for themselves and their animals, and sowed them in vast quantities to plough back into the soil as green manure.

Plants from Europe and Asia were mentioned in the first English herbals and their cultivation in British gardens was recorded as early as the fifteenth century. The discovery of an exotic version, *Lupinus arboreus*, along the coast of California by Captain Vancouver's expedition in 1792 must have caused quite a stir.

The tree lupin is a woody evergreen shrub with compound palmate leaves and short racemes of pale yellow, delicately perfumed flowers. What excitement, bringing home the seeds. And imagine the amazement at their rate of growth.

Tree lupins compete seriously with Jack's beanstalk. Given the right conditions, seed sown in early spring will produce a plant up to 6ft tall, and as far across, in its first year. It bears such a wealth of flower that the foliage is almost invisible from early June until September. It is short-lived, but since new plants can be raised so easily this is neither here nor there.

Because of its instant stature, this is an ideal plant to fill in gaps in a shrub border or even amongst slow-going herbaceous plants.

The great advantage is that it fixes nitrogen in the soil, making it more rather than less fertile as it gets bigger.

In fact, the tree lupin will put up with almost anything as long as the ground isn't waterlogged. It is prone to snapping in richer conditions, but when grown hard it is pliable and strong and will bind sandy soil. It is happy at the seaside and can stand high degrees of salinity, which makes it useful as a glamorous windbreak.

Should the tree lupin exceed its designated boundaries and start to overshadow its neighbours, you can chop it back hard without causing permanent damage. This is amongst the most tolerant of plants.

Growing tips

The one single requirement of all tree lupins is sun. *Lupinus polyphyllus* and *L. nootkatensis*, both forerunners of our modern herbaceous varieties, will take some shade, but *L. arboreus* needs full light and open conditions.

When planting, the ground should be cultivated thoroughly but there is no need to add compost or rich food. A handful of organic bonemeal should be worked into the surface first unless you are vegetarian or vegan and, if the soil is heavy, dig in half a bucket of sharp grit or gravel.

To prolong flowering well into September, cut back spent flowers so that new shoots are produced on the side axles.

Propagation

Lupins are easy to grow from seed sown singly into small pots of loam-based seed compost. Young plants need to be potted on frequently – two or three times, or whenever their large, legumi-nous roots stick out of the pot.

Wait until they are at least a foot tall and wide before putting them out so that you get a good strong garden plant. If you buy one from a nursery don't leave it hanging about in a pot by the back door because it will deteriorate very quickly.

Good companions

Eryngiums, especially those with large blue bracts, look striking next to tree lupins – *Eryngium bourgatii*, *E. alpinum* or cultivars such as *E.* x *zabelii* 'Violetta'.

Green and cream-flowered sedum, such as 'Stewed Rhubarb Mountain' and *S. telephium* subsp *maximum* 'Gooseberry Fool', are ideal partners. A pale-yellow lupin beside our steps has the blue rounded flowers of *Geranium* 'Brookside' mingling with it to great effect.

Yellow day lilies make a good vertical clump in contrast to the broad, spreading growth of the lupin, with the blue of *Anchusa azurea* 'Loddon Royalist' or *Baptisia australis* breaking up the yellow and green.

Elsewhere in the garden, the large and spreading bush of a blue lupin sprawls between clumps of *Geranium psilostemon* with vivid magenta, black-centred flowers against a backdrop of the lovely magenta moss rose 'William Lobb'.

Chapter Six

At Bolton College of Art, I got together a body of work – drawings, paintings and prints – in readiness for the next step, enrolling at another art college for a three-year Diploma in Art and Design course. This was a degree course but it was only years later that its title was changed to BA (Bachelor of Arts).

My acceptance hinged on passing five O levels. Thankfully I just scraped through, satisfying the minimum academic qualifications despite having left school so early. Only twenty-nine colleges offered the course. I took advice from teachers but finally decided I would apply to Newport Art College. Far from making my choice on the basis of research and good sense, I chose Newport because it was the closest place to Cardiff to be awarded the new course and my then-boyfriend John Higgins was going to Cardiff University to study civil engineering. So many of my choices in that first part of my life were governed by other people – always men. Had I been born thirty years later I wonder if this would still have been the case. Despite thinking for myself and being aware of the emergence of feminism, in so many aspects of my life, including making important decisions that would affect my future, I was too often swayed by, sometimes controlled by, my love interest and since I am heterosexual, that was always men.

I distinctly remember the train journey to Newport for my interview. It was a perfect hot summer's day travelling through Worcestershire, Gloucestershire and Monmouthshire. The countryside shimmered, the green of trees was as bright as it could be, in that perfect time between the freshness of spring and the fullness of summer, and everywhere were splashes of colour from wildflowers.

There were meadows, real meadows, only sixty years ago.

At Newport, I was interviewed by the principal, Thomas Rathmell, a figurative painter of some repute, and John Selway, ditto. They both liked my work and I was offered a place there and then. Throughout my three years there, they were very supportive; John Selway even recommended me for a scholarship through his gallery Roland, Browse & Delbanco.

I could hardly believe I had won a place. But outside of college, there were still adventures to be had.

Loretta, Sylvia and I got together on numerous occasions in between classes at Bolton to dream about travelling to Europe. Slowly in the months after Christmas, our dreams evolved into plans and our plans became more and more concrete. Apart from my French exchange at grammar school I had never been abroad.

I had hitchhiked once on my own to London to see and stay with my cousins, John and Glen, and my Aunty Barbara and Uncle Jack in Loughton on the edge of Epping Forest. It was probably a stupid thing to have done but I got there and back in one piece. This sounds far-fetched but it is absolutely true: in the forest I saw a hoopoe and a golden oriole, though not on the same day nor in the same place. I also ate my first James Grieve apple, the most delicious apple I have ever eaten and the only apple I had ever eaten straight off the tree. What strange things you remember, like standing with John and Glen in the kitchen there and us eating a whole sliced loaf between us.

Whilst I had a safe journey that time, the same was not true when I hitchhiked to see John Higgins in Wales and I almost came to grief having accepted a lift in a lorry with two men who turned out to be predatory. I escaped, but it still makes me shudder.

Well, there were going to be three of us hitchhiking through France and Spain. Safety in numbers. None of us had any money and though we weren't very realistic about how much we might need to attempt this adventure, we made a start on saving what we could. During my last term at Bolton, I got a barmaid's job at the pub right next door to Burnden Park, then Bolton Wanderers Football Club's ground. I was only seventeen but the landlord wasn't too worried – he worked me harder and paid me less. I looked older than I was since I had already entered my beatnik phase, wearing mainly black and adopting black eyeliner and loads of mascara – the Dirty Dusty Springfield look. As long as I could pull pints and wash and polish pint glasses that was all that mattered. By the time we left I had enough to cover food – we had calculated that our transport was going to be free, apart from the ferry. We had also invested in a YHA membership that was going to take care of our accommodation needs and planned our route through France and to the south of Spain from hostel to hostel. When I say 'planned' I use the term in its loosest interpretation.

Frankly at that age, certainly at that time, life for young people was all about living in the present. Not long after I had started at Bolton, the Cuban missile crisis terrified the world. After the war, there was for young people a sense of apprehension – not because of any fear that the world was about to change but because we were already in the world of the Cold War and of nuclear weapons. The

H bomb was a cold fact then; though it lurked way off, out of consciousness, it was still a terrifying shock to be brought face to face with what it could mean. The possibility of nuclear war was suddenly a reality. I understood little of global politics and neither did my peers. Plans to travel to the north of Scotland and live in caves were discussed. For once I talked to my dad and all my fears spilled out. For hours we talked it all through and gradually I felt reassured that Armageddon wouldn't happen. Not straight away at any rate.

By the time of this trip, I had finished the relationship with John Higgins. It had cooled gradually during my year at art college, and with his absence at university in Cardiff. There had been some exciting, some joyful and some excruciating times, though.

The previous Christmas, John had decided he wanted to marry me and came, very drunkenly, to my house where, after my father had asked him to leave, he attempted to regain access by climbing a drainpipe. It was a bit of a token gesture since the drainpipe was on the side of the house with no windows. Having reached the top he fell all the way down and broke his leg. As a consequence for months afterwards his leg was in plaster.

Nothing would stop John from going out and having a good time. Sometimes he would take me to hear modern jazz at clubs in Moss Side, sometimes we would visit different pubs in the centre of Manchester. On an earlier occasion we had entered one of the most popular pubs on a Saturday night. It was crowded; people were queuing several deep to be served at the bar. John, never slow to take the initiative, suddenly developed a tremendous limp; clutching his leg, he apologised profusely about his broken leg as the crowd parted and allowed him preferential treatment. When we had finished our drinks, instead of limping out quietly,

John grabbed my hand, laughed as loudly as he could and raced out of the door. Hardly surprising, then, that when he entered the same pub months later, this time with an actually broken leg, he was kicked out. It was like a latter-day Aesop's fable. John was a truly good person. Although he knew how to have a good time, he always seemed to be haunted. His own drinking bothered him, perhaps because his dad was an alcoholic. We went to see him once, a thoroughly funny, bright and beautiful person when sober, but his life had been ruined by drink.

On my eighteenth birthday, John came to see me with a card, flowers and an Art Blakey LP which to my shame I later tried to exchange at the record shop in Bolton Road. After I called it off, John and I didn't see each other again until I went once to see him when our friend Paul Jackson had died. But he wasn't interested in talking to me.

* * *

We left, Sylvia, Loretta and I, the week after my eighteenth birthday. Loretta lived in Ramsbottom, and I met up with her in Bolton where we were also due to meet Sylvia, who lived in the town. After waiting for an hour and anxious to get on our way, we called at her house. We rang the bell, a bedroom window was thrown open and Sylvia's red-haired head appeared. 'With you in a minute!' Ten minutes later she appeared looking as though she was just going off to Blackpool for the weekend. She had on a sundress, was clutching two baskets and a small suitcase and wearing an enormous straw hat which hid most of her red hair. Too late to make any wardrobe suggestions – and anyway it's a free country, isn't it? – we took the bus to Walkden and down to Worsley where we intended to start hitching. It had taken a lot of fibs to persuade my dad to let me go.

He thought we were going to travel by bus and train. We stood on the grass verge outside Worsley Church and started to hitch.

Nobody teaches you how to hitchhike, but we stuck out our thumbs and hoped for the best. One of the first vehicles to come flying past was my brother Pip's drop handlebar bike with him on it. He screeched to a halt. 'What are you doing? Where are you going?' he demanded. I implored him not to tell our parents when he got back. He made no promises. I had nothing with which to bribe him and I felt in any case he would feel duty bound to tell everyone, principally because he was worried about me.

The trip could have ended before it had begun, but thankfully soon after Pip had pedalled off, a car stopped, Loretta negotiated, we jumped in the back and we were on our way. I have no idea what happened when Pip reached home and too many other events passed during the six weeks we were away for that day to create any long-term angst between us.

It was a long time ago and though certain events, certain people, places and plants thrust themselves forward, it is impressions that remain most real: mile after mile of straight roads over flat fields in northern France lined with poplars reminiscent of the journeys in Charles Dickens' *A Tale of Two Cities*, arriving in Paris in the dark with boulevards decked in dappled light through the leaves of plane trees, perceiving it through a psychedelic haze, not brought on by drugs but by lack of sleep, and the smell of it all so different. A kind man with whom we travelled right through France, who paid for our food, proper food too, and for a real hotel for one night! We were never placed under any obligation, far from it, and our French improved enormously, as did his English. It was a privilege to hear about the places we were travelling through; he was a human guide-book and you could ask questions and gather so much information about the geography, the history and the culture of the places we were passing through.

Finally we had to get out and say thank you and good bye; we were confident enough for a '*Merci et au revoir.*'

We headed for a youth hostel in the Pyrenees – I think it was still in France. At first we were told they were full but eventually the folk who were running the place relented and squeezed us in. The young people already in residence seemed to belong there as though they had always lived there. It was such a relaxed place, there seemed to be no rules, just an expectation that everyone would lend a hand picking peaches.

The whole place, the courtyards, the outbuildings, the bedrooms, smelt of ripe peaches. For the next few days so did we. The place's hedonistic lifestyle became slightly overpowering after a few days, not to mention the smell of peaches and, though they were free and delicious, you can only eat so many.

We travelled over the Pyrenees to Barcelona, a place we had all wanted to visit. From our meagre funds we had decided to treat ourselves to a proper meal. Sadly the paella was disappointing but the place was not. We befriended a group of Catalan film students who took us out for several nights to a wine cellar where even though wine was cheap, extra bottles that were even cheaper were smuggled in. Spain was still a dictatorship then and would be for many years to come. At one time Franco had banned the speaking of Catalan. These students were politicised by necessity, and much of their work, it seemed, was clandestine. In contrast we were probably empty headed.

I immediately fell in love with one of the students, Francisco, ironically Franco's Christian name. He was very short sighted and wore thick glasses which magnified his lush black eyelashes. We spent a couple of days with our film students and then were off again. Heading south we arrived in Alicante and spent the day on the beach. Sylvia, who was red-haired and pale-skinned, went to sleep in the sun. Inevitably, she got burned – in fact she got sunstroke.

We moved on later in the day heading for Murcia but Sylvia became more and more poorly. We had been dropped off in a very rural spot and were standing at the side of the road which ran amongst orange groves on either side. It was getting late and we were getting worried. A little group of children came purposefully through the orange trees towards us. They wanted to give us a couple of postcards depicting the local area; we found what we could to complete the exchange, some unopened soap. There were smiles and laughs all round and Loretta's Spanish was good enough to explain what we were doing.

A couple of them ran back in the direction of the long, low, white-washed house in the distance. They returned almost immediately holding hands with a man, their father. He invited us back to the house and we gratefully accepted since Sylvia was really ill and becoming slightly delirious. The house was shared by a brother and sister and their respective families, seven or eight children. This was their orange grove. They chucked out several of the boys who shared a room for us and we put Sylvia to bed straight away.

They fed us and entertained us sitting outside with crickets chirping. Apparently, for thousands of years, Spanish farmers have been using the frequency of cricket chirps to gauge temperature.

The highlight of the entertainment was a visit to the central room where the father's collection of stuffed animals and birds was on display. Taxidermy was his hobby. Perhaps it seemed slightly odd to prioritise stuffed animals over caring for children but then it seems quite odd to stuff animals anyway.

It took Sylvia two days to get well. We thanked our hosts and, probably much to the relief of the boys who had lost their room, we were on our way again. Our journey preceded the package holiday and the popularity of Spain as a place of exodus for large parts of the British populace. The roads along the coast to Malaga, our final destination, were hazardous, positively precipitous especially in lorries with devil-may-care drivers who seemed to pay no regard to speed limits or sides of the road. We decided to stay in Malaga for some time, persuaded mainly by Loretta who unbeknown to us had a tryst with a Spanish boy arranged long before we left England.

The youth hostel was packed with interesting people including an Alaskan called Paul Bates. This time it was he who fell in love with me. As people are wont to do at that age, we spent a long time putting the world to rights. He said England was on his itinerary and vowed he would come and see me. Sylvia was getting concerned about returning home and it struck me that if I was to get back to attend my new college, I had better get a move on. Loretta didn't want to leave so we decided Sylvia and I would hitch to Madrid and Loretta would join us in a couple of days, then we would get back as soon as we could.

There was no way I was going to miss Madrid, and in particular the Prado. Often in my younger life I would fall in love or have a crush on somebody. This was not necessarily confined to people I'd met or knew, nor even to people who were alive – there were painters on the list, for example, who had lived hundreds of years ago but to whose images I found myself deeply drawn. For years I had admired the paintings of El Greco, loving his graceful, elongated figures and his portraits of young men. Coming across these paintings in the dark depths of the Prado made me cry. Then I discovered Velázquez. Although I had seen reproductions of his work, nothing could have prepared me for the impact of his paintings. Like so many people who have seen his works, especially in the Prado, I was spellbound.

I've loved Velázquez ever since that trip to Spain. The painting of his that I most want to see is the portrait of Juan de Pareja in the Metropolitan Museum of Art in New York. Even looking at its image on a computer screen makes me shiver. Sadly, however, I missed it on a trip to New York years later.

I suppose I am old enough now to have favourite painters in the knowledge that I won't change my mind. They both begin with V: Velázquez and Vermeer. The paintings of both are full of humanity. They bring out the best in you; they appeal to your empathy and make you proud to be human. Ironic perhaps that Juan de Pareja was enslaved to Velázquez, but not that he was given his freedom and encouraged by Velázquez, having worked alongside him for many years, to paint and become an artist of repute in his own right.

Loretta missed out on the Prado but joined us in Madrid and we pressed on northwards. By this time we were almost broke and when eventually we reached Paris, Loretta was literally penniless. We went to see the British consul who repatriated us.

Arriving back in Manchester, I had already missed my start date at college. I got myself together rapidly and my dad took me down to Newport. I had nowhere to stay but the college suggested a couple of possibilities. We went round to the first one, a boarding house run by very nice people. My dad paid my first month's rent, and he reclaimed it when the first instalment of my grant came through.

After a meal in true boarding house style around a communal table during which the other boarders introduced themselves, I settled down in my attic room, my first independent home.

The next day I went into Newport College for the first time and met my class and my tutors with apprehensive interest. I was brown from the sun on my travels and still full of the adventures of the summer I had just left behind. My fellow students had already met, chatted and established themselves. They viewed me with some interest. Eventually I was allotted a place, an easel, a table and a cupboard with a couple of screens separating me from the students either side.

Gradually I found my feet. Over the next three years this was my base. The first painting I attempted was a double portrait of me and Paul Bates, who materialised a few days after I arrived. He'd visited the address I had given him in Malaga, appearing on the doorstep one evening in Manchester. My parents gave him my new address, and there he was. I thought it would be a very grown-up thing to do, in the tradition of artists and garrets, to paint in my room. Sadly my landlady was scandalised by the idea and forbade it. Shortly afterwards I moved out.

Paul wanted to see a bit of the country and we hitchhiked to the Lake District one weekend. We took a tent and a camping stove – he said he'd cook. Unbeknown to me, when he had travelled from Malaga across to Morocco he had brought a big bag of marijuana and he incorporated some of it into the mashed potato he dished up just before we went for a walk up the Old Man of Coniston close to where we were camping. By the time we came down (from the fell) I had lost it. I fell down a cattle grid, making a large dent in my shin, but couldn't feel a thing. I made breakfast the next day!

Paul returned to Alaska. He wrote to me later enclosing a packet of morning glory seeds. In my naiveté I planted them, not realising that they have hallucinatory properties, containing a similar chemical to that found in LSD. The Aztecs used it in some of their rituals.

These days, I grow it for its glorious trumpet flowers. There is a wide selection of different varieties; the deep purple varieties give an instant exotic effect and though like its cousin the bindweed, flowers last only for a day, plants produce a succession of them for months. Originating in Central and South America, and spread along Mediterranean coasts perhaps in ships' ballast, the bright blue *Ipomoea tricolor* is familiar to any of us lucky enough to have taken a holiday in that region.

Morning Glory

It would be unwise to eat the seeds of one of the most celebrated annual climbers – Morning Glory, *Ipomoea tricolor* – unless you want to start hallucinating. Anyone who has had a Mediterranean holiday will be familiar with its clambering growth sprinkled from head to foot with caerulean trumpets. If you want to replicate the holiday scene for yourself, soak seeds overnight then sow individually into small pots, separate compartments of a module tray or in toilet roll middles that you can plunge directly into the ground later without disturbing the roots. There are purple, crimson and striped cultivars too. One year we grew one called 'Split Personality' with white-centred crimson flowers. We planted it on the south side of our shed to which Neil had attached a couple of sheets of weld mesh. Just one packet of seed yielded enough plants to smother their supports.

Ipomoea lobata, a close cousin, has clusters of small red, yellow and white flowers and if you want instant height without fuss, sweet peas and nasturtiums can be sown direct in late March or early April.

As with most gardening it's how you put it together that matters. The great majority of these annual climbers are from Central and South America and there is always a touch of the mariachi band about them, ocarinas and flute playing in the background. They are ideal plants for introducing an instant tropical effect but for masses of flowers avoid nitrogenous fertilisers and muck. Many will flower well in quite poor soils.

For a stop-you-in-your-tracks show, try combining different plants – *Eccremocarpus*, perhaps, with one of the climbing nasturtiums.

Even though a few might manage to survive the winter, and *Eccremocarpus* and even runner beans can be mollycoddled and get going the next year, it hardly seems worth it. These flamboyant climbers are so easy to grow from seed and – once they've germinated and got used to the fact that they're in Penge rather than Panama – their growth is so rapid and extensive, why bother?

Chapter Seven

Living away from home for the first time was exciting but often fraught. There were new skills to be learned: how to manage a budget, pay rent, eat properly, cook, clean, be self-disciplined enough to start work each day promptly. I seldom succeeded. There were new freedoms but also new responsibilities. Some of my fellow students went home at weekends; I didn't go back to Manchester until the end of term, Christmas. There were no mobile phones then, so it was harder to stay in touch. My mum had written quick notes from time to time, though I'm not sure I responded.

She was overjoyed to see me, hugged me to her and then, holding me at arm's length, surveyed me in my new entirety and told me I had put on weight. Indisputable. Too much beer had been consumed and, during the space of just one term, I had changed from a fairly slim bronzed young woman into a rather lardy lump. My weight gain in no way discouraged her from feeding me up over the holidays whilst she had the chance. Nor did it put off one of the young men in my class, Geoff Olsen, whose company I shared for the next three years. We only lived together for a short part of this period but we often stayed over at each other's places and spent most of our days in close proximity, working in the same studio and discussing each other's work. Though he had a strong sense of justice and quite a chip on his shoulder about being from a working-class family he was basically apolitical. He was, though, very aware of the landscape both as nature made it and as man had changed it and had a strong sense of the history of his home. It was this that informed his paintings, both then and subsequently, even though some of the destinations where he later lived and taught were far removed from the dark and dramatic South Wales valleys with their slag heaps, pit heads and miners' terraces perched precariously on the steep hillsides. I have only seen reproductions of his later work but it is clear that where he came from was the hub from which all his work emanated. He died in 2007.

Merthyr was built on the back of those who mined the coal and made the steel. Geoff once took me to Vaynor just outside Merthyr to visit the grave of one of the iron masters, Robert Thompson Crawshay. His huge gravestone lies flat on the turf, a piece of granite weighing more than ten tons inscribed with the words 'God forgive me'. Although I visited Merthyr with Geoff, I was not allowed to meet his mother and father and never went to his home but stayed with his sister, her husband and son. His father was feared by them all. A Lawrentian family indeed.

On 21 October 1966 one of the spoil tips from the Merthyr Vale Colliery above the village of Aberfan slipped down the hillside, engulfing the junior school and a row of houses. One hundred and forty-four people were killed, 116 of them children. Aberfan is only five miles away from Merthyr Tydfil. As soon as news of the disaster came through Geoff, along with several other 'local' lads from our college, went to help. They were away for days though no survivors were found after 11a.m. on the first day.

Wales was the first 'industrialised' country in the world. Is that a claim to fame?

For three years I painted pictures. They were figurative and full of colour. There were drawing classes, photography and history of art. Our teacher for the latter was well informed about her subject but involved with it seemingly only on an academic level, with a preoccupation with who influenced whom and how one 'style' followed another.

When we entered our third year of college, we all became concerned about what we would do next.

Although life was hardly idyllic – most of us were broke – we had been given the opportunity to indulge ourselves by expressing our own ideas and creative impulses for more than two years. Soon we were going to have to face reality. It was easier for me than many of my fellow students in some ways since I had already been 'out to work' whilst many of them had gone straight from school to college. There was the temptation, though, to extend this slightly unreal and self-indulgent way of living. There was the prospect of post-graduate study, most probably in the form of an art-teaching diploma course, and for a lucky few a travelling scholarship to pursue their own work – or you could really go for it and apply to the crème de la crème, the Royal College of Art and/or the Slade School of Fine Art. For many hopefuls from most art colleges this is their aspiration. I wanted to try but Geoff said 'No!' What I did do was help fellow students including Geoff to pack up their paintings and artwork for their journey to the capital.

Geoff also didn't want me to apply when my tutor John Selway recommended me for a travelling scholarship with his gallery Roland, Browse & Delbanco. He was horrified. He was very controlling. I didn't take it up. When we both applied for an art-teaching post-graduate year, I was accepted at my first choice, the Institute of Education, part of University College London, whilst Geoff took up his third choice at Swansea. He insisted I also change to Swansea. Meanwhile, unbeknown to me, he had applied for a British Council scholarship in Munich. He took it up, and by that time I had lost my London place, but was lucky enough to be offered a place at Brighton College of Art to study for an art teacher's diploma.

Geoff wrote to me from Germany every day and I kept the faith until one dark December day, when a load of my friends from my course physically transported me to the pub across the road, plied me with drink and freed me at last. I burned all his letters. On his return home to Merthyr Tydfil months later he burned all my paintings and my books. Since he had a store there, he had offered to safeguard them with his own stuff until we got together again. Needless to say, he didn't burn his own paintings. It reminded me of the time my dad burned all my school reports when I left school at fifteen and ruined his dreams of what I might have done.

* * *

It could not have been a more exciting time to be in art college, especially Brighton College of Art. In the students' coffee bar on the Old Steine across from the Royal Pavilion, the jukebox played Jimi Hendrix all day long. We had lectures galore on aspects of teaching from child development to psychology to lesson planning, but the most important part of the art teacher's diploma course was teaching practice. Now I was going to find out whether or not I wanted to teach and, more to the point, whether or not I could. Would I be any good?

There were not enough placements in Brighton itself for all of us to find a position, so each year some students had to go to Crawley and other places with large comprehensive schools to practise our teaching. Four people in my class were bound for Thomas Bennett Comprehensive, a school with 2,000 pupils. One of the four was Spencer Owen, the only person in the class with his own transport, so we all bundled into his van, shared the petrol costs and travelled back and forth each day.

I had not set out to be an art teacher as a lifetime ambition, and was quite apprehensive. But I enjoyed the experience, loved the kids (most of them, at least) and though there was no Damascene conversion, I found that teaching was something I wanted to do and that I would enjoy and might be able to do well. It was 'in at the deep end' but the kids I was 'practising' on seemed to enjoy the ideas and lessons. There were no riots or bad behaviour, though this may have had more to do with my having a 'strange' accent coupled with a loud voice (trained at the Stretford End of Manchester United's Old Trafford). All in all I couldn't wait for the next time. I finally started 'proper' teaching a few months after that, and I continued to teach for the next thirteen years, mainly in comprehensive schools with a couple of forays into junior schools and further education and a year out in Rome.

Teaching art is a privilege. Now, when I watch my grandchildren making pictures, it is such a thrill to see what they make, and I was in the position for all those years of seeing, day after day, the work that hundreds of kids produced: drawings, paintings, collages, pots, models, fabrics, embroideries. It is heartening to see children feeling proud of what they have made. Children have their own style and all their work is valid. It is truly sad to see children lose their self-confidence and thereafter try to conform to what they think is right or wrong. Colouring-in books are anathema to me. For many children, making their own pictures and artwork is their only opportunity to express themselves unfettered by the idea of rights and wrongs or what adults have decided is how things should be done.

We tend to think of schoolchildren's drug-taking as a recent problem, but it was rife at that time too, with dealers peddling their wares, mainly purple hearts and other amphetamines or similar 'uppers', outside the school gates. In my classes there was fairly strong evidence of this amongst a few of the pupils – very strange, disjointed, nervy drawings or children, usually boys, falling asleep as a result of a 'crash' having partied on pills the previous night.

I had very little spare money for drinking; any surplus I had was spent on old stuff, and Brighton was the place for 'old stuff'. The Saturday morning markets were heaven and Joannie, with whom I shared a flat, and I would search for bargains. Joannie is still one of my best friends. Later we shared a flat in London. She has always had my back and put up with me patiently and lovingly even in the most trying circumstances. We had wonderful Sunday mornings, reading the papers and feasting on the best croissants ever from Fogels, the brilliant Jewish bakers on Upper St James Street just round the corner from our flat on Grafton Street in Kemptown. We were just across from the beach and sometimes we would take our lunch, invariably cooked by Joannie, there. It wasn't just sandwiches either. Often it would be a full-blown casserole. She is a really good cook, a kind but very modest and diffident person despite being very creative. Like me she taught art for a number of years, though she went on to teach printmaking at the London College of Printing and later became an art advisor. Throughout this time, for more than sixty years, she has continued to draw, paint and make beautiful prints.

The last term of my art teacher's diploma course at Brighton was a strange and unnerving time. Nothing seemed certain or sure. My three-year-plus relationship with Geoff Olsen had ended. I was unsure about teaching I didn't know where I was going. Whilst barmaiding at a pub called the Dog Tray which then stood close to the police station and magistrates' court (it has long since been demolished), I pulled a pint one evening for a student from the art college who became an important person in my life. He always drank alone, and I assumed he was unattached. We saw each other frequently for many months until one day he told me he had a girlfriend with whom he had been living for a long time but who was in a psychiatric hospital suffering from quite severe mental illness. It was an impossible situation, and after some time he ended our relationship.

One day I saw them walking in the park. They looked happy. He was wearing a suit, a cream linen summer suit I had bought him from the 'dress agency' where Joannie and I bought clothes.

I have always found it difficult to come to terms with situations that I dislike or disagree with, especially when reality differs from the idea I have in my head and I am impotent to control or change it. Much of this is just a question of pride. I was at my wits' end, powerless, distraught, desperate, and one night decided that I did not want to live anymore. I took an overdose of codeine just as I had done almost ten years before. Joannie found out what I had done and acted promptly. I was admitted to Brighton General Hospital. It was too late to try pumping my stomach; there was nothing to be done but to wait a while and then go home. I had to talk to a psychiatrist but it was clear that there was nothing he could do for me. I went home slowly realising how happy I was to be alive and how lucky I was to have the opportunity to be with people, to make them happy and to be happy myself.

Gradually hurt and heartbreak faded. Looking for jobs became a priority. I had other barmaiding jobs including one at a seafront hotel.

Going home from there one night, I came off my moped just around the corner from Grafton Street where we lived. I dashed in with the taste of blood in my mouth, looked in the mirror and saw my mouth was full of blood and fragments of teeth. Once again to the hospital, where they patched me up as well as they could. I had broken one of my front teeth in half. It is not until something like this happens you realise how important your teeth, your smile, your looks, can be. By that time I had started to see Anthony Amies, a student at the Slade who was studying painting and printmaking, and was the best friend of Tim, who had been in our class. The next year I married him, and he paid for some dental repairs as a wedding present.

I loved Brighton, still do; I feel a great affinity with it. This poem, about the possible derivation of the name of the pub where I used to work in Brighton, has always stayed with me:

> On the green banks of Shannon, when Shelah was nigh
> No blithe Irish lad was so happy as I,
> No harp like my own could so cheerily play,
> And wherever I went was my poor dog Tray.
> When at last I was forced from my Shelah to part,
> She said (while the sorrow was big at her heart),
> Oh ! remember your Shelah, when far, far away,
> And be kind my dear Pat to your poor dog Tray.
> Poor dog, he was faithful and kind to be sure,
> And he constantly loved me although I was poor,
> When the sour-looking folks sent me heartless away,
> I had always a friend in my poor dog Tray.
> When the road was so dark and the night was so cold,
> And Pat and his dog were grown weary and old,
> How snugly we slept in my old coat of grey,

And he lick'd me for kindness—my poor dog Tray.
Though my wallet was scant, I remember'd his case,
Nor refus'd my last crust to his pitiful face,
But he died at my feet on a cold winter's day
And I play'd a lament for my poor dog Tray.
Where now shall I go, poor, forsaken and blind,
Can I find one to guide me so faithful and kind,
To my sweet native village so far, far away,
I can never more return with my poor dog Tray.

* * *

Many of our fellow students had moved on from Brighton but a few decided to stay. I had some good friends, some talented friends too, including Keith, who played, repaired and constructed musical instruments. His true love was steel guitars. Keith had developed a brain and nerve condition that was making it increasingly difficult to continue. I wish I knew what had happened to him. How unfair it is when somebody with real talent has their ability to pursue and develop this cut short or compromised. I often think of the waste of creativity that our education system fails to recognise and encourage, and then think further that we are the lucky ones compared to the millions of young people worldwide, especially young women, who through poverty, war, corruption and misogyny will never be able to develop their talent …

It wasn't always gloom and doom for me and Joannie; we had some fun times. I was broke, and I can remember painting my quite spacious room, but having afforded a large tin of very cheap white emulsion, I only had enough money for a very small brush, so I spent three days on a task that could have been completed in an afternoon with the proper equipment.

Joan had a proper job teaching art at Roedean, a posh girl's school. Meanwhile, I'd finished art college in Brighton and realised just how broke I was (my only income was from the bar job at the hotel on the seafront). I rolled up at the Labour Exchange resigned to searching for a local art-teaching job. I was told the nearest one was in Durham and was offered a variety of local 'alternatives', from sales assistant to factory hand, with the instruction that I could only sign on if I started applying. In the event I signed on for one week. The first job I took was at a small 'factory' where they made architects' curves, devices used to transfer or copy curved lines and shapes. The work consisted of encasing lead in rubber and using tetrachloride to seal the ends. This had to be done close to your face. It soon became clear that all the women (all the employees were women apart from the foreman and the boss, who brought round the wages on a Saturday morning and distributed them personally) had coughs. The longer they had been working there the worse were their coughs. Nobody belonged to a trade union. When I made a fuss and tried to organise an element of resistance to the dangerous working practices, I was given a week's notice.

That autumn I dug out my PSV badge and applied to Brighton and Hove Transport for a job. They were short of conductors and they employed me straight away. Though I say it myself, I look good in a uniform and I was pretty good at the job. I was hopeless at two aspects of it though. One was getting up and out for the early shift – I can remember flying up Grafton Street at four in the morning only to see the staff bus hurtling past the end of the road, lights ablaze on its way to the main depot to deposit drivers and conductors who would take out the first buses of the day.

At the same garage at the end of the day, we would pay in our takings squared up with our ticket sales. Most of the time mine would tally, but unlike all the professionals who by the end of the day had rationalised all their loose change into as few coins as possible and took no longer than a couple of minutes to pay in and go home, my money bag would be full of every possible combination of coin in random amounts and would take an age to sort and pay in.

On most of our routes there would be the possibility of a cup of tea at either terminus – but not always. Often you would spend the whole week on the same route. Doing a whole shift without a cup of tea was taxing. More organised conductors would have brought a flask with them. Sometimes there would be a convenient cafe but no time in the schedule for a sit-down cuppa. In such circumstances we would often bring a cup of tea back to the bus and, standing on the platform, we would cool the tea down by pouring it by degrees into the saucer and either drink straight from the saucer or cool the whole cup by pouring it back and forth. Timekeeping had to be precise. If there was no time to return the cups and saucers then, we would take them back on our next journey.

One time I hit on a solution to ensure getting a cup of tea on one route with no convenient cafe. Grafton Street where Joan and I lived ran at right angles to the sea and Marine Parade. Running parallel with it was Rock Gardens, down which our bus passed, and in the middle of it was a bus stop. There was access to Rock Gardens from Grafton Street at both ends. I had hatched a plot with Joannie that she would bring round tea from our flat on one particular journey and we would rendezvous at the aforesaid bus stop. Things did not go according to plan. I stopped the bus in Rock Gardens as arranged. We were a bit early, Joannie was a little late. My passengers were getting concerned when the bus failed to move on. I got off the bus and started to walk in the direction of Grafton Street, towards the sea. Meanwhile Joannie had taken the other route. Our paths didn't cross but when I returned, there she was standing at the bus stop, tray in hand (Joannie always does things properly, tea pot, milk jug, the lot). I think there were even a couple of slices of fruit cake. There were passengers on the platform; everyone was wondering where I had got to. A conductor is responsible for the care and safety of her passengers and should never desert them. Thank goodness this was before the advent of mobile phones!

* * *

I soon joined Anthony in London. We were great friends and got on well. I wanted to get married and despite misgivings on his part, in that he thought we should wait for a while, I won the day.

My dad gave me £30 to buy a wedding outfit. The money was stolen on Oxford Street (no wonder I hate handbags). In the event I settled for a Chinese silk jacket embroidered with flowers that I had bought in Brighton on one of the numerous shopping trips I could ill afford to the Saturday morning market.

Still unsure about whether or not to teach, when I moved to London I took a job with Halien Cleaning Services. Four hours in the morning, four in the afternoon, make your own way from one to the other. Most of my regular clients were Jewish. They ranged from a snobbish woman in Baker Street who, if she gave me a cup of tea, reached down for the Woolworths cups in the bottom of the kitchen cabinet, to Mrs Zack in Hendon who had lived in the same house since she fled Austria in the late 1930s and had retained this house and its contents in exactly the same state since then. I soon learned the routine, including the eleven o'clock break when she would sit me down in her art deco kitchen, get out the best china and make me a most delicious cup of coffee with thin almond biscuits. She would sit down with me, though without a cup of coffee, and ask what I had been doing and how things were going. She never talked about herself but seemed genuinely interested in me and my life. When I told her I wouldn't be coming anymore because I had decided to take a teaching job as she had advised I should, she was sad to see me go but thrilled about the new chapter in my life.

I had applied for the new post of a part-time specialist art teacher at a junior school in Kilburn called Kingsgate. It was unusual to have a teacher in a junior school specifically for art, but I was full of enthusiasm to make it work. Our intake was working class, with lots of kids with Irish heritage and loads of first-generation children with Caribbean backgrounds, but with many other ethnicities represented as well. The headmistress, Miss Richardson, was strict not only with the children but also with the staff. I was called in to her office one day. I had imagined she would be asking how I was getting on, but instead she launched into a diatribe about the unsuitability of my clothes. She had taken particular exception to what I was wearing that day, a cream linen all-in-one culotte. It was my favourite outfit, bought the year before from a dress agency just round the corner from our college in Brighton.

'Most unsuitable!' Miss Richardson declared. 'Don't you realise that all the children are laughing at you?'

I didn't, in fact I knew they weren't. Pupils I have taught have generally approved of the way I dress. I continued to wear what I wanted to. Even if I had wanted to obey her dress code, none of my limited wardrobe would have complied.

At Kingsgate I became aware of how difficult life could be for some children. In one of my classes was a little boy from Nigeria whose family had only been in the country for two years. He was very withdrawn and quiet. One day in the midst of an art session, he rushed over to the table where big tins of powder paint were open, picked up the tin of purple paint and threw it on the floor, shouting, 'I'm hungry.' On this occasion Miss Richardson was kindness itself. Sitting in her office, we discovered he and his little sister hadn't eaten for two days. Their mum had gone off in search of their dad and had left him in charge of his sister. He was nine.

Many of the children I taught had no idea where their food came from. Although they drank milk at playtime, some of them had no idea that it came from a cow. (A few years after this, in 1971, Maggie Thatcher abolished the provision of free school milk for seven- to eleven-year-olds.)

Miss Richardson was generally strict and fair but was terrorised by one group of nine-year-olds and in particular by their gang leader, Eddie Kelly. I don't know how the situation had become so dire, but this small boy ignored her authority on every occasion. She was always in charge at dinnertime, insisting on straight lines, orderly queues and nobody pushing in, but when Eddie and his gang showed up they went straight to the front where terrified dinner ladies would dish up their dinners without a murmur. It turned out that when he was younger he had been locked in a room with his baby sister. She had died. It is very hard to imagine what some children have gone through.

I was becoming more of a political animal and stood on a soapbox on the corner of the Portobello Road and Cambridge Gardens regaling passers-by with an anti-capitalism, anti-Conservative speech starting with, 'Maggie Thatcher – milk snatcher.'

The job at Kingsgate was part time and though I continued with a few of my cleaning jobs, I read in *The Times Educational Supplement* an advertisement for a part-time art teacher's post in

Stepney in a secondary school, Sir John Cass. I applied for the job and got it. I did both jobs for some time, then was asked to go full time at Sir John Cass. I said a fond farewell to Kingsgate.

Although art was on the curriculum in my new school, it was not an exam subject, but by the time I left a few years later it was entering students for both O and A level art. One of my star students was a boy called Michael Hayes. He was quiet yet popular – quite an unusual combination in a working-class school. He became head boy and went on to study art and become a teacher, then later an art examiner. I had a letter from him several years ago, one of the most precious letters I have ever received, and I have lost it. I have tried every way I could think of to get in touch with him but to no avail. If he reads this or anybody reading this knows of his whereabouts I would be so grateful to hear. In the letter he thanked me for what I had done for him, told me of how his life had progressed and that it was because of my persistence in persuading him to make the most of his talents and study art that he had gone on to do just that. Neither of his parents could read or write and both wanted him to get a steady job, preferably in a bank, when he left school.

Many of the fathers of the children worked in the docks, which had been the main source of employment in the area for hundreds of years. That was all about to change with the introduction of containerisation. This required ever bigger ships with which the East End docks could not cope. Gradually the docks were closed down, and unemployment and poverty became rife.

The dad of one of my favourite kids, Elaine Clarke, was a docker. They lived on the Isle of Dogs. I was invited to Sunday dinner there on several occasions. I have never been so well fed, nor so overfed. The works, including pease pudding, and just in case we hadn't had enough to eat, treacle pudding and custard for afters.

I was taken out by some of my older students on a couple of occasions when I had been daft enough to admit I had never tried a few East End delicacies, including jellied eels and pie mash with liquor (which has nothing to do with booze).

Today Sir John Cass's Foundation and Redcoat School has been rechristened All Saints School. Stepney has become Tower Hamlets. The school and its catchment area have changed hugely. It is a C of E school, but the vast majority of students come from other ethnic backgrounds. When I taught there the school's intake was almost exclusively white working class with very few kids of Asian heritage. 'Paki-bashing' was just beginning. Many of the immigrants in and around Brick Lane, now famous for its curry houses and a centre of Bangladeshi culture, were from Bangladesh, then called East Pakistan, rather than Pakistan, then called West Pakistan. Bangladesh only became 'Bangladesh' in 1971.

The Kray Brothers were extremely active in the area and kids would come into school some mornings discussing stabbings and shootings from the previous night. They were wonderful kids in the main, cheeky and with irrepressible energy. They needed it. Sometimes they were a bit too cheeky. As art started to become recognised as a legitimate subject, we took on a new teacher. I knew him already, a pleasant, slightly timid man. This was his first teaching job (not that I had much experience either). The art department had two rooms, one of which was a pottery. Unfortunately the kids had learned that if you throw small amounts of damp clay at the ceiling, it sticks, but as it dries it loses its adhesion. Paul was tormented on several occasions like this. We banned working with clay for a while and resumed pottery later when the kids had got to know him better.

I was lucky enough to teach such a lot of lovely pupils there. One boy in my class had a lot of trouble reading and writing; he was severely dyslexic. Dyslexia was not acknowledged as a condition. 'Word blindness' had been recognised for some time but it was not until the 1980s that the Department of Education officially classified the condition. He was teased sometimes by his classmates and some of his teachers thought him 'not very bright', but whenever we had an end-of-term quiz everybody wanted him on their team. His general knowledge was astonishing. A few years ago I was chatting to a taxi driver en route to a voiceover session in central London. We were talking about schools. He was an East End boy. It transpired that my former pupil was one of his closest friends and though there was a ten-year age gap between them, they belonged to a group of taxi drivers who went on holidays together. By that time Paul was thinking about retiring. It was great to hear that he hadn't just survived but that he was thriving.

Whilst I was at the school, a new English teacher, Chris Searle, was appointed. He was a forward-thinking, progressive sort of man and a brilliant teacher who valued the children's talents and got them to value themselves. So impressed was he by their work he wanted them to share it and published a collection of their work entitled *Stepney Words*. He had previously taken it to the school governors and then to the headmaster who were totally against its publication.

Raising funds from several individuals including Trevor Huddleston, the Bishop of Stepney, and Jack Dash, a poetry-writing, picture-painting dockers' leader, Chris Searle published it – and was dismissed. The kids spontaneously went on strike in support of their teacher. It wasn't until two years later after all sorts of legal wranglings that he was allowed to teach in London again. Meanwhile *Stepney*

Words sold more than 15,000 copies, had excerpts in national newspapers and was even featured on BBC radio.

Brick Lane

Brick Lane is a horrible place
Where everyone has a gloomy face
There isn't one little space to play football
Everyone plays in the dirt
Filling all their hair with dirt
What a place
I always try to be happy and cheerful
Now I begin to get doubtful.

– Tony Hussey

Tony was another one of my students. I remember him well, and can capture how he looked. He wasn't a big boy, his shirt collar always stuck out and his tie was always awry. His grin was the widest you ever saw; it seemed to cover half his face, and his hair stuck out all over the place. If you had just a few words to describe him, they might be 'slightly dishevelled, immensely cheery but with a little bit of sadness round the edges'. He was the sort of boy who would make everyone in the class laugh and spent most of his time trying to do just that.

Inevitably he was sometimes picked on both by fellow pupils and sometimes by staff.

One staff member stood out particularly for all the wrong reasons. He was not only a bully but a paedophile too. After an internal disciplinary hearing following complaints from parents – and it must have been pretty serious since in that context, at that time, parents were likely to believe teachers first, and their children second – he was moved, but apparently years later came back. He was a big, looming man and would pace the corridors wearing a black gown and carrying a cane. He probably had several victims but the one I was most aware of was a boy who he would pursue and harass at every opportunity.

The boy had a sibling in the school, his twin sister. Both of them were tall and good looking with light brown hair, pale blue eyes and dark lashes. This teacher would seek him out wherever and whenever possible and take him away to administer corporal punishment. Several times I found the boy standing in the corridors in tears. Neither I nor his much feistier sister could get him to say exactly what had happened or to go to the headmaster and tell him. Such people think they are omnipotent and do such harm.

I got on well with many of the teachers there including Chris Searle and made a special friend of Carol Johnson, head of English. She invited me to travel with her, her young daughter and her boyfriend to Morocco in their van. The trip was not a great success, and shortly after we had reached Morocco Carol decided to return home. I had two options: to go back straight away with them, or stay in Morocco on my own. I decided to stay. I hitchhiked from place to place and met all sorts of interesting people, including being invited in to meet the family in a Moroccan household in a very rural location. I was fed too. It always seems the less people have, the happier they are to share.

I then started the long journey back to England. I ended up in some strange situations, including being woken up in northern Spain by the first warm rays of the sun and realising that the place I had collapsed with exhaustion the night before was in fact a huge mountain of almonds. It sounds uncomfortable but I had slept like a log! My solo journey continued until I met up with a German lad who was travelling in the same direction. He seemed pleasant enough and his English was excellent, but as we travelled I began to realise he was a control freak. Neither of us had much money and we lived on tomatoes and bread. He persuaded me to travel further north than I had intended, convincing me that I should accompany him back to his home. We went via Switzerland and when we reached Geneva, we made a stop. The idea was that despite my somewhat unkempt appearance, the colour having run from my favourite suede jacket following getting soaked in a downpour, we would have a proper meal in a real restaurant. It would have to be a cheap one, of course, so seeing postmen leaving their place of work at lunchtime, I went to consult them about good places to eat. They were very helpful and I returned to my companion jubilant and very hungry. He had changed his mind and had unilaterally decided that we should not waste our money and should hit the road again. I said no, probably in a very loud voice, and to his amazement, turned on my heels and marched off. I never saw him again. There was a BOAC office just down the road. I went in and asked when was the next flight to London and after phone calls to banks I wrote a cheque and booked a flight for later that day. I went straight to the airport, took a shower and got on my flight where I was treated to fresh orange juice, lunch and a glass of wine – oh, what luxury. I had enough change for my bus and tube fare back to the Angel to tell Joannie all about my adventures.

By this time I was no longer living with Anthony and I had filed for divorce. It was never going to work. We were great friends but there was no real spark, certainly no burning passion. He was a brilliant painter, his landscapes and seascapes so evocative of the feeling of the part of the world from which he came, its hugeness and the patterns and rhythms within it. His paintings, drawings and etchings make their own world; there is no need of people. Anthony was an all-round nice bloke, and it is tragic that his life was so short. He died in 2000. He drank too much and I think it was the drink that did for him.

His mum wasn't keen on me. She had brought him up on her own, his dad having disappeared when he was a baby. Perhaps she resented me. She certainly never approved of me. When we visited once in the winter, it must have been before we were married, I was not allowed to sleep in the house but was relegated to a camp bed in the shed across the garden. It was very clean and spruce, but also very cold. She filled an old-fashioned metal hot-water bottle and I was so cold and probably so drunk that I burned myself badly on my left wrist and the inside of my left knee. You can still see the marks more than fifty years later.

When Anthony's art contributed so much to the world it seems a bit mean to talk about hot-water bottles.

We had drifted apart gradually and some of our mutual friends had also left. Anthony's best friend, Malcolm, had taken up a teaching post at Taunton College of Art and was living there with his girlfriend Jane, who was one of the funniest and most sarcastic people ever, and one of the prettiest. On the plane on a recent working trip to Italy I sat next to a woman who turned out to be Jane's sister-in-law. She told me how Jane's life had progressed and how sadly, two years ago, Jane had died. She'd had motor-neuron disease. I know she would have coped with it with her usual dry humour and acerbic wit. She was a very special person.

I decided to go and visit the two of them, hitchhiking and stopping off at a couple of places I had always wanted to go on the way, top of the list Glastonbury. The place is imbued with spiritual myths and legends. It was not until a few years after this that the Glastonbury Festival got under way.

On approaching the Tor I turned round at the sound of tinkling bells and chanting to come face to face with a huge group of Hare Krishnas. They were on a pilgrimage to the top of the Tor, carrying enormous plastic buckets full of fruit salad. They encouraged me to climb alongside them, which I did, though when we reached the top, having admired the view and partaken briefly of their feast, I continued on my journey and left them to their festivities.

I returned to our flat in London. It was a basement flat and its back French windows opened onto broad steps that led upwards into our landlords' garden. Our landlords were lovely people and he was a keen gardener. Lilies abounded. We didn't use their garden but we did enjoy it, or at least its scents and aromas. You felt close to the earth despite never setting foot in the garden. You were surrounded by scent, especially on long, hot summer evenings. There was jasmine close by, but the most powerful perfume was that of the lilies.

Corn cutters with their scythes. Two of my great grandads were corn cutters in the summer, working on the land throughout the year.

My mum's family: her father Isaac, my mum Jeannie sitting on her mum Sarah Jane's knee and her sisters Catherine and Grace.

My mum proudly holding aloft me and my brother Bill, circa 1948.

My grandma Sarah Jane in the doorway of their new house in Folkestone, with my mum and her brother Maurice.

My grandfather Henry William, my dad in school uniform and his sister Barbara, in the mid-1920s.

Visiting Father Christmas at Lewis's in Manchester. Coats and hats courtesy of Grandma Higham, long grey socks knitted by Grandma Parkes.

Class 2, St. Paul's Junior School. I'm the scruffy one, bottom row to the right of Coronation Year board. Long grey socks and footballing dirty white shoes.

As a teenager in the school hockey team, me on the far right.

Dressed as Robin Hood taking part in the Whit Walk, determined not to be cast as Maid Marian.

Rhode Island School of Design trip, Napoli, making friends with three garage mechanics. Picture by Bernice Mast.

Another of Bernice's pictures with large gap between front teeth, Roma 1969, in a top by Biba.

Teaching at Christopher Wren, White City, probably the day of the swimming gala, at the swimming pool in Bloemfontein Road.

Me, my mum and dad and Bill, my eldest brother, with the ex-police Triumph Saint on which Bill and I rode to Geneva and back.

Bill and Helen's wedding and our family, Pip in foreground with an afro.

Our wedding day, me with jasmine in my hair, Neil with confetti. My lilies courtesy of the kind man in South Molton. September 16 1978.

Glebe Cottage 1978. On the left, the 'garden' with packing cases and assorted weeds. Right, a home of our own.

1981: One up, one down. Taking turns holding Annie and building terrace and a stone wall, the first of many.

Following in my great grandfathers' footsteps, tackling giant weeds on the far side of the track with a scythe.

Annie's birthday present. Cobweb checking on her four kittens, born in the wardrobe drawer. Annie and Alice having a gentle cuddle.

Alice's birthday. Annie standing on 'the lawn', with Alice on the front step. Look at that wisteria! The girls' bedroom was behind it.

That's more like it. The field alongside was much more fun to play in. The girls were outside as often as they could be.

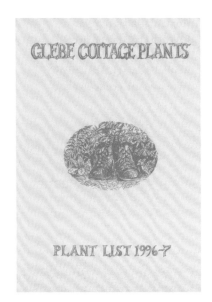

GLEBE COTTAGE PLANTS

Pixie Lane Warkleigh Umberleigh
Devon EX37 9DH

Proprietress: Carol Klein

Here is our long-awaited plant list for 1996-97.

Our nursery is small and intimate but the choice of plants is wide. To get into our list, a plant has to be garden-worthy, interesting and beautiful. We love the plants we grow - each of them is handmade for you - an individual.

We mix our own compost to ensure our plants have the best possible start, we grow them on naturally without heat or forcing, and sell them when they are ready to be planted.

We exhibit at all the major flower shows, where we display the plants we sell. (The nursery won gold medals at Chelsea in 1992, 1993, 1994 and 1995). Unfortunately, we are so busy and cramped for space at these events that we are unable to deliver orders. However, we always have a wide selection of plants for sale at these shows.

We regret we no longer offer a mail order service. We are sorry to disappoint our regular long-distance customers, but we have had to end the service as it has become increasingly expensive, problematical and time-consuming.

By far the best way to buy our plants is at the garden nursery. Here you can see examples of many of the plants we offer growing in the garden. We are sorry to dispel the myth that finding us is tantamount to plant-hunting in the Himalayas at the turn of the century. We are actually quite accessible from all directions and we now have many signposts around locally. We give exact, easy-to-follow directions on the back cover.

We are close to many fine gardens including R.H.S. Rosemoor, Marwood Hill Gardens, N.T. Knightshayes and N.T. Killerton.

The prices quoted are for guidance, being new plants in 9cm pots. As they are potted on, they may be repriced.

We at Glebe Cottage Plants produced a new catalogue every year. Neil drew the boots. Our ethos inside!

Also courtesy of Neil, who created all sorts of artefacts for shows, a picket fence and sign in the colour of the moment, and an obliging paeony.

Our first Chelsea in 1990. My darling friend Sonia explains about a plant to a visitor. Kind, compassionate and mad about plants. I miss her so.

Every Chelsea show was different, plants, props and design. Here we used cob structures. Suit by Jean-Paul Gaultier.

I loved selling plants and always wanted to know about people's gardens, checking out the suitability of their new homes.

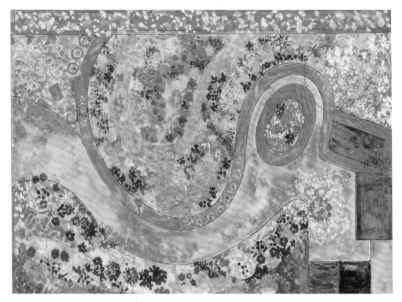

21 Century Street, 1999. A plan of the garden: curvy walls, oak capped to sit on, herb table, wave planting, sweet pea obelisks and native hedge and the first ever cow parsley at Chelsea.

Grinning between sweet pea obelisks (emphasising using vertical space, especially in a small garden) and glorying in the planting.

Jon Snow, Germaine Greer, me and Rory Bremner. Channel 4 sponsored the garden and commissioned 'Wild About Chelsea'.

My most important Gold Medal awarded by the late, great Valerie Finnis VMH, inscribed on a banana – only the photo survives.

Tessa Traeger's sublime image of our Chelsea 2002 show in The Great Pavilion.
Note Dick Thornton's labels. © Tessa Traeger

Somebody's birthday on a sunny day. Cobweb has just finished the ice-cream.
The beech trees on the horizon now touch one another.

Tessa's portrait of me amongst plants just returned from Chelsea. Both these images from her epic *A Gardener's Labyrinth*. A huge honour to be included. © Tessa Traeger

Glebe Cottage Plants, our first nursery, with ramshackle greenhouse and a lorra, lorra lot of plants. I wonder how many plants we've grown?

Contender for the 'Best travelled mossy log in the world'. Returning from the Hampton Court Garden. Taking shows down is the least glamorous of all aspects of exhibiting.

My two best gardening friends Veronica Cross and John Massey celebrating my VMH award. In my hand is the bone china pot Veronica hand-painted and awarded me to commemorate the day.

A pile of medal cards and some medals including VMH.

In the garden at Glebe Cottage, with a clump of *Geranium psilostemon* that has been dug up from Annie's border and is ready to divide before replanting. © Jonathan Buckley

My two husbands, John Massey on left (a husband according to *Hello* magazine) and Neil Klein (according to The Registrar, Barnstaple Registry Office).

My brothers Bill and Pip on the occasion of Pip's 65th birthday. I am so lucky to have had such lovely brothers. My classmate Fergy Bailey is on the right.

With my friend Roy Lancaster at Hampton Court, celebrating my winning the RHS Iconic Horticultural Hero award.

Showing our grandchildren Sydney and Bill around our Hampton Court Garden. They are both enchanted by the natural world. I hope they will continue to garden.

Lilies

My first recollection of lilies is of their scent on a sultry summer's evening. It drifted down the broad steps that led up to my landlord's garden, filling the whole place with their heady perfume in the first flat I rented in London.

Although there were many gardens and thousands of plants in my childhood, there were no lilies.

Art history lectures with images of Renaissance paintings of the Madonna depicted her lily, *Lilium candidum*, and I yearned to see not just Botticelli's beautiful painting of *Madonna and Child with Eight Angels* with its background of tall stems of *Lilium candidum*, but the lilies themselves.

This lily is one of the oldest in cultivation and is featured in the art of many ancient civilisations. Portrayed in Assyrian bas-reliefs, there are artefacts dating back three and a half thousand years showing clearly that it was known and prized. Its association with purity remains to this day.

It is grown here in the UK but has fallen out of favour, perhaps because it does not fit the commercial template to which lilies nowadays have to conform. It is unusual in that it makes a tuft of leaves in the autumn which stay all winter and from which the flower stems arise, sometimes reaching two metres tall.

It is unusual in other ways too, in that it loves to be baked and thrives in alkaline soils. A true cottage garden plant. If you can grow it, do. It will not grow at Glebe Cottage; when I cadged a few bulbs from a kind cottage gardener, they sulked and died. If you are lucky enough to find it, plant it shallowly, only a couple of inches deep.

Once upon a time, apart from *Lilium candidum*, lilies were seldom seen anywhere but in the gardens of the rich. It is only in the last fifty years that they have become truly popular. During the last few decades there has been a revolution in the lily world, with the breeding and selection of hundreds, perhaps thousands of new hybrids aimed both at the cut-flower trade and their cultivation as garden bulbs.

In his *English Flower Garden*, the main plant reference tome for Victorian and Edwardian gardeners, William Robinson lists and describes several species of lilies along with their countries of origin, but very few hybrids are mentioned. Nowadays new varieties are introduced constantly by lily specialists, commercial and amateur. They have to hand, as their source, lilies from all over the world to come up with new colours, patterns, habits and perfumes. There are double lilies now, which I eschew – to me the beauty of a lily is in the shape of its flowers. Work is being done to breed lilies that have no pollen – yes, it's a nuisance if you get pollen on your clothes or your person and it can be a killer for cats, but the way in which pollen-laden anthers protrude or dangle is part of the lily's personality and its grace and beauty.

Nor do I understand the emphasis on trying to produce short, stumpy lilies, often with upturned flowers, 'for the small garden'. Most lilies for such gardens – the great majority of our gardens are small and getting smaller – are grown in pots, and since lilies tend to be vertical, why should we not grow taller, more elegant varieties which respect and cherish what a lily is? To me it is always a mistake to assume that small gardens must have dwarf plants and that everything must be miniaturised.

Breeders have made such leaps and bounds and some of the lilies available today are truly breathtaking. To wander around the stands of lily specialists at the big flower shows is a rapturous experience.

It isn't all plain sailing though. Some lilies just won't hybridise, but methods have been devised to fertilise them and take off the embryo before it is aborted, growing it on and nurturing it till maturity. Dr Chris North experimented with pioneering techniques during the sixties and seventies and laid the groundwork for much of the lily breeding that goes on now.

What is it about lilies that makes them so special? They are surely the most glamorous of flowers, and most combine their wondrous colours and patterns with a grace and elegance unmatched by any plant in our gardens. The majority have a scent powerful enough to make you weak at the knees.

To find a bulb that is so easy to cultivate and reliably produces such spectacular results, one that often goes on year after year and brings a touch of mystery and exoticism wherever it is grown, is horticultural happiness itself.

To gild the lily, they are unparalleled as container plants. Since the advent of garden centres, more and more gardeners have used ornamental containers and pots to create features in our gardens and ring the changes. There have always been urns, cisterns and other imposing containers in grand gardens but now we all have the wherewithal to use pots and containers. They can be either planted directly into the containers in which they will flower or in plastic pots which can be either dropped into decorative containers as the lilies begin to flower – at Glebe Cottage we substitute them for fading tulips which are grown in the same way – or the pots can be placed in borders behind or amongst tall perennials to enhance the display.

At ground level they are a versatile group of plants. As with all other plant ingredients on your garden menu, remember Nicola Ferguson's maxim, 'Right plant, right place.'

If you have shade, choose woodlanders – martagon lilies will thrive and naturalise under trees or between shrubs in humus-rich soil. They are best autumn planted and put in at least five inches deep. To create a natural effect, scatter the bulbs so they grow randomly.

Lilium regale, which is the most widely grown lily in the world, looks wonderful in pots or in the ground. It likes an open situation and like most lilies prefers to have its roots in the shade but its flowers in the sun. It is unlikely you can duplicate its natural habitat! This is the lily that the famous plant explorer Ernest 'Chinese' Wilson discovered in the Min valley in western China growing in rock crevices and beside raging torrents high in the mountains. He brought it back in 1904 after years of unsuccessful attempts, but not before acquiring his 'lily limp', sustained when his leg was broken in a rock fall. He used his camera tripod as a splint and had to be carried for three days to find medical help.

We should all take his advice 'not to ruin its constitution with rich food'. Check the requirements of the lilies you want to grow to ensure they will thrive in your soil and that they will be happy in the place you intend to plant them. Most hybrid lilies including the Oriental Trumpet hybrids are happy in the majority of situations, whereas the Oriental hybrids need soil with an acid pH.

Lilies make superb cut flowers and are immensely popular. Each year a quarter of a million weddings use them as a cut flower and they are used at twice that number of funerals!

I'm not having a funeral, but when Neil and I got married my bouquet consisted of several stems of *Lilium speciosum* tied up with a slatey-blue velvet ribbon. We were late with arrangements and the day before the wedding I realised I had no flowers. Driving past council houses in South Molton, I spotted a huge pot of *Lilium speciosum*, screeched to a halt and rang the doorbell. The gentleman who'd grown them cut them there and then and refused to let me pay. All he got for his generosity was a piece of wedding cake and my eternal thanks. I'll never forget him, nor the scent of those beautiful crimson and white blooms on that very special September day.

Lily beetle is the scourge of all lilies. They can be collected as adult beetles (put paper on the ground beneath the plants before you start as they are inclined to drop down from the plants when they realise they are under attack). The larvae won't try and get away – they look like squidgy bird poo so it's not a pleasant task to remove them, but it must be done if your lilies are to do their best. Vigilance is required; we need to conduct beetle patrol every day.

L. speciosum rubrum

If you want delightful, perfumed Turk's cap lilies to flower right into the autumn, try these. They prefer acidic soils but are wonderful container bulbs if your soil is too alkaline to grow them in the open ground. Wonderful with autumn foliage colour and asters.

L. 'Mrs R.O. Backhouse'

I've been lucky enough to visit Sutton Court, where this lily first arose, a Backhouse cross between *Lilium hansonii* and a martagon lily (the garden still boasts clumps of martagon lilies). Its colouring is exquisite; you never want the buds to open but when they do you wonder how you could have waited.

L. tigrinum

Several lilies come under the umbrella title of tiger lilies, but the one most commonly called by this name is *Lilium lancifolium*. The tiger lily was once one of the most frequently grown of all lilies. There are yellow and dusky pink forms too. They share the ability to produce bulbils in their leaf axils which can be detached, grown on and will eventually make proper bulbs.

L. 'Carbonero'

This Oriental Trumpet lily is happy in most soils. In common with all lilies it likes humus-rich conditions with adequate moisture though resenting wet conditions. It is highly scented and flowers from July onwards.

L. pardalinum

One of the few lilies that enjoys damp conditions, the 'leopard' or 'panther' lily comes from the west coast of the USA in the woodlands and mountains of Oregon and California. It makes clusters of bulbs and individual flower stems can attain 2m plus.

L. martagon 'Album'

Martagon lilies have a widespread distribution from France through to the Far East. They are essentially shade lovers and the one that looks better than any in this situation is this, the pure white form.

L. nepalense

Surely one of the most strikingly seductive of all lilies despite its subdued colouring. It grows at the woodland edge in damp soil and often moves itself around via stolons. During the day there is no scent and the flowers are camouflaged. At night it pumps out intense perfume to attract nocturnal pollinators.

L. 'Firebolt'

A short Oriental hybrid up to 75cm tall. Glowing dark colour in late summer and scented to boot. Must have soil or compost on the acid side. Difficult to mingle – better on its own.

Regardless of your soil and site, or even if you have no garden at all, as long as you have some outdoor space, you can grow lilies in containers. Terracotta pots are ideal since they're porous and allow excess water to drain away – lilies hate sitting in wet compost. Use any good proprietary potting compost, but if you're potting up acid lovers like the Orientals use ericaceous compost. As for the size of your containers, the bigger the better is the rule to allow plenty of room for root development and to accommodate lots of compost for nutrient and water uptake. Shallow pots aren't suitable. You can pot lilies up individually but make sure each pot is roomy. They make a quirky feature down steps or along a path. A mild liquid feed high in potash can be applied intermittently once your lilies have come into growth.

1) Use damp compost and if your clay pots are new, soak them first so they don't suck out all the moisture from the compost. Half fill pots with compost. I prefer loam-based compost because sometimes my lilies are in their pots for years and soil

holds nutrients better than peat and peat substitutes. Nobody uses peat or peat-based composts anymore, we hope. Sale of them will be banned from the end of 2024.

2) Ensure your bulbs are plump and firm. Discard any scales which show signs of disease. Gently push the bulbs into the compost, spreading out any new roots as you go. Old roots should be pulled off. Pot up bulbs as promptly as possible. Bulb size varies from species to species but always go for the biggest on offer!

3) Top up your pots with compost. Sometimes, especially if you're keeping your lilies under cover until later, you can just cover the bulbs when planting and then top them up as their shoots emerge so they are never in danger of rotting. Water once but then leave them alone until compost begins to feel dry.

4) Finish off the surface with grit. This will stop weeds, moss and liverwort growing on the surface of the compost, and it will help retain moisture in the compost and protect the lilies' stems from rotting. Because it is heavy it prevents wet compost splashing up when you're watering or feeding. It can also look pretty!

Chapter Eight

After Anthony and I had split up, there had been disastrous efforts on my part to find somewhere to live and to find someone I wanted to live with. I met up again with Donald Taylor, whom I had known at both Bolton and Newport Colleges of Art, and we started to see each other frequently.

I left Sir John Cass in 1969 to travel to Rome with him; he was a talented artist who whilst studying art at the Slade had won the Rome Scholarship. He came from Bury, close to my home. He pursued his painting, but though I had every intention of taking up my own drawing and painting again, that being the pretext under which I had given up my job, I spent more time exploring the grounds of the British School and beyond, enchanted by the flora and the formality of the gardens. On one memorable trip, soon after we arrived, Donald and I travelled to the Abruzzi mountains, due east from Rome. We both loved the great outdoors and this was a chance to be in nature. I had never seen cyclamen growing before, though in the markets in Rome I was entranced to see bunches of these dainty flowers offered for sale.

I needed to make some money and was employed by the archaeology department for a couple of months making reconstructive drawings of Roman pottery from fragments they unearthed on their digs. There was a lot of measurement and precision involved, not really my style though I got the hang of it; it was tempting sometimes to employ a bit of artistic licence to complete the curve of an urn or re-invent a handle. By far the most interesting part of the job was talking to the archaeologists about some of the seeds and grains they found and how some of them, as much as 2,000 years old, had germinated.

My sojourn at the British School did not last long. During a Bonfire Night party where huge branches of recently pruned bay trees fuelled the fire – the smell was wonderful – I was attracted to a guest from the Rhode Island School of Design, which had an outpost in Rome. Many American art and design/architecture colleges had branches in Italy where students could come and study for six months or a year, imbibing the culture and practising their art. Robert was studying architecture. We met on several occasions and I decided to leave Don and begin a relationship with Robert. Feeling it would be too hurtful and amoral just to move out, move across Rome and move in with Robert, I decided that to sate my conscience I needed to travel back to the UK and then return to Rome to my new relationship and my new home. I had no money so I hitchhiked, spent a few days with my family, turned round and hitchhiked back. It was midwinter and cold and I took a strange route through the Netherlands and ended up somehow in the Black Forest where on a night colder than any I can remember, I was picked up with two other hitchhikers, taken to a police station and fined for illegally hitchhiking. The fine just about cleaned me out. We asked the police from where it would be legal to hitchhike and my journey continued. Amazingly I got a lift from an English lorry driver whose destination was Rome. He was from up north and seemed glad of the company and all went well until on a stop in Switzerland, he made it clear that he expected sexual favours from me in return for his kindness. I got out of his cab immediately; he chased after me and apologised and asked me to return. The rest of the journey was uneventful but quiet.

RISD had their headquarters at Palazzo Cenci in the Jewish Quarter of Rome. In their premises on one floor of the palace, there were studios, some living accommodation, a kitchen and a communal area. I was made welcome, and they found me somewhere to work. I completed just one piece of work there, a pencil self-portrait. One of the tutors there, Barry Kirschenbaum, arranged for me to have a job there, cleaning up, washing up and generally helping out, which paid very little money but entitled me to live and do my own work there day to day. Also, and much more excitingly, I was to be allowed to travel with the students on several trips. By far the most memorable of these was a trip to Sicily, taking in the Valley of the Temples of Agrigento. Our route took us to Pompei and Napoli. The history, geography and culture of the areas we visited was fascinating but what stood out for me then and now were and are the plants. Through the coach windows and each time we stopped there were plants I had never seen before, vegetation and landscapes unlike any in my experience.

It was when we reached Agrigento though that my excitement turned to overwhelming delight. Our coach had stopped at the top of a wide slope above some of the temples. Most of the students walked down to see them, but I was overwhelmed. Before me, basking in the bright morning light, thousands of anemones turned their faces up towards the warm spring sun with petals in jewel-like colours, red, purple, mauve, lilac, pink and pure white, each with a centre as black as coal. I sat amongst them feeling part of them, part of the earth from which they sprang. They and the generations before them must have grown in just that way since time immemorial, long, long before the Ancient Greeks landed from the turquoise sea below and built their temples. People come and go but, if we do nothing to stop them, plants go on forever.

* * *

Although I failed miserably in learning Italian, I immersed myself in taking in as much I could. Not in any highfalutin culture-vulture way but just in terms of day-to-day life, especially food and market shopping. The markets were glorious; the one closest to Palazzo Cenci, Campo de' Fiori, was an entertainment in its own right. Produce galore, fat purple artichokes, bundles of skinny wild asparagus, tomatoes and peppers of every shape, size and colour. There were stalls that sold nothing but different kinds of dandelion leaves, each with its own name.

In France dandelions are called *pissenlit*, and we used to call them 'wet the bed'; children would tease each other mercilessly when they picked the flowers or broke off the clock to tell the time. We have a fieldful and it has crossed my mind that we might investigate the commercial possibilities of harvesting them. They are diuretic and, both historically and in contemporary herbal practice, are often used in medicinal remedies.

It is the flowers that are the most fascinating aspect of this plant. Members of the daisy family, which they are, have two sorts of florets, disc florets and ray florets. Dandelions have only ray florets.

* * *

When I came back from Rome, having parted from Robert Leigh and decided to make my own way in the world, I was jobless and homeless. It was summer, not a great time to find a teaching job, but

I applied for a job as a playleader in an adventure playground – a new phenomenon – in a London park. It was a great job, organising all sorts of activities. The two women I was working with didn't like me much, they seemed to think I was too full-on and that my yin-yang balance was badly awry, and they advised me to steer clear of aubergines. Perhaps they were right for the wrong reasons. Because aubergines, alongside tomatoes and potatoes, belong to the *Solanum* family, some say I should avoid them because I have mild arthritis (in common with most people of my great age), though there is no conclusive evidence to suggest this is the case. I love eating them too.

Having stayed briefly with friends, I managed to get a small room in a flat near Primrose Hill, sharing with four girls, all friends and all much younger and posher than me. I kept looking for teaching work and applied for a job at a big boys' comprehensive school in White City, Shepherd's Bush, as a full-time art teacher. I went for an interview and got the job starting that September. From the outset I enjoyed it immensely.

Almost all the teachers were men; one of the main contingents were older men who had taken up teaching immediately after the Second World War. Happily for me a couple of other younger women joined the staff later and there were a few young, more politically aware and forward-thinking men to share conversation and ideas with. One of them was Safder, whose family, Gujarati in origin, had moved to this country from Tanzania. Safder invited me to come to a political meeting. I went along to the meeting, the first of many over the next seven years, though I am not sure that initially at any rate Safder was not more of an attraction than the politics.

Although Donald Taylor and I were both card-carrying members of the Communist party, I had never previously engaged in any political activity other than a bit of door-to-door canvassing. Meetings were often held in people's flats and I was asked if I would offer my room for one such meeting. About twenty people packed into my tiny room; many of them smoked. It was not ideal and only happened once.

A much more salubrious venue was a house in Hampstead on Pilgrim's Lane, which by strange coincidence was right next door to the house where Anthony Amies and I had lived. In the meeting were several new people, including two brothers, Peter and Neil Klein. They were Hampstead residents and friends of the couple, Lina and Wowo, whose house it was. Peter had come along out of curiosity and persuaded Neil, his younger brother, to accompany him to compensate for arriving late. During the meeting Peter and I had argued and after it was over we had carried on the discussion, all three of us walking onto Hampstead Heath.

When I saw Neil for the first time I fell for him. He was a tall, well-built young man with a beard and matching long, wavy locks of vivid auburn. I should have been concentrating on politics, but instead, as you do, I was wondering about this beautiful young man: where was he from, what did he do, how old was he, did he have a girlfriend or even, heaven forbid, a wife? I think it is fair to say the attraction was mutual. Since we finally got together, we have been together non-stop. I love him without condition. He is by far the kindest, most selfless person ever and just about the funniest too (this is from someone who knows Tom Allen a bit and has met Joe Lycett and Josh Widdicombe and Graham Norton). He is the best thing that has ever happened to me, and I feel so lucky to have spent so many happy years with him and intend to spend many more. Our girls could not have had a better dad, nor I a better partner. I just wish I could have done as much for him as he has done for me.

We realised that I was eight years older than him, or that he was eight years younger than me, and at the same time we both realised that it really didn't matter.

We were 'just friends' for the first year of our acquaintance. We saw each other frequently at political meetings – I am not convinced Neil would have attended if I had not been there.

He is a brilliant cartoonist. His drawing is spot on and he has the facility to understand the crux of the matter and get to the nitty gritty, whereas I digress and cannot always see the wood for the trees. I get waylaid sometimes and fail to prioritise what is important. One of my favourite Neil cartoons was stuck on the side of a jar of yogurt he made for me when he came to see me in hospital after my cone biopsy op at the Samaritan Hospital for Women on Marylebone Road. It portrayed Marx, Engels, Lenin, Trotsky and Stalin with a couple of hammers and sickles for good measure.

Later on we went out together a few times. There was a picnic in Cookham, Stanley Spencer being one of my favourite painters. But we never could actually take the big step from a friendship to a love affair; he was too shy and I was too wary, fed up with men after several discouraging misadventures.

Then one night, friends of ours were having a party in Notting Hill Gate. I wasn't stringing Neil along but had refused to commit to anything full time or long term when I looked up to see him leaving the room in the wake of a very beautiful woman. That did it. I rushed after him, grabbed him and smothered him in kisses. We left the party soon afterwards and walked back the long way to my flat in Kensal Rise. It was already late when we left the party. It was one of those June nights following a hot sunny day when the temperature seems to be maintained throughout the night. The air was sultry, perfumed with the scent from roses and lilies. We walked and walked and when we opened the door to my flat it opened the door to the rest of my life.

* * *

Teaching art was a much easier proposition than teaching maths. Some of the teachers with whom I taught were splendid, passionate about their subjects and committed to the pupils. Robert Tannitch was an inspiring head of English, full of energy and enthusiasm and the desire to acquaint the boys with the richness of their literary heritage. Some of the boys in my class and I helped in a school production of Oscar Wilde's *The Ballad of Reading Gaol*, directed and produced by Robert. We mass-produced papier-mâché masks for judges, first modelling moulds from clay. We helped with sets and programmes; we worked after school with great gusto.

Tom Burke, Bill Harper and Ian Barnard were three of the leading lights – all in my form, I am proud to say, and all lovely boys. Ian was brilliant at art and hugely interested in the natural world. I wanted him to take up horticulture, but his stepdad wasn't keen. Ian now lives in Lincolnshire amongst the wildlife that he loves. I recently received a letter from him, addressed 'Dear Miss (Carol)', where he reminded me about our gardening club where he and I were the only participants. It is good to hear how happy he is.

There had grown up an unofficial art club most days after school in my art room where a motley collection of lads would come and paint, draw and craft. One little boy who attended regularly was called Colin Shimhue. He had not been in the country long. We made tea and coffee and the boys would take it in turn to go across to the shops on Bloemfontein Road to buy milk and occasionally biscuits. I paid. On this particular day I gave Colin some money and off he went. I glanced out of one of the windows of my art room on the second floor, which faced the road, and saw Colin coming along, milk bottle in hand. As he got towards the door I could hear an altercation and saw and heard what happened next. One of the teachers stopped him as he was about to enter and demanded to know what he was doing and where he was going. Colin told him. The teacher told him not to answer back and promptly hit him and knocked him over. I could hardly believe my eyes and ears. I opened the window and leaned out and shouted for him to stop. The teacher went into the building, Colin got slowly to his feet, I rushed down two flights of stairs. The teacher had disappeared but Colin was still standing outside the door dazed and dismayed that the milk had spilled over the grass beside the path. We made our way back to the art room. Later on my way home I called in at the staff room looking for the teacher, but he had gone. The next morning, first thing, I went to see the headmaster and told him what had occurred. He said he would look into it. The next thing I heard was that I was to be hauled before the NUT executive to face a charge of unprofessional conduct. I went along to it with my well-informed colleague, Maggie Majumdar, and after a hearing that lasted an hour and a half, the committee, which seemed to be composed of the whole NUT executive, found that there was no case to answer. I was exonerated. But why was I there in the first place?

Perhaps it was because I belonged to a small political group called the Women Workers League which tackled local issues and supported working people fighting for their rights. We were particularly active in a local girls' school where many black girls had been suspended indefinitely. We waged a campaign, leafletting the school and fighting individual cases of unfair suspension alongside the girls and their families.

There was a Black Workers League too, and an Unemployed Workers Union. Many left-wing groups were active in the area. On one occasion we held a meeting in the community hall on Talbot Road just down the road from the Mangrove, to discuss joint action in demonstrating against a meeting the National Front were about to hold at the old Kensington and Chelsea Town Hall. The police were informed that our meeting was to take place since there had been talk of the National Front trying to disrupt the proceedings. Eventually they turned up shortly after a mob of National Fronters had broken into the meeting and started to attack participants. They came in armed with knuckle dusters and various weapons but got more than they had bargained for. There was a fight during which one older bloke, 'The Colonel', attacked me and I retaliated by picking up the stool I had been sitting on and hitting him with it. I hate violence and kept reliving this for months afterwards. We threw them out. Instead of the police coming to our aid they allowed the invaders to disperse without taking any names or making any arrests.

Our meeting continued with more determination than ever despite a suggestion from a senior policeman that we disband it and go home.

We demonstrated against their event at the town hall. In his job as steward I saw Neil in a new light, marshalling us to ensure that the agent provocateurs who had infiltrated our crowd found it impossible to stir up trouble and start a fight. Nonetheless the National Front meeting went ahead.

* * *

These years of teaching were rewarding but politically tumultuous. In 1975, I was the first person to bring a case of sex discrimination under the Sex Discrimination Act. I took my employers, the Inner London Education Authority (ILEA), to court when they gave the job of head of the art department at Christopher Wren School to a man less qualified than me. I had already been doing the job during the previous year. Our case went to court; I represented myself and Neil was my McKenzie man. Our case was impeccably researched and well presented but in the event the judge reserved his judgement to decide whether or not the act was retroactive.

The school had brought forward the interviews due to be held in January 1975 to October 1974. I will leave you to form your own conclusions. Needless to say it was decided that the act was not retroactive and the court could only hear any cases occurring after its passing into law on 1 January 1975. The job itself was not important, but the injustice of the decision and the cynical move on the part of the ILEA and the school to move the interviews to avoid jurisdiction meant I was duty bound to pursue the case as far as I could.

It was probably more a case of political discrimination anyway. The powers-that-be within the school did not like the fact that I and several other younger teachers were willing to discuss with the boys any issues they thought important. We all had a form period for an hour once a week and this was an opportunity not for me and the others to fill kids' heads with left-wing propaganda but for them to bring up any issues and for us all to say what we thought. It was a great opportunity for them to air not just their tolerances but also their prejudices.

The National Front were 'big' at the time. The parents of a few boys in my class were in sympathy with their views and a few of them were members. I can remember one boy in my class, who had two good friends of Irish and black descent. He was already influenced by his parents' views and when asked how he squared that with his friendships with these boys, replied that they were different. Contradictions abounded in school just as they did and still do in the bigger world outside. All three of these boys and the rest of our form went to Kew Gardens on an art outing. I arranged these trips from time to time, taking just one class at a time with sketchbooks and pencils to draw and explore, but mainly to surround themselves with plants and nature. The school had one camera, so everyone got a chance to take one picture. Theoretically whatever information they gathered would be used during their next art lesson as the starting point for a piece of artwork, a painting, print or, in a few cases, an embroidery.

Our trips to Kew were suspended because of an unfortunate though nonetheless amusing incident. The group were sitting drawing beside the water-lily lake when one of the boys said, ''Ere, miss. Ain't that Dean and Mark?' It was; they had commandeered the boat the gardeners used for maintaining the water-lilies and were practising their oarsmanship. On this occasion they were completely in control, pretending they could not hear my order to come back to shore. It was some time before we were allowed back.

Soon after the sex discrimination case, we left London, and I took up a job as head of art – not a whopping department, just me and two others – at a school in South Molton. It was advertised as being on the edge of Exmoor, and I was excited at the prospect. I had imagined a romantic, rustic stone building covered in ivy or perhaps Virginia creeper – it was September and the leaves would be reddening up by then. What a glorious picture I held in my mind. Instead, on a preliminary fact-finding tour the evening before my interview, Neil and I were somewhat dismayed to be confronted with an ugly, large white 1950s monstrosity that looked more like a stranded liner than a school. But by then I had fallen in love with the countryside we had glimpsed on our journey there, especially the ferns. My eyes could hardly take them in.

They are one of the reasons I will never move from here.

Cyclamen

One of my most abiding memories is coming across colonies of *Cyclamen hederifolium* growing in the boles of beech trees in the Abruzzi mountains outside Rome. It was early September and they were at the beginning of their flowering season. The immensity of the trees emphasised the fragility of the cyclamen's tiny pink flowers, which, at close quarters, are intriguing at every stage. Their scrolled buds are long and narrow. The petals gradually unfurl and as they do they draw backwards as though surprised to find themselves upside down.

There are few plants which offer both such exquisite flowers and such ornately decorative foliage as the ivy-leaved cyclamen, *C. hederifolium.* Like human fingerprints, every plant has unique markings, no two ever the same. A mass planting in the late autumn or winter is more fascinating than the most intricately detailed Persian carpet. In late winter they are joined by the foliage and flowers of *C. coum*, which in its typical form has round, leathery, dark green leaves and flowers with the same intriguing propeller formation as *C. hederifolium.* The usual flower colour is vivid magenta. Seedlings are pale pink and occasionally white, but even the white-flowered varieties are stained with pink at the base of their petals. At one time *C. coum* was described as always having plain green leaves, and

varieties with silver markings were classed as a separate species –
C. orbiculatum. Now bulb firms list distinct silver-leaved and silver-
marked varieties as forms of *C. coum*.

Nature is always ingenious and nowhere more so than in
the distribution of cyclamen seeds. As the petals fall after pollination, the seedpods swell and the stem begins to spiral, ending
up as a tight coil. Eventually the seed-head descends to ground
level, where it fattens up and, on ripening, splits apart to reveal
a collection of small round seeds, each one of which looks like a
tiny tuber. Meanwhile their starchy coating has changed to sugar,
attracting ants, which move in and carry them away, thus ensuring
that young plants are not competing with their parents. Sometimes
the seeds are carried even further afield by wasps, also attracted to
the sugar. As flowers fade, leaves begin to appear.

This is the process responsible for the large colonies of
cyclamen which often establish themselves under trees. You can
allow nature to take its course or intervene by taking seed just as
the pods begin to split apart and sowing it on the surface of any
seed compost. Cover with grit and stand the seed tray or pot in
a bowl of shallow water. Put in a sheltered place and prick out
individually into cell trays or small pots when the first leaf is properly developed. Alternatively, one seed can be pressed into each
individual section of a module tray which helps prevent root disturbance when potting on. Young plants will flower for the first time
in their second or third year and, if the conditions suit them, will
get bigger and better year by year. In gardens where they have been
established for a long time, you can sometimes come across huge
tubers the size of a dinner plate producing hundreds of flowers each
year. During the summer, tubers lie dormant, dry amongst the tree
roots yet protected from desiccation by fierce sun. As leaves fall,

tubers are exposed to autumnal rains and as the soil becomes moist they plump up and spring into life.

Although the flowers of *Cyclamen hederifolium* are reason enough to grow it, it is its foliage which constitutes the major attraction. Each plant has unique leaves and a whole colony in full leaf provides a rich tapestry of intricate detail in countless shades of green. This foliage lasts throughout the winter and spring until fizzling out in early summer when the tubers gather their strength for flowering. In Italy (it used to be called *neapolitanum*, from Naples) it grows under trees up in the mountains and this proclivity for shade makes it an ideal plant for the darker parts of the garden. Under deciduous trees its foliage makes a brilliant patchwork during the winter months and when the canopy fills in overhead it offers the shade which the plant needs. Some of the silver-leaved forms, especially those with white flowers, make a splendid feature in the darkest corners of the garden. They are a fitting foil for dark-leaved, black-flowered hellebores which are at their peak at the same time.

Cyclamen coum is in full flower from January to March. Its rounded, slightly dumpy flowers are borne at the same time as its foliage. They are often a particularly vivid shade of magenta that shines out from the surrounding dreary brown and buff of midwinter's dross. The leaves are rounded and usually very dark green and shiny, but recent breeding has given a fine selection of pewter-leaved forms, some edged in green. One particularly fine cultivar is *Cyclamen coum* 'Maurice Dryden'. Its white propeller-like flowers are stained purple at their base and the rounded leathery leaves are silver outlined in green. None of these selected forms necessarily breeds true, but when we have sown seed here from silver-leaved plants, the great majority have been close to their parent plant. In the wild both these cyclamen come from Mediterranean regions. Whilst *Cyclamen hederifolium* is a shade-lover, *Cyclamen coum* prefers a more open site. It is an ideal addition to a trough or container planting but will spread itself around in an alpine bed or on a rock garden.

Although it can be grown on its own, it is also a good mixer, ideal with the small winter irises, forms of *Iris reticulata* and *Iris histrioides*. For a striking picture, underplant it with *Crocus tomassinianus* – the two will happily self-seed and make trouble-free ground cover.

Scillas, chionodoxa and muscari also make good bedfellows, but the classic accompaniment for both *Cyclamen hederifolium* and *Cyclamen coum* is snowdrops. There is no more beautiful winter picture than drifts of snowdrops mingling with the patterned, ivy-shaped leaves of *Cyclamen hederifolium* or the vivid magenta flowers of *Cyclamen coum*.

Chapter Nine

When Neil and I lived in London I yearned for a garden. In Keslake Road, where Neil and I had our first flat together, I had my window boxes. In Ladbroke Grove where we lived next I had window boxes again but this time with dwarf conifers rather than sweet peas and nasturtiums. I grew a tomato plant and a bean on the tiny square of roof, where there was just enough room for them and me to sit and enjoy the sun. I would walk around the square where we lived peering into people's gardens and ply them with questions. I can still remember talking to one elderly couple at the top end of the square who were digging up and replanting their bearded irises. They showed me what they were doing, breaking off and discarding the old spent rhizomes, and replanting younger, fresher ones on the surface of the soil facing the sun so they would ripen and produce flowers. I can remember asking them how often they did this. 'Every five or six years,' they told me.

When our landlord, Monsieur Martin, generously agreed to my taking over one of the two beds at the front of the house, I was overjoyed. On my way home from school on my bike I raided the gardens of derelict properties, untended and overgrown. My panniers were full of soil. I found white Siberian irises – I felt such excitement when they later flowered, since they were just shoots and roots when I first liberated them. I brought back *Dracunculus vulgaris*, the dragon arum, with its striking, almost black spathes which stink to attract the flies that pollinate it. M. Martin objected to this – he couldn't see it, as he was blind, but he could smell it!

I persuaded Neil, whom I had only just taught to ride a bike (under the Westway), to accompany me on jaunts to Syon Park, to Kew Gardens and on one exhausting trip, to RHS Wisley. How fortunate I am that Neil has loved me and loves me still so much that he has not only tolerated my gardening mania but positively encouraged me in it. In some ways I feel I have given him no choice but to sublimate his wishes and desires to my gardening. He is the one who has made it possible for me to do what I love. Only through his sacrifice have I been able to do what I wanted.

* * *

The garden I have lived in, and loved, longest is the one at Glebe Cottage. As much as I made this garden, this garden made me. I have a lot to thank it for. It was as though my life had been leading up to this but also in some ways my life got going from the time when I started to make this garden.

I first saw this place on a February morning in 1978. I saw it from afar, across snow-covered fields, down the valley and up again, a small cottage halfway up the hill opposite. There had been severe blizzards cutting off the south-west for weeks.

The farm where I was staying, Little Stone, was completely snowed in. I had got back from an art-teachers' course in Dartington when the snow started, and it didn't stop. The *Mahonia japonica* that I couldn't resist buying on South Molton market the week before had to be rescued and brought into the porch. In fact it would probably have been fine outside, not endangered but protected by the snow.

Gardeners need to be optimists – I didn't even have a garden, but the scent of those pale yellow flowers was so seductive, pure lily-of-the-valley. That plant is now a huge shrub in the garden here and each day for the last couple of weeks, bringing Fifi back from our walk, I have made a diversion to enjoy that perfume as the long racemes of flower begin to open.

I digress again.

Little Stone was a small dairy farm and, during the blizzard, milk had to be taken out in a tractor and trailer across snow drifts. I helped a little with milking and with lambing which was just starting. Neil had not moved down permanently yet, as we were still looking for a place of our own while I stayed at the farm. I hadn't seen him for weeks, and when he finally got through on the train, he'd had to push his bike much of the way from Umberleigh station, pursued by sheepdogs. We were determined to find somewhere to live and went out on our bikes to survey a couple of properties, one of them at Deason, a cluster of cottages close to where we are now. Coming away, slightly disheartened, I saw a fingerpost sticking up above the snow pointing down a lane with a little passageway cleared between towering hedges, made mountainous with crystalline snow. Walking to the end of the lane, I saw Glebe Cottage – the name on the signpost.

Later that year we moved in.

For a few weeks, we had to share the cottage with the people from whom we had bought it. By the time they left it was school summer holidays. There was no garden, just going on for an acre of rough grass, weeds and brambles. A TV show would have called it 'a blank canvas'.

The track ran through it and broadened out to make a wider turning area for cars. Some of the cars on the plot would never turn round again! There were five or six of them that Billy Prout, the lovely JCB driver who we managed to afford for one day only, pulled out of the garden to be collected by a scrap metal dealer later on. I knew Billy, having briefly stayed with his family in South Molton when I had to vacate Little Stone for summer lets.

There was one car, a Morris Minor, which had come to rest in one of the many gullies, a feature of the land on one side of the track. Billy was going to move earth and rubble from a mound close to the cottage, probably there from when foundations were dug for the bathroom that the church had added when they owned the cottage, and use it to fill in some of these capacious holes. Since he was only there for the day, we all agreed it would be expedient for him to squash the car with his biggest bucket prior to filling the hole.

A few years later I planted a *Cornus* 'Norman Hadden' above it that has become the most important tree in the garden. It was a poor specimen when I first bought it, a layer from the tree in the garden at Rosemoor which was given to Lady Anne by Norman Hadden himself. Since it is doing so well, it is tempting to suggest that other gardeners follow suit when planting the same tree, except there are probably even fewer Morris Minors around than *Cornus* 'Norman Hadden's.

Billy used lots of the rubble to fill in the hole above the car, and he used most of the residue to make the foundations for paths that I imagined would eventually divide the area into separate beds. There was a lot of imagining at that stage of making the garden and there would be a lot of graft before such dreams could become a reality. One of the most immediate jobs was to clear not only the cars but a series of ramshackle sheds our predecessors had left us. They had been used to house rabbits, kept for breeding. Thank goodness by the time we arrived no rabbits were present.

Reverend Charles Napier was our next-door neighbour at the rectory, Glebe Cottage having been built initially to house the gardener-cum-gamekeeper for the incumbent rector. He was a keen gardener himself and only too pleased to teach me how to use his Austrian scythe and, once he thought I had got the hang of it, to lend it to me. Before I could borrow it though I had to become proficient not just at using it but also at sharpening the blade. Once you get into it, there is a beautiful rhythm to it and it was by far the most effective way to cut through grass and undergrowth. Perhaps using a scythe was in my blood, two of my great-grandfathers having been corn-cutters.

All this was happening on the east side of the track. There was no getting away from the fact that the track chopped the garden in half, and it still does. Because all the garden here is in front of the cottage, once you come in at the foot of the hill you are always heading up towards it. Short of creating obstacles across the path, the only way to lure you from it and into the garden either side is by employing diversionary tactics – enticing you away from the straight and narrow onto paths that might just take you on an altogether different journey.

Not that this was what was planned initially. I have always been deeply interested in plants, whereas garden design has never been my strong suit. For sure, experienced garden designers coming into my garden for the first time might find it lacking in any kind of design principles. They might find it incoherent. Yet they might be wrong – or to put it another way, in some respects, the garden has designed itself. It has grown out of itself, it is what it has made itself and we have just assisted.

As you looked out from the cottage when first we had the place to ourselves, beyond the nasty wide but shallow concrete steps that led down to the rest of the site was a wasteland, first of hardcore flattened by countless car manoeuvres which joined up with the track and then a wild area, not of delightful wildflowers but of rough grasses and assorted weeds which seemed to be competing with each other for dominance. There were three spindly Scots pines along the western edge, but they were the only evidence of any deliberate planting within the garden. On the other side of the track, plants, especially nettles, docks, brambles and field hemlock, were having a heyday – this is where my scything talents came into play. My theory was that the soil beneath their roots was nourished by the overspill or underspill from our septic tank. Neil bravely cleared the blockage and the weeds grew back less vigorously.

We had no mains drainage nor any mains water. Our water was supplied from a well way up in the field behind the house. It was not reliable and when we had it tested it fell well below acceptable safety standards. We decided mains water was a must – mind you, when we did have that installed and sent off samples for testing, the results showed that it was even worse than the well water.

One of Billy Prout's many other skills was divining water, dowsing as it is called. He identified several places in the garden where there were springs. If you look at the Ordnance Survey Map for this area, several springs are marked, and though they seem to move position slightly, there are always areas within the garden that are particularly damp. I am not sure what Billy's dowsing had to do with where he decided the trench for our mains water should run, but he dug it out across the fields and up to the road, pipes were laid, it was connected and it has worked well ever since. Billy was a little chap, especially in contrast to the giant JCB he manoeuvred so effortlessly. He was always cheerful, always smiling, always happy and he passed on this feeling to everyone around him. He made you feel that everything was possible and probably easy too. His favourite comment, regardless of the context, was, 'This is it.'

The only drainage we have ever implemented in the garden was to lay drainage pipes diagonally across the area where we later made a short-lived lawn when our children were young.

Back to the drawing board. In fact I didn't use a drawing board but I did engage in quite a lot of drawing. Having measured up the plot on the west side of the track, a long tapering triangle about 300 feet on its two long edges by about 40 feet at the top, I set about drawing a plan I thought might work.

I am pleased to say it would never have worked and none of us would have liked it if it had. It was full of all the worst gardening clichés. There were great sweeping lawns surging between voluptuously curving flower beds with places to sit here and there. It almost felt as though it was falling down the slope. Probably the most geographically striking feature of the site (it was a long way from becoming a garden) was that it slopes, quite dramatically – a fact of which you become even more aware as you become older, especially when you are walking up the hill.

This place has told me what it wants to be and as it has grown and developed it continues to tell me. Once I realised that it was a question of evolution rather than imposition I have been at ease with my garden. It has been a gradual process rather than an epiphany; it has become a discussion. I have never had an overall vision of how this place should be. Should does not come into it. There are no rules or regulations here imposed on the garden. Our only condition was and still is to respect natural laws – you plant your bulbs the right way up.

There must be thousands of ways I could have treated this patch of land, and who is to say whether or not what we have done here is right. When it comes to gardening, my philosophy is that there is no right or wrong – what is needed is an empathy with the surroundings and the willingness to help the garden to be as welcoming and easy as can be, as though it had always been there, as though it is meant to be.

All gardens are artifice, however naturalistic they purport to be. Every garden is artificial: it is us imposing our will on a piece of ground and controlling, to a greater or lesser extent, what grows there and how it grows. The more in tune we are with our plot, the more we recognise the prevailing conditions, the more likely we are to succeed.

Nobody can change the topography of a garden, but the place itself, the location, has to be consulted. We must have empathy with its surroundings and let them advise us how our garden can fit in with them. It is as Alexander Pope said:

> Consult the Genius of the Place in all;
> That tells the Waters or to rise, or fall,
> Or helps th' ambitious Hill the heav'n to scale,
> Or scoops in circling theatres the Vale,
> Calls in the Country, catches opening glades,
> Joins willing woods, and varies shades from shades,
> Now breaks or now directs, th' intending Lines;
> Paints as you plant, and, as you work, designs.

Perhaps it could have been done differently. Had I had the mindset of a landscape contractor, I might have made an all-encompassing plan and thought of making the garden as a finite project with a beginning and an end. But for me making a garden is a process and it can never be construed as a product, something that is finished.

It cannot be seen in the same way as interior decoration where there is an aim, work towards achieving that aim and a completion. Gardening is an organic process; everything within it is related to everything else, the plants to each other, the plants to the soil and situation, the weather, the passage of time.

* * *

The main asset of this garden is its situation facing south-west, halfway down a hill. It is fairly open yet protected on all sides. To the north is the cottage and an old hazel hedge plus the slope of the hill to nestle into; to the east a tall, straggly hedge of mixed oak and beech with a smattering of hazel, then further down the slope a dogleg bordering on the rectory's garden and lined with beech, probably an ancient farm hedge which is now 60ft tall.

Since it tapers down to nothing, there is really no boundary to the south but beyond a field rises gradually, part of a little valley. Heading west up the hill from there you come to a ridge and along it is a series of old beech trees, our horizon on that side. We use them as a calendar to read just where the year has reached.

The soil is heavy clay, fertile soil, but as an old farmer who came here in the early days commented, ''Tis hard-working soil.' We have constantly added organic matter over the years, home-made compost, leaf mould and quantities of cow dung from our very obliging near-neighbours the Thornes.

Initially there was an enormous amount of hard, physical work with little or no mechanical aid. One of the first things I wanted to do was replace the ugly steps down from our front door. I became a dab hand with a pickaxe and soon had a pile of rubble sitting at the foot of what had been the steps. Around the garden was scattered a quantity of large stones. They may have been left over from when the cottage was built between 1900 and 1904, which we know from our chimneys, both of which were dated in the concrete around them. Soon after we came here, we were lucky enough to meet a lovely lady called Connie whose father had been in charge of building Glebe Cottage. Stone for it was quarried in a tiny quarry at the bottom of Broden Hill close to where we live and Connie's cottage was just down the road. She could remember stone being loaded onto a horse and cart from the quarry and pulled up the hill. The ultimate in recycling, some of the stones I had used had already been used, cut and trimmed and later when my slightly uneven steps were replaced by Neil's far superior brick steps, the stones became part of a retaining wall further down the garden.

How many aeons of labour and energy must have gone into preparing and laying the stone for the cobbled roads in many of our cities?

The sloping ground beside the steps was odd and difficult to plant and though Glebe Cottage is on the modest side, it seemed important that the face it presented to the world should be proper. A fairly level bed at either side of the front door seemed appropriate, supported by low walls; it would have to be stone too. Whilst I was at it we could do with a level paved surface at the base of the steps but the surrounding area would need to be lifted to the level of the base of the bottom step. The demolished steps were a start but it was going to take much more hard core.

Meanwhile, back indoors, the walls between a pantry-cum-coal hole-cum-tiny bathroom were being demolished to make a bigger bathroom – more rubble, excellent! From the bottom of the steps I moved outwards and, having acquired a few slates, I paved as far as I could. A further retaining wall was to stop the rubble and flagstones moving down the hill. The effect worked: we now had a platform from which we could view the garden when there was one, perhaps even a place to bring out chairs, maybe a table.

In a garden I've always found that there's a particular thrill in the connection between the ancient and the new, the materials and species that have been with us for millions of years alongside our recent introductions. In Glebe Cottage, we're deep in fern country. These mysterious and magical plants occur throughout the British Isles, but it is surely here in Devon that they are most in evidence.

Ferns are amongst the oldest plants on the earth. They have been around for 500 million years and they make flowering plants look like newcomers. Although fern species may have evolved continuously during this time (there are up to 10,000 species but only 50 in the British Isles), their sex life has stayed the same; they have never developed into flowers.

Wandering through the woods near the cottage at the end of April or early in May fills me with an excitement that is almost primeval. The cerebral is forgotten; you don't think it, you feel it, you immerse yourself in a landscape that must have changed little for thousands of years. And the plants that contribute most to this sense of immediacy, of the visceral as opposed to the intellectual, have been around much longer, not thousands but millions of years. During that time they have hardly evolved, having carved out for themselves a niche and developed a survival strategy that is indestructible. There is a smell attached to them, an indescribable odour of earth and all that is fundamental about the soil and what grows in it. At once it is the smell of decay and that of life. We must always have recognised it.

Ferns

In one corner of our garden underneath a line of tall beeches planted as a farm hedge long ago, very little sunlight gets through, yet this is one of the most green and alive parts of the garden. Apart from spring cinderellas that appear before the canopy fills in overhead, snowdrops, celandines and primroses, there are few flowers. Not only is there not enough light to support them but they would be out of place anyway. These same sort of conditions must exist in so many gardens, not necessarily underneath giant beeches but often by buildings – houses, garages, sheds or the overhanging branches of 'weed trees' or *leylandii* hedges.

Ferns of all descriptions thrive in such dark corners, but from November onwards the evergreen varieties come into their own. They persist through the winter and provided they have some shelter from the coldest winds their fronds will look as pristine on New Year's Day as they did in midsummer.

Many of them are native to the British Isles, some are from Europe and Asia, South America and even Australasia. They combine perfectly and the variety of their individual fronds, from solid and shiny to soft and lacy, adds a wealth of textural interest.

Devon, where we live, is famous for its ferns. During the Victorian era, fern trains would leave regularly from the North

Devon coast for London, their wagons packed with ferns stripped from the north-facing slopes and hedgerows to satisfy the fern craze that swept the capital. Thankfully ferns are survivors and there is little evidence now of these former depredations. The high Devon banks positively drip with polypody, one of the most enduring and most useful of evergreen ferns. It spreads slowly outwards, establishing large colonies. On a bank its stoloniferous roots bind the soil together and create pockets where mosses and primroses can make a home. The individual fronds, about 30cm long, are deeply cut and a bright, fresh green. Even when this fern is butchered by mechanical hedge trimmers, its fronds quickly resprout, repairing the bruised and battered hedgerow. One variety, *Polypodium vulgare* 'Cornubiense', has finely cut fronds. Sometimes it reverts and the typical plainer fronds reassert themselves. When this happens they should be removed promptly.

Polypodium is often accompanied by the upright shuttlecocks of *Asplenium scolopendrium*, the harts-tongue fern. Although it is not much taller than the polypody, asplenium creates a much more architectural effect. It contrasts well with low, clumping plants and the lacy filigree of many other ferns. It appears frequently at Glebe Cottage, usually at the base of stone walls, making a living 'skirting board'.

There are several variations on the theme including *Asplenium scolopendrium* 'Crispum', a highly prized variety whose undulating edges give it a frilly look.

If you need a bold fern with glossy dark green fronds which stands up for itself and achieves a metre in height then *Blechnum chilense* should be ideal. It comes from Chile and under normal conditions in a British garden will gradually colonise. Under trees or in a sheltered corner it has protection from the worst of the weather, but might turn its toes up in a really cold garden. It has been frozen solid here from time to time, but has always managed to get going again. *Blechnum spicant* is a native plant, half the size of its Chilean cousin but just as beautiful. Sometimes it is adorned with taller, slimmer fronds which bear the spores.

The famous gardener Gertrude Jekyll wrote that 'green is also a colour', and ferns cover so wide a range of greens, no two ever seeming the same.

But there are a few evergreen ferns whose fronds are definitely not green.

When *Dryopteris erythrosora* unfurls its new fronds they are decidedly orange – it almost looks autumnal although this new growth pushes through during April and May. Its fronds are glossy and eventually the orange changes to rich green. They are beautifully arched; just one plant set against a tree stump makes a fine picture. This is an exceptionally beautiful fern and it comes as no surprise that it originates in China and Japan.

Dryopteris dilatata, our native 'broad buckler-fern', is just as graceful but herbaceous.

The shield ferns, *Polystichum*, contribute several very varied species to the evergreen ferns available to grace our shady corners. *Polystichum setiferum*, the soft shield fern, is one of my all-time favourites, especially *Polystichum setiferum* 'Acutilobum' and *Polystichum setiferum* 'Densum'. Both are elegant and very finely cut, creating in *Polystichum setiferum* 'Densum' a frothy effect. The central midrib of each frond is covered with shaggy brown scales and the fronds themselves are of a lovely soft green.

No matter whether you have room for just one of these beautiful ferns or a stumpery with numerous examples of each species, once they take up residence in your garden they give an air of timelessness, an echo of the primeval. Over millions of years, their sex life has remained unchanged. And a very esoteric sex life it is. Flowering plants reproduce each generation from seed; ferns have no flowers and set no seed. They use spores to procreate and there are two distinct stages in this fascinating ritual. The first is the frond stage, where no sex is involved and the fern spontaneously produces spores, then releases them from the reverse of the fronds. In the second stage, the prothallus stage, the spores produce small scale-like growths, which in turn produce male and female cells. These cells move around in the water on the reverse of the prothallus. It is their union that creates the new fern.

This dependency on water in the reproductive cycle leads scientists to believe that ferns are descended from aquatic plants. All manner of magical properties have been attributed to ferns, mainly because before the invention of the microscope, nobody understood how they reproduced. Folklore had it that spores could bestow the gift of invisibility to those who believed in their magic power. Now that we know what really happens we may no longer believe in these fairy stories. The myth that persists though is that growing new ferns from spores is wreathed in mystery and fraught with problems. Although it takes time, and therefore also some patience, it is an exciting and rewarding process and full of an ancient poetry.

Growing from spores

Spores can be collected from June through to September. There are no hard and fast rules. Watch the plants and check the reverse of the fronds. Some of our native ferns set spores prolifically – sometimes the ground beneath them is covered with their spores, and spiders' webs suspended nearby take on a fine brown film where spores have been caught.

Carol Klein

Sever a whole frond with scissors or secateurs at its base. The whole frond can either be plunged into a large paper bag or laid on a piece of cartridge paper. The latter is more fun because you can actually see the spores and after a few days on a warm windowsill the fallen spores will make a print of the fern frond on the backing paper. Fold the paper in half or cover it with another piece of paper. The spores can be gathered and stored until the following spring or sown promptly.

Everyone who grows ferns from spores has their own special recipe for compost. It should contain no fertiliser and it should be sterile.

Some people use John Innes potting compost (which contains a certain amount of fertiliser). Our mix was equal parts sterilised loam and leaf mould with some coarse sand added. Incorporating crushed charcoal prevents stagnation and helps keep the compost sweet.

Fill a clay pot or clay pan with the compost, leaving a 'breathing space' of about 1cm between the top of the firmed compost and the top of the pot. To sterilise thoroughly, cut out a circle of newspaper that fits on top of the compost and pour boiling water on to its surface. Keep on pouring until the whole pot feels hot and the compost is saturated. Cover with a piece of clean glass.

Allow to drain and cool. Cover the surface of the compost with a fine layer of brick dust to provide a sterile surface. Tap the spores into the fold of the paper on which they have been collected and sow them as evenly as possible on to the surface of the brick dust, either straight from the paper or on the end of a knife blade. Replace the glass and leave in place until the fernlets are separated to keep out foreign bodies and maintain moisture levels – vital if fertilisation is to take place. The pot must be placed in a shallow dish of rainwater or distilled water and must always be topped up. Drying out will put paid to the process.

Place the whole caboodle in a warm, shady place. After several weeks a green film should appear on the surface of the compost. This is the developing prothalli, the in-between stage. Eventually tiny fronds will begin to appear. The glass can be removed at this stage although a warm, moist atmosphere must be maintained around the developing plants. When they are big enough they can be carefully lifted in small batches, separated and pricked out into seed trays. Later they can be potted individually into small clay pots into loam-based compost. Top-dress the pots with grit to keep the surface cool and ensure good drainage and even water distribution. Ferns are essentially shade lovers – always ensure that young ferns are kept out of direct sunlight.

Plant out hardy varieties into the garden when they are big enough to fend for themselves. Pot on tender species and keep under cover, although many are perfectly happy having a summer vacation outside in a damp, shady spot.

New plants from division

Large clumps of established ferns that form separate crowns, such as the male fern *Dryopteris filix-mas* and the lady fern *Athyrium filix-femina*, can be separated in exactly the same way as clump-forming perennials. Cut back the fronds in March, lift them and either pull them apart with your hands or if that's too tough a proposition use two garden forks back to back. Break up into chunks, each with at least one crown and adequate roots, and replant, directly adding leaf mould or home-made compost.

Some ferns have running, stoloniferous roots and this habit can be exploited to make new plants. *Onoclea sensibilis*, the sensitive fern, and *Matteuccia struthiopteris*, the shuttlecock fern, are two good examples. Simply sever the stolon, which joins one plant to the next, lift the furthest plant and pot up individually. Water well, allow to establish and plant out when well rooted. Alternatively the offsets can be planted out directly if they have enough roots to sustain themselves independently.

Ferns from bulbils

A few ferns form bulbils along the midribs of their fronds. Sometimes these develop spontaneously into new plants, sometimes they need extra help and encouragement.

In the case of *Polystichum proliferum*, the frond develops a whole series of separate plantlets and the classic fern form of the frond is barely distinguishable. Once a frond has reached this stage, the whole thing can be severed and simply laid on top of compost in a seed tray or large pot. To ensure that each of the bases of the new fernlets is in contact with the compost, use short pieces of florist's wire or staples to maintain intimate contact between them and the compost. Water well and keep in a warm, shady place, frequently spraying with a fine mist to maintain moisture levels. After a few months each tiny fern will have made its own roots and at this stage they can be separated and potted up individually.

Some ferns make only one new bulbil per frond (*Asplenium lamprophyllum* x *A. bulbiferum*). In this case the frond can be bent over pushing the new fernlet and its bulbil gently but firmly into a pot of compost. Again it can be held in place with a staple. The mother plant together with its satellite pots should be kept in a moist, warm, shady place and once rooted the new plant can be cut from the frond, launching it on an independent existence.

Polystichum setiferum, or the soft shield fern, is certainly one of the most graceful and refined of our native ferns. Some varieties make bulbils all along their midribs. Choose a frond where these are clearly visible and pin down the whole frond laying it down on top of a tray of compost or directly on to the ground, having first prepared the area, forking it over and incorporating grit and leaf mould. Sever the frond from the plant when separate fernlets have developed and then pot up individually.

Propagating ferns takes a little time and trouble. It is a wonderful reminder that gardening is not a question of turning out a product but rather of engaging in an ongoing process. In the case of ferns the process had been going on for hundreds of millions of years before we were even aware of it.

Chapter Ten

Not long after our arrival at Glebe Cottage, much more important events transpired. There was another member of the household. Our daughter Annie was born on 29 June 1980. She and her younger sister Alice have grown up with this garden and the garden has grown with them. There have been so many wonderful events in my life but by far the most momentous have been the births of our two daughters. They are just beginning their forties now and have been constantly in my thoughts throughout this time and always will be. I am immensely proud of them.

All births are memorable. All pregnancies too. We had never been as happy as we were when it was confirmed that I was pregnant. Scans were not automatically given in those days. I knew it was a girl though – both times.

Halfway through my twenties abnormal cells had been detected in my cervix, and I underwent a procedure called a cone biopsy. They called it pre-cancer in those days. The procedure is both diagnostic and curative. They decided to keep a close eye on me when I became pregnant. As well as having had this earlier surgery I was considered to be quite old, both concerning factors. I was just thirty-five when Annie was born. Nowadays it is quite usual to give birth for the first time in your thirties, even in the second half of your thirties. Then it was unusual especially in more rural areas.

Later on when I used to go and collect my children from school, all the other mums seemed to be much younger. Not that it mattered; the real concern for my children was that I always turned up in my gardening boots – how embarrassing.

I worked up until a couple of weeks before my due date. I tried to eat well and would take packed lunch, though a couple of the hungry lads in my class doing lunchtime art club would give me a helping hand. Even though they stole my food they looked after me, carrying heavy things and moving furniture.

Carrying things that are too heavy has always been a bad habit of mine, probably born of the need to show how strong and independent I am – it has always been important to do things myself. A ridiculous example of this was when, living in London, I went to see an expensive osteopath, felt much better and passing by a very good art shop on my way back, went in and bought a large, heavy bag of clay which we needed at school and carried it back on the bus.

We were lucky to have a lovely doctor, Dr Rosemary Doddington, in South Molton. She was so caring all through my pregnancy and throughout her time in the South Molton practice was beloved by all her patients. She and her partner Sheila were also keen on gardening and from time to time would come over both to check up on my health and to talk gardening. They came one boiling hot Sunday and, not seeing me in the garden, went up to the cottage and talked to Neil who explained I was next door; the rectory was empty at the time. We met up on our track where I, clothed only in bikini and gardening boots, was pushing up a barrow of the most wonderful duck manure, beautifully rotted, from the shed next door where the vicar's Muscovy ducks had hung out overnight. Of course my barrow was overloaded – another fault of mine is to be incapable of pacing myself. Rosemary was not pleased but we soon changed the subject. I was fortunate in being fit as a fiddle throughout my pregnancies.

I took maternity leave intending to return, but I fell so deeply in love with my baby, we decided I would not go back.

We were pretty soon broke but we managed and the happiness we all enjoyed was unmissable. Alice, our youngest daughter, was born two years minus two weeks later. Throughout this time I gardened merrily and propagated round the clock. Bringing up babies and gardening can go hand in hand though there were occasions when gardening had to take a back seat. I can remember feeding Annie one day in the autumn, looking out of the front window, watching a pride of goldfinches laying waste heads of thistles and watching thistledown floating off to land I know not where. But much more vividly and enduringly I remember the feeling of holding my babies in my arms, of dancing and singing with them.

When Alice was due, my mum came to stay with us to look after Annie whilst we were away, hopefully just overnight. The 15th of June was a close, thundery day. I was dividing primulas, clumps of a delightful dainty primula 'Lady Greer', more than a hundred years old now and hailing from Co. Leitrim, when my waters broke.

I walked from the bank where I was planting the primulas round to the other side of the house and straight into the shower, shedding wellies and clothes as I went, then got dressed and left immediately in our Land Rover. Neil was driving. En route we encountered an old couple driving at a leisurely pace in front of us. They stayed in front of us all the way to the hospital probably averaging about fifteen miles per hour. When we got there, Alice was being born. We made our way to a delivery room where I had intended to give birth in as natural a position as possible. The young nurse in attendance took a good look, told me not to push and scurried out of the room, returning moments later with two other nurses and two doctors. Alice, in what we were to come to recognise as her typical enthusiastic 'let's get on with it' way, had managed to wrap the cord round her neck. When she was born minutes later the nurse had to catch her. She was fine. I have always thought that people who drive ridiculously slowly have a lot to answer for.

We are all summer birthdays in our house – three Cancerians and a Gemini. Alice is the Gemini. She has to put up with our moodiness, our always being late, our over-sensitivity and our general crabbiness especially at full moons. We have had to get used to her always being early and changing her mind frequently, though she does always see both sides. Annie and Alice have always loved our garden. When Alice was just a few months old she accompanied me when I sold my first plants. St John's Garden Centre in Barnstaple bought twenty *Helichrysum* from me. The next year I took a stall in Barnstaple market and on my first day I sold out. It has never happened since. I had a tray of a plant I've now forgotten and half a hundredweight of rhubarb.

Our rhubarb was particularly lusty. It was planted in one corner of the fruit cage, not that it needs any protection, I was just trying to keep our fruit together. There were several plants all with lavish amounts of well-rotted muck under them. In the fruit cage, quite an early installation, were rows of raspberries, gooseberries galore and masses of redcurrants, blackcurrants and even whitecurrants. It was a big structure and we collected our fruit in buckets and washing up bowls. Despite this the birds also benefitted.

My mum called it 'the bird cage'. I made jam, I baked bread, I grew vegetables and sold them alongside plants on our market stall.

All through their childhood, the girls helped out with the garden. It was always at their behest; I know too many people who have been put off gardening by having to do gardening 'chores'. Yes, there are always a few boring jobs that have to be done, but repetitive jobs like weeding or watering are not only essential, but because they are semi-automatic, give a gardener an opportunity to think of other things, bigger more creative plans or daydreaming – such an important pursuit. Also, when you are engaged in either of these activities you look closely at plants. This allows you to see problems but also appreciate the beauty in the detail of flowers and leaves. It is important, though, that children are encouraged in all the most exciting parts of gardening, particularly seed sowing and planting.

We designated two of the terraces within the garden to them – Annie's garden and Alice's garden. Though there have been consultations over the years, neither of them has played an active role in planning or planting. They both love colour and it is in respect of their colour preferences that many of the plants within their gardens were chosen, subject to the usual considerations about suitability for soil and conditions. In fact Annie's garden has exactly the same orientation as Alice's, her terrace being the one below with a supporting wall and a path between them. When I am working there they both come to mind, but then like most mothers I think of my children often.

Alice favours pinks and whites with a dash of crimson, Annie veers towards more bluish pinks and purple. Foliage plays a hugely important role and both gardens have the same allure for wildlife. Year-round interest is an important factor in both gardens, as it is throughout our garden, starting off in January with snowdrops which take over from the russet grasses and the last of the dwindling perennial foliage. In Annie's garden there is a large crab apple, *Malus* 'Golden Hornet', that is smothered in blossom, abuzz with bees in May and heavy-boughed with a crop of amber fruit in late autumn and into winter. It is older than Annie; it was planted before she was born and seems to exert a caring, maternal influence over her garden. At the other end of her plot, an apple, Cox's Orange Pippin, is another protective presence.

A note. Cox's Orange Pippin is best suited to the south-east. It loves deep, rich soil. In heavy clay soil like ours it is prone to canker and ours suffers from that – but it still does well and produces loads of apples. In some years we have to thin the fruit substantially. Ten or so years ago, we had a debate about whether or not it should go. I was quite surprised when Annie talked about it philosophically, about what a good life it had had and about everything having its time. I know she loves the tree and it is a sight for sore eyes when smothered in blossom.

It was a present from Eve Jeffs, a friend and at that time our local postmistress, so it would have seemed churlish to take it out. Any cankerous twigs and branches are pruned out regularly and its flowering and fruiting do not seem to be affected. It is vital though to thoroughly clean my beautiful Niwaki secateurs afterwards. Apples are not its only offerings!

We were filming in the garden one day with a lovely director, Emma, and several contributors. They had come to the garden to learn about different propagating techniques and plants. We were up close to the cottage, but looking down the garden you could see several boughs of the apple tree and we could all hear a noisy buzzing coming from that direction. We investigated. On one of the lower branches, a swarm of bees had gathered, buzzing and moving within this great clump. What is the right verb – wriggling? Seething? No: swarming. We called Neil, who quickly donned his beekeeping outfit and, suitably dressed, knocked the branch hard with a club hammer and the bees fell into a winebox that I was supporting. Astonishingly we already had an empty beehive ready and waiting. As part of our *Life in a Cottage Garden* series we wanted to keep bees and one of our producers had prematurely sent down a very modern top-bar hive. The bees seemed quite happy with their new residence.

There have been many changes within the garden, but none of them has been arbitrary. They have all been a result of what the garden has told us and occasionally been prompted by circumstances beyond our control.

The terrace down from the front door was enlarged. It had to be extended, its original width and length being decided by the materials we had to hand. We had run out of rubble and hard core to build up the height and all our flagstones had gone. Nowadays, there are quantities of slate used for the terrace, as well as on either side of the house where two paved areas now exist. There are also two broad slate paths within Alice's garden, plus one below it separating the girls' gardens, and below Annie's garden another broad slate path that turns to gravel where we ran out of the stone. Our paving came from several different sources and they all have their stories. If we were to attempt to start this enterprise now, neither our bank balance nor my back could take it. More stone was needed too as I came to the conclusion, learning from what we had done close to the house, that the best way to deal with our sloping site on the west side of the track was to build a series of terraces divided by paths, thus creating level beds and borders that could be worked on without requiring the nimble-footedness of a mountain goat.

Neither Neil nor I could drive when we arrived here; when we were living in a city there seemed no need. My father taught both my brothers to drive; they both passed their tests soon after they were eligible for a licence. I was the eldest, and though I would have loved to learn to drive then, my father refused to teach me. He encouraged my footballing and my athletics, in fact he trained me, but when it came to teaching me to drive – nothing doing.

He did, however, teach me to ride a bike. I was probably five or six, and I was given a two-wheeler – no stabilisers in those days. My dad pushed me round and round the block of terraced houses on Church Road, holding on to the saddle. It wasn't until I almost rode into him on one circuit that I realised he had let go. I could ride a bike.

Twenty or more years later Neil had the same success when I taught him to ride a bike under the Westway on a big black sit-up-and-beg police bike bought from a shady bloke on Portobello Road Market. Another twenty years after that, Neil taught both our daughters to ride their bikes on our hazardous tracks, holding on to their saddles then letting go. Recently Alice taught Sydney, our granddaughter, to ride a bike employing the same method.

I'll bet we all had the same triumphant look on our faces when we finally took off.

Not too long nor too many driving lessons after I came to Devon, I passed my test and my youngest brother Pip brought us a very old Land Rover. He drove down from Manchester with his then girlfriend, with a motorbike in the back for the return journey. They encountered heavy snow over the top of Exmoor and the windscreen wipers could not cope, which necessitated her leaning out of the window and clearing as much snow as possible.

Our Land Rover was very dear to us but very temperamental. To start it we had to use a starting handle – heavy work and even when you managed to get it going you had to double de-clutch, a complicated manoeuvre. It had a gearstick with a long shaft and when I once lent it to someone at school, he walked into the staffroom with the gearstick in his hand.

If it weren't for that Land Rover our paths and walls might never have materialised. I heard of one farmhouse where the flag floors were being replaced and a deal was struck. My poor vehicle was severely injured by my optimism in carrying far more than I should. The terrain didn't help either. Access to the somewhat remote farmhouse was up and down two steep dips. In Devon steep can mean almost vertical and I broke two sets of springs carting my new paths back home.

On another occasion when the old hospital in Barnstaple closed down they were selling some of the fixtures and fittings including lots from the morgue. On the off chance, Neil stopped and asked the foreman about slate slabs and was told he could go and rescue whatever he could find from the mortuary in the basement in the dark. He was stopped by the police on the way back – the vehicle was overloaded. He was nearly home by then so they allowed him to carry on. A few extras came from a nearby churchyard where they had been laid as a path (not gravestones, I hasten to add).

Ian Tucker, the farmer from up the road, had more land further down the valley which included two old stone-built cottages, totally derelict and with only vestiges of the walls remaining. They were completely out of the way and overgrown but he said I could help myself to any of the stone. It was a challenge. The cottages were not quite inaccessible – clearly at one time whoever dwelt there had to get in and out – but even with co-operation from my friend who lived nearby, the closest I could get my Land Rover was twenty-five yards away and the terrain in between was difficult, treacherous even, overgrown with roots and ivy.

Wheelbarrows were a non-starter so I carried each stone individually and loaded them into the Land Rover. This time no springs were broken but progress was slow. Sometimes there would be weeks in between a cluster of stone-collecting forays as I would build the next piece of retaining wall, digging out soil to make paths and loading it behind the wall as I went along to make level beds. It was hard work but immensely satisfying and the stone was a perfect match for the stone from our cottage leftovers. It might have come from the same quarry, but if so it would have been at a much earlier date. However many years earlier it might have been, it would have been as nothing compared to the age of the stone itself.

It is such an honour to handle natural materials: wood that was a tree, thank you tree, stone that was formed millions of years ago, soil that is comparatively recent but nonetheless formed by natural forces, by the interaction of millions of micro-organisms that we cannot even see. When mankind and nature collaborate, what beauty ensues. Clay is ancient and mankind's use of it to make pots is one of the earliest indicators of civilisation. There is evidence of clay being used as pottery in what we now call Japan from 14,500BCE and every ancient (and modern) civilisation has used it.

Before the introduction of plastics, clay pots were used extensively to rear and nurture plants. They are the ultimate in recycling. I treasure our collection of clay pots, big and small, and press them into use at every opportunity. I feel like crying if one gets broken, even though it will have further use as crocks to provide drainage in its fellow pots. When you see the evidence of those who made them in the shape of a thumb or fingerprint, a gash or a wobble, you can imagine their being made: the clay prepared, thrown hard into the centre of the wheel, its revolving, water, thumb and fingers giving it form, no longer a lump of clay but a pot. Every one is unique, an individual.

* * *

Some time ago we bought the field next to our cottage; it must have been a good year. Sadly we spent so much buying it, there was nothing left to do anything with it nor has there been ever since. We dream about planting trees there, replacing the copse that the farmer destroyed. There should be wildflowers and a big pond and a boggy bit.

Before we bought it the farmer who rented it from the church used it exclusively for cutting for silage, winter food for his cows. We often used to sit at the top of it, just through from the cottage, and one day Annie was sitting reading a book in the early evening sun. Alice was around too and at one stage she, Neil and I had ambled over to have a chat. As I walked through from the garden I noticed something moving fast along the hedge, then bounding up the field towards us. It was a hare. It stopped and sat a couple of yards from Annie. She sat stock still and we froze, hardly daring to breathe.

I have always loved Dürer's watercolour of a hare painted 500 years ago, but here was the real thing, with soft fur and amber eyes and tall ears, tufted at their tips. I don't know how long we stayed there, transfixed, the spell only broken when he gently moved away to continue his circuit of the field. It felt like a visitation from mother nature herself.

There have been so many spellbinding appearances by wild creatures during our time here. We mark them as special memories, though for the wild creatures they are everyday occurrences, just getting on with the job of staying alive. Knowing that they take for granted the garden, the field, the sky above and the trees below, and that we are incidental, puts you in your place.

Birds are some of the most easily visible and audible residents and visitors. Tiny birds, goldcrests and firecrests and little wrens whose perfect, spherical nests we have found occasionally. What a performance; the cock bird not only takes his prospective mate to see different locations but starts several nests, and when she chooses one, she perfects the interior decoration with moss, lichen and feathers. To complicate matters further he may have more than one mate – small wonder that wrens dash about so much, though we only catch short glimpses of them. I know quite a lot of Latin names of plants, but few of birds, but the wren's I could never forget – *Troglodytes troglodytes*. Troglodytes are cave-dwellers or hermits; I wonder if it got its name because it likes to hide and stay out of the limelight, though its trilling song is as loud as loud can be.

There are small birds, titmice galore, blue tits, great tits and coal tits and gangs of long-tailed tits, gossiping and twittering as they move up the hedge, snacking in the bird cherry, then off again on their garrulous way. There are warblers, willow warblers and chiffchaffs with their repetitive call that gives them their name. There are chaffinches, goldfinches, greenfinches too. We have seen bramblings recently and once upon a time when we came here there were linnets, though they seem to have disappeared. We no longer hear the curlews whose curling plaintive call made you shiver then smile, so wild and free. We saw snipe darting off from the grass when you walked too close and even a woodcock or two, their eyes in the side of their heads.

Big birds, ravens nesting in the pine trees behind the cottage, buzzards with their eerie cries, a heron, prehistoric, en route to the little lake next door. In the summer every year, though in steadily decreasing numbers, swallows turn up, swishing through the sky at the end of their momentous journey. Since they nest here I always feel this is their home, they've just been on a winter holiday. Once upon a time a cuckoo would arrive at a similar time. The cuckoo is such an iconic bird, symbolising the coming of spring. Although its arrival has dire consequences for some hedgerow birds, it is welcomed by humankind.

When first we came to Glebe Cottage, we heard a cuckoo every spring, just as the hedgerows were greening. In the field, lady's smock or cuckoo flower was opening its pale lilac flowers. Orange tip butterflies were on the wing – lady's smock is their preferred food plant, with its flower providing nectar for the butterflies and its leaves as the caterpillar's staple diet. Pigeons enjoy the leaves too – cardamines are related to cabbages! I once discovered that leaves pecked off by a pigeon from a very special double cardamine had taken root in the surrounding moist, leafy soil. Food for the pigeon but an excellent lesson in how to propagate the plant for me. Three double-flowered forms were listed in Glebe Cottage Plants' Plant List 1996–7. Being double they set no seed so can only be propagated vegetatively.

Glebe Cottage is our home. I should be loath to have to leave it. The girls flew the coop long ago but they still return from time to time. I hope our grandchildren will get to know and love this garden, and maybe they will have happy memories of it too. Gardens need people – to maintain them and nurture them, yes, but as a raison d'être too.

It is a privilege to welcome anybody into the garden, but especially children. Our grandchildren, Sydney and Bill, love sowing seed. Once or twice at their nursery (and hopefully this will continue at school), I have planted bulbs and sown seeds with them and their friends and playmates. I wish everybody got the chance to do this. For our garden at the Hampton Court show in 2023, Sydney and Bill sowed some peas here in old module trays. They loved it. Sydney was very organised, she is a particular sort of person, and Bill gave them a good watering, he is a very good waterer. When their peas grew on, I potted them on and later squeezed all those pots into trays with hazel twigs from the twiggy pea sticks (I always want to call them piggy twee sticks) cut from our native hedge. Eventually we packed them into one of the two trucks alongside our other plants and assorted chattels, taking them to the grounds of a royal palace. Then began the hard work.

A fortnight later, with the garden complete, their peas were the highlight of the little vegetable garden that formed part of the bigger garden. When they came to visit the show with their mum and dad, not only did they see their peas and the notice written in chalk on slate – 'Bill and Sydney's Peas' – but they got to pick, pod and eat some.

Primrose

To call a flower the epitome of spring may seem a bit of a cliché, but in the case of the primrose, *Primula vulgaris*, it is perfectly apt. No other plant gives the same feeling of spring's inexorable progress. It is such an elfin plant, a wild spirit, and it has its own ideas about how and where it best likes growing. It is keen on a west-facing site where, with a bit of luck, it will get warm afternoon sun. Its pale flowers with their egg-yolk centres shine out even on dull days and no doubt attract moth pollinators in the dusk, but when the sun shines their gentle perfume pulls in insects from all around. On steep Devon banks, you can study it face to face, each wan flower balanced on a fine pink stalk – the colour of baby birds. Rosettes of crinkled fresh green leaves turn each plant into a posy, sitting comfortably in hedgerow or ditch or smothering the ground at the woodland's edge.

It is the 'prima rosa', the first flower of spring.

The primrose is the county flower of Devon, but there must be many people throughout the country who feel such an attachment to this joyous little flower, considering it particularly special to their area and to them – their own primrose.

Essentially an edge-of-woodland plant, along with man it has moved out to the banks and ditches he has created. Where I live in the Devon countryside, hedgerows are alive with its pallid flowers and, on a sunny day, the air is filled with their sweet scent, available just where it is needed – at nose level, and just at the right time.

In its natural habitat it seeds itself around, each new plant becoming an established clump spreading itself out gradually in search of nutrients amongst the debris of leaves and moss.

It has always been picked, little bunches of it, tied with soft wool and presented as gifts or love tokens. It has special associations with Easter.

Unlike so many of our native flowers, resilient primroses seem to be adaptable to man's encroachment. Nowadays more of us get to enjoy their sunny presence, even if it is in our own gardens or on motorway embankments as we hurtle by.

No doubt wild primroses have found their way into gardens from the very first time plots were set aside to cultivate food, and though they can be eaten and drunk (primrose wine must be a delicacy), it is for the joy they bring to spirit and soul that they are prized. They and their offspring are celebrated in *Gerard's Herball*, published in 1497, and for centuries people have cherished both the wild primrose and its multifarious cultivars.

One of the oldest of these, *Primula* 'Wanda', has been a popular plant for decades, possibly centuries. Its strident magenta flowers are a familiar feature to town and country dwellers alike. It was the first primula I ever saw. When I was little it used to fill the tiny front gardens of the miners' and millworkers' terraces, sometimes travelling right up the street. It is an easy plant to 'pass around', and since it is almost indestructible it offers encouragement to new gardeners.

Recently it has lent its genes to a whole range of 'Wanda' hybrids, short, stocky plants often with dark leaves and richly coloured dark flowers with a little yellow in their centres, an inheritance from another contributor, *Primula* 'Cowichan'. At Glebe Cottage we grow a version of this we call *P.* 'Black Magic'.

The Cowichan group were developed by Florence Bellis, an American concert pianist who, having no work at the time of the Great Depression, decided to earn her living breeding primulas and trying to sell them. She settled as a 'haylofter' in a barn in Oregon with two pianos and a tattered trunk and called her house and her new enterprise 'Barnhaven'. Originally all her seed was from England and over a period of more than thirty years she worked on perfecting different strains including the cowichans. 'Striped Victorians', 'Chartreuse', 'Desert Sunset' and 'Grand Canyon Strain' are examples of her work.

Later she succeeded in developing a seed strain that regularly produced double-flowered forms of the primrose. Using pollen from an exquisite old French primrose, *P.* 'Marie Crousse', she crossed and back-crossed her plants. Double primroses are sterile, producing very little pollen, so it was no mean feat that, after years of patient work, she achieved her objective.

Many of the modern double primroses owe their existence to her perseverance. Cultivars such as 'Miss Indigo', with its navy blue flowers touched with white, or *P.* 'Dawn Ansell', a pure gleaming white 'jack-in-the-green', are probably descended from Barnhaven primulas. Modern doubles are often micro-propagated in their thousands nowadays. Some still retain some of the grace of old varieties, like *P.* 'Lilacina Plena' and *P.* 'Alba Plena', although others are decidedly dumpy. Because double flowers cannot set seed, their flowers tend to last long on the plant, which makes them a particularly attractive proposition in the garden.

Their cultivation is exactly the same as that for single prim-roses, in fact all primroses thrive in the same conditions and on the same diet.

As gardeners we can help guard against the demise of the primrose by growing it ourselves. It is most suited to naturalistic settings, happiest in the sort of surroundings it would choose in the wild – carpeting the ground between shrubs or under trees – but it is such an amenable soul it will fit in almost anywhere providing it has ample moisture, a bit of shade and humus-rich soil. That goes for the whole primrose and polyanthus clan. Modern, more garish primulas have been bred to put up with anything and to brighten things up all winter. They are not my favourites.

Two other strains in which Florence Bellis took particular interest were the gold-laced polyanthus beloved by the old 'florists' who grew them for competition, and the 'Elizabethan' primroses, all manner of bizarre polyanthus and primroses with extended calyces or one flower inside another. This last group are named after types of Elizabethan hosiery – hose-in-hose and pantaloons.

1) **Primula 'Wanda'**

   As already described, a popular and vigorous primula with striking magenta flowers and sunny yellow centres.

2) **Red Tomato**

   A good example of some of the modern polyanthus that capture the daintiness of older varieties with unexpectedly vivid coloured flowers. There was an old primrose called 'Tomato' of just this colour.

3) **Gold Lace**

Gold-lace polyanthus have flowers like black velvet with each petal ringed in bright yellow. The flowers are held symmetrically at the top of a straight stem. Together with the precisely gold-edged petals this creates a very formal impression. These intriguing flowers find favour with many gardeners who love the quirky and the whimsical.

4) **Lady Greer**

Some of the sweetly named polyanthus, their flowers clustered on top of the stems, are very desirable. *P.* 'Lady Greer' is one of the most understated, with dainty pale cream, slightly belled flowers, sometimes touched with pink.

5) **Blue modern polyanthus**

There are several old varieties of deep blue primulas. *P.* 'Blue Riband' is ground-hugging with vivid blue petals rimmed with crimson; 'Ingram's Blue' is a polyanthus. This modern variety captures their colour.

6) **Orange monstrosity**

Breeders have created a seemingly endless array of polyanthus in a kaleidoscopic range of colours. Given careful combination with other plants, the effect can be eye-catching. This would be great with early euphorbias.

7) **Garryard Guinevere**

An outstanding old Irish primrose, probably dating back pre-First World War. A dark-leaved beauty with pale, lilac-pink flowers. Thankfully she has a robust constitution and increases well. Loves to be well-fed!

8) **Miss Indigo**

   Much breeding of double forms of primroses has been undertaken in past years. Flowers last a long time because they're
   sterile. Lovely in the garden but hopeless for bees who can't
   penetrate the plethora of petals.

Primroses are opportunists. In the woodland or edge-of-woodland
setting that is so often their home they live happily amongst the leaf
litter, moving steadily outwards to take advantage of the humus-rich
leaf mould around them. Often the centre of the clump dies out but
the colonies it has established on its perimeter grow and flourish. In
the confines of our gardens they may need a little more help.

Gertrude Jekyll said that primroses should be divided 'When
the bloom wanes, and is nearly overtopped by the leaves'. From
summer through to autumn is probably best but you can try this
with newly bought plants too if they're of sufficient size.

Primulas need to be divided fairly frequently and single crowns
of a nice, chunky volume will establish well. Within a couple of years
they will make good clumps and be ready for splitting once again.

The same method can be practised to keep most cultivated
descendants of *Primula vulgaris* and its close alpine cousin, *Primula
juliae*, in vigorous growth indefinitely.

1) Lift your plant from the ground or empty it from its pot. The
   best policy is to do this on a cool, moist day. Gently tease
   clumps apart discarding the old, non-productive centre.

2) Trim back the roots to 10cm, the length of your palm – this
   will encourage the formation of fine feeding roots. Never fold
   or wrap the roots or plants will struggle.

3) Plant them in soil enriched with home-made compost and/
   or leaf mould or pot them individually in loam-based potting
   compost. In either case, make sure roots are not folded or they
   won't establish. Water well.

Chapter Eleven

It was an easy choice to elect not to go back to teaching. Easy in that it seemed right to be at home with my girls, not so straightforward living without my wage.

Alongside learning about how to look after babies and small children, I was learning about gardening and plants. Thankfully most gardening is common sense and whether or not we recognise it we all have an innate sense of how to do it. The mystification of gardening by some TV pundits and gardening writers is disingenuous. You often find they have more to say about themselves than about plants and gardening.

Good advice abounds though, most often from people who have done it or are doing it themselves. There are so many people who are only too keen to offer advice.

Geographically, we are not at the centre of things here, which of course is one of the main attractions. It is rather wonderful to go outside on a fine, sunny day and sing as loudly and joyfully as possible. A few birds and small mammals may be frightened and our dog and cats may look askance but nobody is unduly put out. It is also good to be able to shout profanities when things are going badly without fear of anyone taking offence.

We have always had to go out into the world, although on a few occasions the world has been happy to come to us. If our girls were to socialise, we had to make that happen. We took them to local playgroups and I even attended an evening class to become a playgroup leader. Most enjoyable.

Our circumstances also meant that we had to go out and meet the world if we were to earn a living. Almost immediately after we had come to Glebe, I had started to grow plants, the only way we could possibly stock the garden. A greenhouse was a necessity and we redirected part of our mortgage meant for replacement windows (we still have the originals) to buying a splendid cedar greenhouse. It has long gone but I now have two excellent metal-framed Rhino greenhouses. Our friend Hilary who made cheese and ran a successful business from selling it suggested that since I seemed to have a surplus of plants, the obvious way to make money was to sell some of them.

I applied to our local pannier market, South Molton, but was turned down. I had been exhibiting at The RHS Chelsea Flower Show for several years before the South Molton Pannier Market apparatchiks deemed me worthy of a stall there. Unsuccessful in South Molton, I applied to Barnstaple Pannier Market, further away but bigger and with two markets per week. For the next several years that was where I sold my wares. Plants were my main trade but plant sales were supplemented by selling excess produce from our garden, including vegetables and soft fruit and jam made from that fruit. Each week though, the first thing I sold out of was bread. Throughout the week I would make several batches of wholemeal bread and freeze them. The night before I was going to market, I would defrost them then give them a few minutes in the Aga before I left for market. The van smelled wonderful en route.

Selling the bread was easy and gradually I also built up a clientele of gardeners who came each week to see if I could tempt them. It was lovely to talk to people about plants; I had grown the plants I was selling so whatever I told them was from experience.

Because the world of plants and their provenance is so fascinating, I have always wanted to find out about them and often try to imagine them in their natural surroundings. I have visited quite a few places in actuality but have travelled to so many other parts of the world in my head, exploring numerous geographies from the forests of Sichuan to the towering slopes of the Andes.

I have always wanted the plants I have sold to people to thrive for them, so welcomed as many questions as possible to ensure both plants and people would be well matched.

One day at market, I got talking to a lady called Sonia, who was very knowledgeable in an unassuming kind of way. Although we began either side of my sales table, we ended up sitting side by side on the bench behind it talking plants non-stop. We became good friends. I learned so much from Sonia. She was in her element talking about plants, so I didn't just learn about plants from her but also how to talk to people about plants. Though she was so diffident herself, she always made you feel you could do anything.

After many markets and numerous plant sales, many of them organised by the wonderful Hardy Plant Society to whom Sonia introduced me, eventually we decided we should branch out and try our luck at some shows.

Selling plants is one thing, but going to shows and being required to put on a display is a different ball game. Sonia excelled at this. Come to think of it, she had probably never made a display as such before. She was a virtuoso flower arranger, though not necessarily in a NAFAS (National Association of Flower Arrangement

Societies) sort of way, and her own garden was a scene of peace and tranquillity where nothing jarred or felt out of place.

I can remember the way she tilted the foliage of a *Rheum* 'Ace of Hearts', a rhubarb relative, so that as well as being able to appreciate the scale and shape of its leaves, you could also admire the rich ruby colouration of their reverses. By now I have made several hundred displays and throughout creating them, Sonia's soft, calm voice has advised me. Sadly she died the year after we started going to shows. Her garden was a reflection of her personality. She preferred children, animals and plants to grown-ups. Sonia had a tough upbringing. She was orphaned at an early age and passed around, staying with different relatives. She had desperately wanted to have children but had a series of miscarriages. She persisted and eventually gave birth to Jan, whom she adored. Jan is a keen and an accomplished gardener. Sonia would be so proud.

She and I had several adventures, all involving plants of course. Sonia didn't drive but you would have thought she had visited all sorts of places, so intently would she read about them and study their catalogues and guides. I thought it would be a great idea to visit a few of these places so that Sonia could see them in real life. It had to be a realistic itinerary – we were both broke. But I had a car, a very old purple Mazda. On several occasions, Sonia had shown me her copy of the mail order catalogue of Washfield Nursery, from Hawkhurst in Kent, well-thumbed and frequently reread. We would both drool over some of the plants listed. Visiting Washfield was top of the list. Great Dixter, Christopher Lloyd's wonderful garden in Northiam, East Sussex, was next, but we thought we could start at the Savill Garden at Windsor. John Bond was the curator there, a brilliant plantsman with a reputation for being no-nonsense and rather strict. I did not know this at the time and wrote him a very polite but possibly over-familiar letter, asking if Sonia and I could visit and if possible spend some time with him. (I also wrote to Elizabeth Strangman and she too said we were welcome to visit.)

John Bond answered saying that would be fine. We looked at the map, plotting our route. No doubt other unrealistic people have also worked out journeys with a map in front of them with no clue as to how long it might take to travel from A to B. Distances look so short on maps! Barnstaple to Windsor, 177 miles, Windsor to Northiam, 77 miles, Northiam to Hawkhurst, 8 miles, Hawkhurst to Diss, 130 miles, Diss to Barnstaple, 321 miles … well over 700 miles, and that was without detours, which we inevitably made. Come to think of it, didn't we also go to John Coke's wondrous Green Farm Plants, then based near Farnham? The marvellous Marina Christopher had just started there. Later the nursery was to move to Bury Court; Piet Oudolf designed part of the garden there, and Marina planted several areas full of sea hollies, other umbels and scabious relatives. Inspiring.

Heedless of the distances involved, or perhaps just plain ignorant of them, we set out on our trip. As we travelled Sonia produced the fare with which she also sustained us on later trips going to shows: banana sandwiches on brown bread. When we reached our first destination, John Bond gave us a tour of the heart of Savill Garden, answering questions. Mine were probably too naïve for words. He showed us rare, tender mahonias that were only just in the country. He gave us cuttings galore, most of which survived despite having to spend several days in plastic bags. Sonia knew a lot, John Bond knew a lot more and I knew practically nothing but I think he recognised how intent we both were in wanting to learn, and just as importantly how we both loved plants. Many years later Savill Garden were our next-door neighbours at the Chelsea Flower Show and made a magnificent display with tip-top plants.

Naturally on 'Royal Day', this garden was the first port of call for the Queen, accompanied by Prince Philip. They strolled around for a few minutes. After they had moved on, I asked John what they had thought. He replied in a somewhat dispirited fashion, 'Prince Philip asked if there was anything left in the gardens.' A team of people had been working for the best part of a year, growing well-nigh perfect plants to clothe and enhance that show garden. Some people don't have a clue.

When we arrived at Great Dixter next morning, the gardens were closed; at that time they only opened in the afternoon. You could see into the nursery and only a short fence separated it from the car park and the outside world. Sonia and I had such a tight itinerary, I elected to climb the fence, not with any dishonourable or dishonest intentions but just to try and find someone with whom I could plead our special case: that for us this was a pilgrimage and we needed to enter the hallowed ground as soon as possible. As I was exiting the nursery in a quest to find someone in authority, who should I come across but Christopher Lloyd. Before he could throw me out I rapidly explained, introduced him to Sonia through the fence and he allowed us in. It was a warm, sunny September day, and for a short while we had the place to ourselves. This was years before Fergus Garrett joined Christopher Lloyd at Dixter. It had long been a much-venerated garden but Christo, Fergus and his team turned it into one of the most exciting and forward-looking gardens around, full of positive energy.

I have visited Great Dixter on numerous occasions and even been lucky enough to stay there a few times and eat a couple of meals cooked by Christo – he was a great cook. He was also wry, extremely witty, opinionated and sometimes outspoken. He never let good manners get in the way of saying exactly what he thought. One time when a well-known gardener was about to start a new garden, Christo, who had hated the cheesy slogans and pious quotations strategically placed in the garden from which he was moving, declared that he trusted he would not repeat in the new garden the mistakes he had made in the old. Forthright as always. One of Christo's best qualities was never to rest on his laurels and always to encourage other gardeners, especially the young, to experiment, find out for themselves and be adventurous. Though he had a very comprehensive horticultural training at Wye College, improved upon and enlarged by a lifetime of practical experience, his ideas never stood still and when his partnership with Fergus grew and blossomed, those ideas moved on apace. It must be wonderful to work alongside someone with whom you are on the same wavelength and spark ideas and inspiration from one another. To see their friendship develop and then to see how in later years Fergus has continued to encourage and inspire young gardeners (and some old ones too – I am one of them) is one of modern gardening's best stories.

On that first visit, one of the features at Dixter that made the biggest and most long-lasting impression was the meadow. Christo was way ahead of his time in recognising the part that gardens have to play in conservation. He was an extremely knowledgeable botanist with a deep understanding of which plants grew where and why they did so, and the relationship(s) of the creatures and plants that evolution has formed.

When visiting gardens even the British talk to one another, although the little group of visitors with whom Sonia and I had a most interesting conversation on the day we visited Dixter were American, from Seattle. They asked us if we had visited Sissinghurst. We hadn't – they insisted we should. They absolutely raved about it. Since it was less than half an hour away we decided we must fit it in. We arrived late in the afternoon. The majority of visitors had vacated the garden and were ensconced in the cafe – correction, tea room – having their tea and scones. Fast-forward forty years and no doubt the place would have been teeming. Sissinghurst is hugely popular now with National Trust visitors although it probably had its heyday in terms of sympathetic garden maintenance when Pamela Schwerdt and Sibylle Kreutzberger were joint head gardeners there (1959–1990). Vita Sackville-West 'was rather tickled by the idea of employing two young women at a time when female gardeners were rare'. They met when they were both in training at Beatrix Havergal's Waterperry Horticultural School. I met both these brilliant women, but wish I could have spent more time talking with them. Perhaps some of their brilliance might have rubbed off on me.

There are so many women who have made such an enormous, often unsung contribution to gardening and horticulture. A few of them were famous, usually by self-representation, Vita Sackville-West amongst them.

The tower in the midst of the garden from which you get an aerial view of all the garden's sections and famous features was cordoned off, but we asked one of the gardeners, since the place was deserted and it was so late, whether it might be possible for Sonia and me to sneak up there. They said yes. It was almost sunset and a full moon was already in the sky. We felt the whole scene had been orchestrated just for us. It was balmy, and scents drifted up from the garden below. Neither of us spoke.

When eventually we descended, the white garden was at its zenith; there could not have been a more perfect time to drink it in. We saw the cottage garden, its hot colours turned down to a simmer as the light gradually faded, and the nuttery transforming into something elfin. We were the last to leave.

The next day we were to meet one of our gardening heroines, Elizabeth Strangman, reserved though extraordinarily talented. She is an extremely intelligent woman who has devoted her life to gardening and producing plants of the utmost beauty. All this despite having to face discouragement and sometimes downright antipathy from her father who wanted her to study law, not to mention the general prejudice against women in horticulture, especially when they were audacious enough to set up in business. Her 'eye' for a plant is unwavering. Her passion for her chosen life is unmatched. If a person can be a benchmark, then as a nursery-woman she is mine.

We looked around her nursery, literally running backwards and forwards between cold frames with excitement, squealing with delight. Despite carrying on with her propagating work, not only was she happy to answer questions, but she initiated discussions about particular plants, their provenance and how to propagate them. Not for her the mechanistic, repetitive, humdrum production of large numbers of the same plants answering 'popular demand'. She observes, experiments and though she recognises that it is the plants that create new plants, she is the most creative of nurserywomen. Her hellebore crosses, along with those of Helen Ballard, so considered and inspired, laid the groundwork and the direction for all the work that has been done subsequently in the last couple of decades by breeders of *Helleborus x hybridus*, which then we called *Helleborus orientalis*. John Massey, Kevin Belcher and their team are foremost amongst them and the beautiful plants that they have produced grace many a garden.

As I write this I cannot resist rushing out to my garden to see how my hellebores are doing. I especially want to see the flowers on any of the plants that are flowering for the first time, a result of crosses I have made. Although none of them will be disappointing, because I don't discriminate enough, an occasional one might be good. One of the qualities Elizabeth has, which makes her so special, *is* her ability to pick out what is special. She has a good eye. When I think of some of the talented people I know or have known, I sometimes feel overawed.

Her nursery Washfield is named after Washfield near Tiverton in Devon, not far from Glebe Cottage. I understand that a nursery-woman, Nellie Britton, famous in her day, ran a nursery there and on moving to Kent, took the name with her. Elizabeth took over the nursery and its name. Washfield is closed now, but Elizabeth continues to garden.

In complete contrast to Washfield, on the next day Sonia and I visited a nursery on a totally different scale, though one where respect for and love of plants was equally at its heart. In Diss in Norfolk, almost in Suffolk, Howard and Kooij's, now Howard Nurseries, is a massive wholesale nursery, but one unusually where they grow the great majority of their own plants. This is an area where every other person has some close connection to the soil, through agriculture mainly but also through horticulture. Though it is not alien to me, I am not familiar with that side of the country and find its huge flat landscape and never-ending skies slightly daunting. With its fertile silty soils though, plants do well.

We had gone to meet David Howard, one of the partners in the firm. I had bought open-ground plants from him, plants like *Anchusa azurea* 'Loddon Royalist', which are short-lived in my heavy clay soil but thrive in their deep, sandy loam. David eventually took over the whole firm when Nicholas Kooij left, and he ran it together with his daughter Christine, who continues to run it since her father's death. David and Nick worked for a time for Alan

Bloom who had initially head-hunted David. They left to set up on their own specialising in vincas – ground-cover plants were all the rage then – but they expanded exponentially, eventually growing a wide range of perennial plants.

The site covers about 150 acres. David treated us to a tour of it and we were blown away by flat fields full of flowers stretching endlessly into the Turneresque distance. I have been lucky enough to film there on several occasions since and to experience row upon row of irises in kaleidoscopic colour (Iris was the Greek goddess of the rainbow), or peonies in their thousands, is mind-blowing.

We walked and walked and gazed and gazed, the weather had changed, it poured and poured with torrential rain, yet still we walked.

By the time we got back home to Devon, you might have expected us to have had plant overload. Not a bit of it.

On these travels I learned as much from Sonia as I did from all the splendid people we met. She taught me so much, including being a bit more tolerant with my own children. She made me realise more than ever what a huge blessing they are. As well as travelling around together and exhibiting at our first shows, she came here many times and saw the garden begin to develop. On one occasion she had arranged a Hardy Plant Society visit to my garden. I can still remember the booming voice of Else Lacey, a warm and wonderful Dutch woman who ran the group, as she entered the garden and started to ascend the track. She didn't get very far very fast, progress prevented by meeting too many special plants. What a joy it is to share your garden with other people and to see others of all sorts of different persuasions and preferences enjoying the place and the plants.

Later we were to open for the National Garden Scheme; we opened for them for more than twenty-five years, sixteen or so times per year. In addition our garden was open alongside our nursery several days per week so visitors could see the plants we sold growing in the garden and thus get a better idea of their habit of growth as well as some inspiration about what to plant with them. People's observations and comments have been helpful too; sometimes you get so close to your garden, just as can happen when painting or writing, that you can no longer see it clearly.

* * *

Most of my life has 'happened' rather than following some pre-determined course. I knew that I wanted to grow plants and recognised that would necessitate selling them too. When I decided not to go back to my teaching job at South Molton, I didn't decide to set up a nursery. It was much more of a feel-your-way-along process, growing too many plants, deciding to sell some of the surplus, then gradually expanding the operation, step by step. During this preliminary period I did some supply teaching just to keep the wolf from the door. One of the schools I went to was Chulmleigh, not very far from us, where I covered a teacher named Maggie Reilly's maternity leave. Whilst there, at a parents' meeting, I talked to the mum of one of the boys I was teaching, Gary Buckingham, who she told me was very interested in gardening and hoped to take it up when he left school soon afterwards.

Gary came to work at Glebe Cottage. He had no training, no more did I, though by that time I had taught myself a few things and established a rudimentary business. Gary stayed for many years; we enrolled him in an OND horticulture course at Bicton which he attended one day a week. Gary was soon better quali-fied academically than me. He was always conscientious but more importantly, thoroughly involved with gardening and plants. We worked together well, and we got a lot of work done. It was a good partnership; after several years I even managed to get him to come along to a show. Sadly, immediately after that show – one of our biggest and most important, the Gardeners' World Live Show at the NEC – Gary didn't turn up for work on the Monday morning. The day you come back from a show is hard work, unpacking lorries, resuscitating sales plants that didn't sell, ensuring that display plants are cosseted and cared for. It was a hot day too. Gary turned up with his mum in the afternoon whilst the rest of us were struggling to unload and get the rented hire lorry back. She told me he was having the rest of the week off since he had had a tiring time. I made it clear I wasn't impressed.

Nowadays Gary is running his own nursery, Millwood Plants, concentrating mainly on plants for shady places. To run a small specialist nursery and to keep it going for any length of time takes a lot of guts and determination. It is a full-time commitment – and then some. During the last few decades it was seen as an easy option by many people, a lot of them baby boomers, retiring from other jobs, who were interested in gardening and to whom it looked a pleasant proposition. The full-time aspect of running a nursery means all-the-year-round, and whilst the prospect of showing off your plants and selling them during late spring and summer is attractive, the only way those plants will be there is when there have been long hours of toil, often in cold and uninspiring conditions, through the preceding winter. Costs are high and profits are low and as in every other area of commerce, there are big companies with highly organised mail-order departments who can rely on the scale of their operations to succeed at the expense of the small producer. Often they do not produce plants themselves, but buy in from specialist growers. So many of the plants that end up on the shelves of our garden centres and supermarkets already have a huge carbon footprint. Many start their lives in China or India, some are grown on in Holland and then exported to the UK. Vast resources of energy for heat and transportation, and water, are used in the production of these 'green products'.

To succeed on a small scale and grow with love, it is your passion, a helping of luck and the goodwill of family, friends, colleagues and customers that must carry you through. There are enormous numbers of practicalities to contend with and year on year these are becoming more and more prohibitive.

We were lucky in many ways. When we first started exhibiting, herbaceous perennials were becoming increasingly fashionable. Thanks to pioneers like Elizabeth Strangman and Beth Chatto, the beauty and diversity of perennial plants were becoming more and more appreciated, with an emphasis on their suitability for their site. Nicola Ferguson's Book *Right Plant, Right Place*, published in 1984, gave a title to a concept that is used at every turn by gardening pundits up to the present day and is at the common sense heart of all successful gardening. In parallel with this the movement in landscape design as typified in the public garden planting of Hermannshof and a more naturalistic and relaxed approach across the board, later taken up and commercialised by Piet Oudulf and others, became accepted by the gardening elite.

For me, with no formal training, much was experiment and observation, trying seed from firms like Jelitto (well, actually no other firm is like Jelitto – they are the bees' knees). I looked for plants that suited my garden. If you grow a plant, you get to know it. I visited local gardens – we have two of the best quite close, Rosemoor in Great Torrington, which before she gave it to the RHS was the superb garden of Lady Anne Palmer, and Marwood

Hill Gardens north of Barnstaple. Both Lady Anne and her eventual head gardener Richard Lee and Dr Jimmy Smart and his head gardener Malcolm Pharaoh were incredibly encouraging – on most occasions anyway. Once when heavily pregnant with my second daughter Alice, I was visiting Rosemoor with my daughter Annie and my mum and I was chatting to Lady Anne when, glancing down at my bump, she enquired when my baby was due. 'Last week,' I replied. She swiftly brought our chat to an end, saying we should probably leave, and ushered us towards the garden exit.

By this time the business had grown and we'd given it the name 'Glebe Cottage Plants'. We needed more room. A farmer neighbour asked me if I was interested in renting a huge old greenhouse, sixty feet long and pretty ramshackle, that his son's girlfriend had put up on a piece of his land before deserting the scene. I was all for it, especially since there was also the possibility of making use of a large agricultural building on the site. There was enough room to turn round vans or a lorry. There was running water and quite a lot of space between and behind the buildings, with the possibility of standing out plants. The greenhouse was a bit of a liability, but beggars can't be choosers. There was never any capital behind the business so rather than follow a strict business plan it was always an impromptu affair. Our overheads were low and friends were always so kind when it came to putting me up when we went to shows.

I have been so fortunate in so many ways, both in running my nursery and in my 'career', as people call it. I have never really thought of what I am doing as a career. When I ran my nursery, I had the best help: Gary, Barbara and Sheila, who worked alongside me for years, committed to our aims and were totally conscientious about achieving them. Several other people have worked here and at the shows too and almost without exception they played an important part in the growth, development and success of Glebe Cottage Plants.

What wonderful characters, what beautiful and fascinating people I have met through running the nursery, exhibiting at shows and taking part in telly. I'd like to end this chapter with tributes to two such people who have been particularly important to me.

A tribute to Alan Street

by Chris Ireland-Jones

Alan Street was head nurseryman at Avon Bulbs 'forever'. That position was initially with Walter Stagg, who had bought the assets of Mars of Haslemere and combined those businesses at Bathford a few miles west of Bath in 1980. Having recently started work for Colonel Mars, Alan moved to join Avon Bulbs as well. Trouble with the access, to what was a domestic property at Bathford, led to the business being moved to rented ground at Upper Westwood near Bradford on Avon. In 1987 Chris Ireland-Jones bought the business and again, Alan came with it as one of the key assets. In 1989 Chris bought a field and moved the business forty miles south-west to Mid Lambrook in South Somerset where the business began to flourish under more suitable circumstances.

A plantsman to his fingertips, Alan constantly used his knowledge and empathy for plants to develop and bring to the attention of keen gardeners some bulbs that were then not so well known. His enthusiasms have included the historic and very largely lost forms of Narcissi that were grown extensively prior to the First World War and which went missing in the upheavals of that time. Eucomis and Agapanthus also took his interest when the heavier South Somerset soils allowed them to be grown more successfully.

This eventually led to him organising and co-ordinating the RHS trials of Eucomis at Wisley beginning in 2017. All the while he was nurturing a passion for Galanthus, but it was only when there was more shade cover and space at Mid Lambrook that the extent of that interest could be developed and the collection grew.

That coincided with the resurrection of an infamous circle of like-minded galanthophiles, meeting for snowdrop lunches every weekend in February each year to pass on and share both plants and knowledge. His remarkable memory for detail came to the fore – the salient features of the plant in question, who had found it, when and where, and the quirky tales that came with those finds. That knowledge was shared at lectures and talks to many interested groups in a wide range of countries when he could be persuaded to tackle the IT issues involved with lecturing. Peppered with witty asides, his talks were amusing, informative and encouraging to the listeners and a thoroughly appreciated tour de force.

The growth of Avon Bulbs was mirrored at the shows, particularly at RHS events over the past forty years. The glory days of the then frequent shows at the RHS Halls in Vincent Square brought in like-minded enthusiasts for particular plant groups in their season and cemented bonds of mutual interests. Avon Bulbs often attended five or six shows a year in the spring and autumn, generally failing to quite manage a gold medal. A breakthrough to gold came with displays concentrating on only one genus – snowdrops – pointing to the difficulty of putting together a mixed display in a very small exhibition space. The highlight of all these was a circular display in 2010 where more than seventy varieties of snowdrop were displayed together, all still growing and flowering perfectly in their pots. That exhibit was a contender that year for the Williams medal for the best single genus exhibit at any show.

Avon Bulbs also showed at the Chelsea Flower Show every year up to 2017. The first gold medal was won in 1986, followed by another every year save for 1992 when it was adjudged a silver gilt with too much of the flower still in bud – a small error in timing in what was a very hot May. This long record saw the transition from very formal displays with regimented isolated plant groups under the old canvas tent to the much less tiered and more open displays (arranged under the new, higher marquee with better light transmission), the plants arranged more gracefully to provide an informal look that included more annuals (seed sales were now possible at the event). All this involved timing the growing and flowering of hundreds of varieties so that they all peaked in the third week of May, which in some cases was six weeks later than they would normally. To achieve this required the plants under-going time in cold stores and a great deal of effort spent attending to each variety's needs. Achieving such a consistency of result over thirty years at the world's premier flower show using such basic resources as Avon Bulbs owned is testament to Alan's skill.

Apart from Chelsea, Avon Bulbs also attended many other shows and events from Harrogate (in April) to Hampton Court (in July). No records of the medals won at these shows remain, though there were many gold medals. Perhaps a culmination of this was the spring show at the Malvern Flower Show in 2018 when Avon Bulbs were the RHS Master Growers with what seemed like a huge exhibit.

Avon Bulbs' success followed the trajectory of the boom in the supply of plants by mail order. In all that time Alan was the core plantsman at Avon Bulbs, identifying plants that would be suitable to grow and sell and leading the way with new plants that could be of interest to the gardening public. That has resulted in a number that have been named for him by others – *Agapanthus* 'Alan Street',

Primula Alan Street and *Galanthus* 'Alan's Treat' included. Many more precious Galanthus have been identified, named, propagated and released along with other widely varied bulbs such as *Gladiolus* Thunder and the *Camassia* Avon's Stellar hybrids. His work has also led to a concentration on increasing the production of such plants as *Tulipa sprengeri*, the range of ornamental *Hedychium* and *Cosmos peucidanifolius*, plants that were not readily available 'in the trade' but which he felt should be more widely known and as a result are now more widely available.

Alan trained to be an RHS judge, although he was never called upon to perform – which may have been a relief to the exhibitor fraternity, as his standards were very high and he was very opinionated as to how standards should be maintained. He was for years on the RHS Bulb Committee and a keen-eyed assessor at the trials ground at Wisley. He wrote a number of articles for the horticultural press including the RHS's *The Garden* magazine.

That is just the potted history of a life cut short but well lived and hugely appreciated by his friends and colleagues. His half-hour programme in January 2021 on Radio 4's *Open Country*, 'Snowdrop Country', encapsulated his passions and interests and his ability to put those over to the public. It is well worth a listen.

* * *

Alan Street was one of the loveliest people you could ever meet, charming, generous, naughty and clever as could be. He taught me and so many people such a lot, always in an enchanting way which would leave you spellbound and feeling as though you must grow whatever was under discussion.

His knowledge was truly encyclopedic, in fact it was better than any encyclopedia because it was always based on practical, first-hand experience. His thirst for knowledge and his curiosity were insatiable. He was born under the Chinese sign of the monkey and was inquisitive to the end, sociable, mischievous and witty as could be. I learned so much from him.

One of our favourite times for meeting up was when we exhibited at the Malvern spring show. Always held in May one or two weeks before the Chelsea Flower Show, it was a favourite for both of us. Visitors were there because they were gardeners, and they wanted to see inspiring displays, buy plants and bulbs, anticipate the summer and engage in the now. There is so much to see and adore at this time of year. Everything is fresh, new and energetic. Against the backdrop of the beautiful Malvern Hills there could not have been a more positive start to the show season.

Alan and I had several mutual friends but none dearer to both of us than Veronica Cross, who lived at Stoke Lacey in Herefordshire, and with whom Alan and I would stay every Malvern show. We always travelled back from the show to her house when we were setting up and for most of the show days too. Alan would drive me in his van and we would use the opportunity to catch up with the gossip. Always plenty of that! Veronica looked after us admirably – always. Whatever time of year you were lucky enough to visit, there would always be a little arrangement of fresh flowers from the garden by your bedside. Even when you were inside, you were outside.

Following a welcome gin and tonic, served by Giles, Veronica's husband, or one of her sons, Ben, and having had a chance to clean up and get changed, we would be treated to a delicious dinner, sometimes with other invited guests in the dining room, sometimes in the kitchen, a warm and hospitable space sitting around a farmhouse table. There were dogs too, Dandie Dimmontish, all girls and all related. One, Miss Tilly, had a snowdrop named after her and was delighted. Snowdrops were high on Veronica's horticultural and social list. Her 'snowdrop lunches' – where all the *Galanthus* cognoscenti gathered on chill February days to explore and exchange views on the snowdrops in her garden, and thence to the dining room to feast on pheasant (Giles thoughtfully provided me with a veggie samosa since I was the only guest who didn't eat meat) – were one of the go-to events in the horticultural world. Outside, guests would instantly acknowledge each other, recognising familiar rear views since everyone was bending over, better to appreciate the finer points of each small white flower.

Had there been a few servants around, there would have been hints of P.G. Wodehouse or early Agatha Christie except that here, Veronica did the lot herself.

To say she was multi-talented is to grossly understate the case. She was a brilliant garden designer with successful commissions completed at some of the best gardens in the British Isles. She had trained at the Inchbald School of Design, only discovering and exploiting her talent after the death of her first husband.

Veronica bought a new house and whilst major works were undertaken there she and her sons lived in a caravan in a friend's orchard.

Veronica never knew her mother. She was adopted at a young age by two women, well-to-do female companions whom she called Granny Dar and Granny Gardie. She was brought up as a Roman Catholic. She had horses, rode and show-jumped and she was good, at one time competing at Badminton Horse Trials and winning at Castletown in Ireland as well as achieving success in the show ring and on the point-to-point circuit. She went up to Oxford, purportedly to study painting though I suspect her social life was more appealing than her artistic activities. She was incredibly chic when dressed up but even in her wellies and her jacket that was so patched you could not distinguish the original, she had style.

Right up to becoming poorly in her eighties, she would go out into the garden every day, constantly creating more beds and adding more plants. She always wanted what was rarest and most special – a true collector. Most plant collectors – by which I mean people who collect plants in their gardens, not those who go out in the wild and bring back treasures – are men, and for most of them the overwhelming desire is to tick off plant after plant, usually with little regard for its arrangement amongst other plants. For Veronica, the acquisition was the first step, but then whatever it was, a rare paeony, a one-of-its-kind shrub, an unusual climber, a new snow-drop, had to be put in exactly the right spot with aesthetic and cultural considerations (for its neighbours).

She had real artistic prowess, both in her design work and in drawing, painting and decorating fine bone china. On the occasion of my being awarded the Victoria Medal of Honour by the RHS she was there with our good friend John Massey (I suspect he was one of those who put me forward for the medal). After the formal ceremony, Veronica presented me with a small box. It contained a delightful Royal Worcester lidded pot which she had hand deco-rated with depictions of mice, leaves and snowdrops and inscribed 'Carol, A day to remember. Love V. March 14th 2018'.

I am so proud of my VMH, but I treasure this little dish even more.

Although we had very different class backgrounds and upbring-ings, Veronica and I got on brilliantly well. She was one of the best friends I have been lucky enough to have, a true friend who, though she had a reputation for being curt, would do anything for you. I remember her coming with me to the Malvern show on the first day, which she always did, except on this occasion instead of dashing off to bag all the best plants, she helped me out behind my sales table, because someone had failed to turn up. She was hopeless with money but a brilliant saleswoman. When you are selling at flower shows, some first-day customers will buy several plants, usually a selection, one of each they have chosen. Veronica, however, exhorted them to go to town. 'How many would you like, three, five or seven – you must always plant in odd numbers!' We did particularly well that day.

Veronica was a one-off. On top of creating a wonderful garden and collecting an enormous range of extraordinary plants, she was a horticultural magnet, attracting all the best people in gardening and plantspersonship. She was responsible for bringing together all the leading lights in the plant world. I first met her at our first Chelsea Flower Show. She was there on press day – she was helping out on the Hardy Plant Society's exhibit and as usual was anxious not to miss a thing. She walked around our small island site several times (arranged as a part of a garden on the ground rather than elevated). She then came and cross-questioned me about a number of plants that were new to her. She came back several times during the day. On her last visit she introduced me to Giles, who not long afterwards became her husband. She was fed up because he had promised her lunch but turned up late having already consumed his lunch in liquid form. Veronica asked if I ever came to the Malvern show. I hadn't done it then, but intended to. She gave me an open invitation to visit her soon-to-be garden and to stay if Glebe Cottage Plants was to exhibit at Malvern.

The next year I took her up on the offer and she took me to see the place where she was going to make a garden. The sale of the property and land was yet to go through, but she didn't let a minor detail like that cramp her style. She had already planned the garden in detail and took me round the four acres or so describing what would go where – for some areas she had already composed the plant list.

It is one of my biggest regrets that Veronica and Alan were not captured on TV for posterity. Neither of them minded – on the contrary perhaps, neither of them were particularly keen to put themselves forward. They were the opposite of those talentless, pushy people who try so very hard yet have so little to contribute.

Alan did have a bit part in *The Great British Garden Revival*, where I visited him at Avon Bulbs and we talked about daffodils and did a bit of cross-pollination. He was splendid. He had such style.

They have both gone, and I miss them both more than I can say. They got on with each other so well; neither of them would tolerate hypocrisy and Alan in particular always had some funny but biting aside to puncture pomposity. It is easy to imagine them in some other reality continuing their discourse, poking fun and giggling whilst inevitably ending up discussing plants.

Both Alan and Veronica taught me so much. It was Alan who showed me how to take root cuttings from Japanese anemones.

Taking Root Cuttings

Taking cuttings from a plant's roots seems an unlikely thing to do – dividing it with roots, shoots, stems and leaves intact is an obvious way to make more, but using roots on their own? How can that work? Even experienced gardeners shy away from growing new plants from root cuttings. Chances are if someone in the family has passed on their skill in propagating plants, their forte will be taking stem cuttings or growing from seed.

Expertise in taking root cuttings has generally remained within the domain of professional gardeners and, like other more 'specialised' techniques, is surrounded with an aura of mystery. Unforeseen difficulties are hinted at, and many of us are inclined to leave well enough alone and not to trespass into the areas of the expert or the specialist. Yet just like most methods of propagation, the practice of growing new plants from roots is very simple.

The hardest part is identifying subjects that can be successfully increased in this way. In every gardening textbook there are lists of plants that lend themselves to this technique, but as a starting point our own personal observations give us a fair idea. All propagation is based on emulating nature, and observing what happens in our gardens and in the wild gives us clues about which plants to use and how to transform their roots into viable plants.

For example, who hasn't tried to move an oriental poppy, digging down to a great depth and making a really thorough job of it, only to find it reappearing the following spring with even more vigour and determination? It doesn't take any expert knowledge to realise that these opulent beauties need no trace of leaf or crown to regenerate ad infinitum. They make perfect candidates for this method of reproduction.

There is a big double bed (double flower bed, before you get the wrong impression) at Glebe Cottage that we call the hot bed, which bisects the light, bright, open side of the garden. Since our garden is terraced, the hot bed's north edge is level with the brick garden but its south edge has a retaining wall about 1.2m high made of sleepers to make the whole bed level, so the soil is deep. A number of plants of *Papaver orientale* (Goliath Group) 'Beauty of Livermere' were planted through the border to make bold splashes of red right at the start of summer. All had been propagated from root cuttings, and there was great excitement when we put them out. The best laid plans ... by some mix-up one was pink, and since most of these oriental poppies look similar at the leafy stage, the intruder wasn't discovered until it started to flower. Beautiful flowers, too, of pretty pale coral with frilly edges to boot, which really rubbed it in.

After several attempts to remove it, we decided that it was just meant to be there; a bronze-leaved elder that lives nearby has flowers of the very same colour, so we have submitted to the garden's will. Since it seems so persistent, so determined, a few of its roots are borrowed each year to make more plants – but nowadays they are clearly labelled and are planted out where we decide they look best.

Japanese anemones, cultivars of *Anemone hupehensis* or *Anemone x hybrida*, are also notoriously prolific once established, so much so that when they have completely overrun a garden, bundles of their roots are often proffered as gifts to those just starting or moving into a bigger garden. Perhaps it's just as well that these donations are usually great woody chunks that seldom settle down. The young, slender roots stand the best chance of establishing themselves. However much they spread, colonies of the beautiful pink *A. x hybrida* and the elegant *A.* 'Honorine Jobert' with its exquisite white petals make one of the most uplifting of autumn's pictures – not just in the shady reaches of the garden at Glebe Cottage but wherever they gain a foothold in the front gardens of city streets or suburban back gardens. In nature the Japanese anemone is a woodlander, often growing in thin soil over rocks. Its stoloniferous roots spread themselves far and wide, gaining a foothold wherever they can. All along those roots are a series of tiny, embryonic leaf nodes, each one of them capable of making a new shoot and eventually a separate plant. This ability to proliferate spontaneously is extremely useful when conditions are hostile.

Only a select group will grow from root cuttings: the European eryngiums with their bristly bracts play along, for example, but the South American types like *Eryngium agavifolium* just rot away. The plants that lend themselves to increase by root cuttings have often evolved a survival strategy which enables them to come back fighting when top growth is damaged or destroyed. Even when plants have been grazed, or trampled, or subjected to disruption from the erosion of soil, they can still hold out to grow again another day. Many herbaceous plants look best in groups or as a recurring theme in a border: when planting for dramatic effect, it is exciting to have a large number of the same plant for maximum impact and thrilling to think you grew them all from a few pieces of root.

Choosing and collecting material

Taking material for root cuttings couldn't be simpler. Gently delve into the soil on one side of an established plant until you come across young roots, then cut them and carefully extract them – or lift the whole clump, shaking off some of the earth and severing the best roots close to the crown of the plant.

Alternatively, if you want to propagate a new variety, buy a good, healthy, well-established plant and when you get it home tip it out of the pot to expose the roots. A well-grown plant will have several roots running around the outside of the compost, which can be detached without doing the parent plant any harm; often nascent shoots will already have started to grow along the root.

One very organised school of thought suggests digging up prospective donor plants the season before material is due to be taken, cutting off most of their roots and replanting them. Just as pruning a shrub will stimulate vigorous new growth, pruning back old roots will also encourage the formation of strong, new roots, ideal material for root cuttings. But if you dig up a plant to prune its roots, it is difficult to resist using those prunings for new cuttings, especially if they seem robust, so if I followed this practice I might end up with more cuttings than I needed. It's always difficult to throw anything away when you know there is a chance it will make new plants. Should you dig up a plant that has been in the garden for a few years, there will be roots of different ages; most of them will make viable root cuttings.

Not all roots are treated the same way: if you want them to work, you have to do what nature does. There are a few plants – mostly woodlanders – that send their roots creeping along close to the surface, ready to pop up new plants. These are fed first from the parent plant and then by the roots along the way, so they can travel until they find a patch of light and then really get going on their own. The growth starts from little nodules, which you can feel if you run your fingers along the roots; keep these roots horizontal as cuttings and they will reward you by producing new growth from all the nodules. But if a plant has roots that grow down, as most of them do, keep your root cuttings vertical, even if you can feel nodules along them. These roots will only produce new roots from the bottom and shoots from the top.

Although taking root cuttings is a long-established method of propagation, very little research has been done on the when of it. Pundits now think that the optimum time to take root cuttings is in the middle of the plant's dormant season. With most herbaceous plants this would be around the turn of the year, but some spring flowering plants such as *Pulsatilla vulgaris* start growth early in the year, so would be at the depth of their dormancy in mid-autumn. At Glebe Cottage we take root cuttings from autumn through to spring, and most are successful.

All our root cuttings are kept on heated benches, and this speeds things up. A small heated propagator will take several pots of cuttings, and can be used throughout the rest of the year to promote rapid rooting of stem cuttings and germination of seed. It will never be empty and soon pays for itself. In fact you may very quickly find yourself investing in another one or a bigger one – or both. Even if you have no bottom heat (always a sad prospect!) you should pick out a warm, bright windowsill or greenhouse shelf, as cuttings placed in a cold frame will soon rot.

Chapter Twelve

I have never had a romanticised picture of gardening. Other people may have imagined me in that ideal 'cottage garden' setting, trug in hand, snipping perfect roses, probably dressed in something appropriately floaty. The reality has been very different, lots of dirty knees and muddy boots.

When we won our first gold medal at the Chelsea Flower Show, Stephen Bennett, then RHS show director, left me a little note beside my medal card saying 'Well done Mrs Muddy Boots x'.

By then, doing shows had become a way of life. Who knows whether or not it was the right course to take. Glebe Cottage Plants, my nursery, did either sixteen shows for seventeen years or seventeen shows for sixteen years. Even I with my shaky grasp of mathematics know that is the same number – 272. There were the big shows, Chelsea, Hampton Court, Tatton Park, Malvern and Harrogate, and the smaller shows, most of them at Vincent Square in the RHS Horticultural Halls. All demanded a huge amount of work and effort.

It was my darling friend Sonia who persuaded me – or it may have been the other way round – that we should try our luck at a flower show, a step on from selling my wares at local pannier markets. This was a totally new departure, fraught and challenging, but if I was mad enough to think I might make a living doing what I loved best, then it was time to broaden our horizons.

At one time the RHS, the Royal Horticultural Society, held fortnightly shows in their two 'Horticultural Halls', grand art-deco buildings just off Vincent Square not far from Victoria in Central London. In their heyday, exhibitors and customers would flock from far and wide to attend these shows which were for all the world like mini-Chelsea Flower Shows. Many specialist nurseries attended and each was obliged to put on a display stand and given a small area for their sales table. Back-up plants were stored under the display. Dark green hessian surrounded the table and was referred to as 'the skirts'. Every so often you would see an exhibitor diving under the table to fish out plants for a customer.

Glebe Cottage Plants first exhibited at these shows in 1990. I had attended the Great Autumn Show the year before to see how things were arranged – and to look under everybody's skirts! Having had a practice at the Cannington College flower show we decided we were ready to hit the big time and off we went in March 1990 to try our luck at an RHS show. Our first display was a mixture of hellebores and primroses in as naturalistic a setting as we could accomplish given the whole exhibit was on a tabletop. We made much use of moss and mossy logs. It was well received. Our display was fresh, organic and quite different from the other exhibits. We had a couple of glowing mentions in the papers but the best accolade was from Valerie Finnis, who found our little exhibit 'enchanting' apart from having to read our vertically written labels with her head on one side.

For all these early shows Neil made me beautiful cherrywood labels (everything has to be labelled with its full title and Latin name) though they would have been easier to read had they been horizontal rather than vertical.

Until fairly recently, small specialist nurseries – who for many flower show visitors are the most important lure – couldn't actually sell anything at the RHS Chelsea Flower Show. When we started exhibiting there, you could only sell catalogues and seeds and take orders. In recent years, however, the RHS have implemented schemes to help small-scale exhibitors and plants can now be sold.

It is a difficult business. The amount of graft and grind that goes into creating an exhibit may be difficult to appreciate unless you have actually been involved in the process. But you are working with plants, which is in itself life-giving, and you are working with people. Ever since the nursery and the shows began I have been incredibly lucky to have worked with like-minded people who have identified with what we have been trying to do and who love plants. Of course if we won a gold medal we were thrilled, but it has always been the working together that has been important. And as Beth Chatto so wisely said when we were lucky enough to interview her in 2017, 'It isn't the achievement, it is the achieving that is important.'

Putting on one of these exhibits is no mean feat. Whether or not you are selling plants (and that is one of the main objectives – making a living), your exhibit has to be the very best you can make it. Before any other considerations about design, it is the plants that matter. The 'P' in VIP stands for 'Plants'. Many of our show plants became old friends, real veterans, and must have been amongst the best travelled plants ever, attending show after show, year after year. Some of our hostas became so heavy they needed two strong people to lift them.

We never ever had a formula, though. We never did the same thing twice. Throughout the show season different plants took centre stage; the idea of our displays was to give gardeners a realistic idea of how plants would grow in maturity and hopefully inspire them to use such plants in their own gardens in their own way. We always laid great emphasis on choosing plants you could grow, plants for the situations in your garden where they would thrive. On several occasions I refused to sell customers plants I knew would never make it in their gardens having heard what conditions they had.

There is great joy to be had through creating a display; crashing sadness too when after a few days it had to be disbanded, or as it felt, 'torn apart'.

These shows gave us an opportunity to come face to face with the gardening public and to talk to them about plants. Gardening can be a solitary business, and to have the opportunity to be amongst like-minded people and talk about what we loved was a privilege. Making a display or show garden is poles apart from making your own garden. With the former you are fashioning a product, with the latter engaging in a process.

* * *

Going to flower shows also had its problems, starting with our first Chelsea. We had been asked to exhibit with just a few weeks' notice. Torbay Council had cancelled, unable to afford exhibiting at Chelsea and implementing poll tax. We pulled out all the stops, hired a seven-and-a-half-ton lorry and duly began to load it the day before travelling to the show. Glebe Cottage Plants was never over-capitalised, and we had none of the professional Dutch trolleys and the other paraphernalia that bigger nurseries took for granted. It wasn't until dusk began to descend that we realised our lorry had no internal lights; the lead we took from the house only reached halfway down the track so we ended up lighting candles to complete our packing. The next morning my friend Sally and I drove into South Molton to park her car and await the arrival of our lorry, driven by Neil. It didn't turn up and eventually we discovered (this was before the advent of mobile phones) that the lorry had broken down just a few yards from where we'd left it. It was a hot day. When the hire firm opened, they offered to bring out another lorry and suggested we move our plants from one to the other. I declined. Eventually they collected the lorry, changed the gear box and away we went. There were two and a half tons of stone in it to build a dry stone wall. I'm glad we didn't need to transfer it.

Looking back, I suppose it was enough to put you off but we ploughed on. Although we had very short notice for the show, we had spent every minute from its being confirmed preparing. Normally you have months to get ready for Chelsea and if you are a big concern you almost certainly have a huge stockpile of plants to make use of. With six weeks' notice and little or no experience, we had to improvise. Most of what we took was already in pots but we added to this by digging up stuff from the garden, some of which succeeded. Sadly some plants didn't make it, but they were looked after and replanted. My friend Joannie, her bloke Nev and two other friends met us at the gates and helped us unload – and Joannie lent us her jasmine for our obelisk.

For those of you who don't know, the RHS Chelsea Flower Show is held in the grounds of the Royal Hospital, alongside the Embankment. At these shows you are allotted a space which Robin and his merry men (the team who do all the groundwork for all the RHS shows, including building stands) mark out. There is space around the edge of your stand to unload all your gear. When we started this was limited – in fact on a few occasions, space was so tight, we would find other exhibitors had purloined our space to deposit all their stuff, but in recent years when exhibitor numbers have declined there has been much more room. This marquee, according to *The Guinness Book of Records*, was the biggest tent in the world. It was first erected for the show in 1951 and annually until 2000. Weighing sixty-five tons and using 274 miles of yarn, initially it took twenty men twenty days to put up.

When first you step into the Great Pavilion at Chelsea, there's a sense of excitement unmatched anywhere else in the horticultural calendar. There are vivid colours, enticing scents, glimpses of wondrous plants, some of which you never in your wildest dreams expected to come across even at a distance let alone face to face. There are exotic orchids, gingers from the Caribbean, strange pitcher plants hanging from mossy logs as well as the crème de la crème of more familiar subjects – paeonies, irises and roses.

At first the stands are obscured by Dutch trolleys full of plants and all the paraphernalia needed to build an exhibit, then gradually the whole marquee begins to clear, you're able to walk down pathways previously taped off as no-go zones and the mastery of the exhibits begins to emerge. Vistas previously obscured are brought into full view as the public spotlight is turned on them.

It is an overwhelming experience to walk into the Chelsea marquee for the first time before build-up; there is just a vast expanse of grass. When we first started exhibiting it was the old canvas marquee that I walked into, just the hugest tent you've ever seen and so quiet. Nowadays this has been replaced by a modern plastic structure, taller and brighter. It was rather wonderful to be in that old marquee on a very windy day. You could almost imagine you were on a huge ship with sails billowing in a force ten gale.

We were lucky to be taking part in flower shows in their heyday. The aisles in between the stands were heaving. It was so crowded once the public flooded in that you were rushed off your feet from eight in the morning till eight at night. You were inundated with questions and comments and it was so thrilling to be face to face with fellow gardeners asking and answering questions non-stop about plants. In later years, when my television work overlapped with our exhibiting, it was good to hear what these visitors had to say about our coverage of the show. It is equally enlightening to talk to people now at the shows – the one chance you get to know what people think instead of just talking to them through the lens of a camera. Some folk are very forthright. A few years ago on Members' Day at Chelsea, a northern lady came rushing over and grabbed my arm saying, 'Ee Carol, we love you on t' telly, we've got no time for them pretty ones!'

Although it is hugely hard work to put on one of these displays, during build-up, most of the work has already been done. For the previous year, exhibitors have been thinking out their display. Which plants will they grow? How many of them? When should they be potted on? Will they need to be held back or pushed forward? What about hard landscaping and props? Are there paths in the display? If so, what are they made from? On top of this are administrative questions. Who is going to man, or woman, the stand? Who will look after the nursery? What about transport, or catalogues?

Every year we attended Chelsea was different – and memorable. That first year we learned a lot. I am always a bit over-ambitious about what can be achieved, which has probably resulted in extra stress for those I have been working with. I apologise. Always better, though, to set your sights too high than go for the lowest acceptable level.

Each display was unique. Just as with anyone's stand, anyone's painting, anyone's poem, our exhibits were instantly recognis- able. They were quite unlike any other displays. On the medal card that is left by your stand on Tuesday morning, the day after judging, there is a medal, bronze, silver, silver gilt, gold, and a brief description embodying the character of your stand or the genera of plants you are displaying if it is a specialist display. When we were awarded our first gold medal in 1994 the inscription was 'For Cottage Garden Plants'. This was not on our initial application but the RHS decided to characterise our stand with that title. It is also the inscription on the actual Gold Medal that Glebe Cottage Plants was presented with. It is a lovely thing. The first time you win any of those four designated medals, you receive the medal itself. After that you just get the card. I have the full set, although my gold medal is a replacement. Later on when presenting, I was daft enough to take my medal into the show. There is always a 'medal day special' on the BBC TV coverage and stupidly I thought it would be great to show our viewers a real medal. It was stolen, but Stephen Bennett, then shows manager, and Bob Sweet, his colleague, managed to get me another one.

As for the medal cards, they are delivered by hand to each stand and to every garden exhibit. When we first started Chris Hulowitz from the RHS shows department used to cycle round the marquee and drop off everyone's medal by their stand, not quite in the manner of an American paper boy. Nowadays for the gardens, it is a TV presenter accompanied by an RHS aide who does the job although what we as TV presenters have to do with it, I have no idea. This year they did not do it.

Quite often we were delayed by TV crews during build-up; no doubt I have contributed to delaying exhibitors from time to time since I have been a presenter, though, being aware of the inconvenience, having had it happen to me, I tried not to delay them too long.

Every one of our exhibits was unique. My memory of some of them is sharp and detailed. Some exhibits stand out, usually for the right reasons although disasters also come to the fore.

One year we snatched victory from the jaws of defeat. It was going to be an extra-special display, and though building our stand would be as spontaneous as ever, we had put in a lot of planning as far as the quality and readiness of our plants was concerned. The small 'Discovery' apple tree given to me by one of my ex-pupils who was working at a famous nursery that specialised in unusual and heritage varieties was going to be the star of the show. Flowering of apples often coincides with the Chelsea and Malvern flower shows, but sometimes just misses. This year it was perfect. I had been nurturing the tree, talking to it every day, and it was full of pink-tinged buds that would hopefully open for judging day. Nobody dared breathe on it. It was to be surrounded by *Convolvulus cneorum*, a silvery leaved semi-shrub with glorious trumpet-shaped flowers; we had propagated loads of them and were able to choose the crème de la crème.

Our hostas, some of them ten years plus, were magnificent. Amongst them were three big clumps of *Hosta* 'Halcyon', my all-time favourite with elegant grey leaves covered in a grape-like bloom. Everyone at the nursery was terrified of approaching them because I had threatened them all with dire consequences should that bloom be spoiled by anyone handling those leaves. I might even have had the fingerprints forensically examined.

Our plants were not like other people's plants. Many show plants have been grown under strictly regimented conditions. They are uniform and well-nigh perfect. Ours were far more au naturel, grown without forcing or heat, looking just as they would in a garden. There were no holes in the leaves – after all, this was the Chelsea Flower Show – but there were often wayward stems, verbascums with slight inclines and similar touches of reality. A time or two such things worked against us with the judges, but we deliberately included them for a touch of authenticity. People often commented that our plants were strong, robust and healthy.

On the day in question we had had a difficult journey, so it was a relief when our lorry was allowed to back right into the marquee. All hands on deck, Neil, our friend Dave and I rushed round to the back where two or three friends were already gathered ready to unload. The shuttered door was lifted and I screamed. The extra shelves wedged in between the apple tree and the back row of Dutch trolleys had collapsed. They had done one of those cartoon tricks, where the top shelf falls at one end then the next shelf down falls the other way. I was running up and down sobbing and swearing. The tail lift went up with me on it. Plants had fallen forward into the tree. Others on the shelves were surely squashed but as I began to extricate plants and pass them down to the willing hands below, expecting to see further horrors unfold, we realised that very little had suffered at all. The goddess was with us. When we finally took out the tree standing in its big copper cauldron, it was pristine and a few of its buds had started to open.

* * *

Making a show garden or display is not the same as making a garden. Nonetheless, at Glebe Cottage Plants we always endeavoured to make our exhibits truthful and informative as well as inspirational. Plants that we put together would have got on well with each other in a real garden. We were always guided by what happened here at home.

Having said that, especially on displays where we were trying to illustrate the idea of 'right plant right place', there would be areas in our display that didn't exactly copy or even emulate specific parts of our garden. There is shade and sun, well-drained to boggy soil, open and enclosed. Although we are blessed at home by having a panoply of areas with varying conditions, I didn't always get it right.

Christopher Lloyd always used to visit our stand. Often he was on a judging panel, though I don't think he ever judged our exhibit. After Fergus became part of Dixter, he would come along too. Now he is a Chelsea judge. One year we had made a display that went through several different habitats as you travelled around it. In the hot and dry area, I had very proudly included several kniphofia, red hot pokers, in the belief that they loved good drainage. Christo, who had seen kniphofia growing in the wild in Malawi in quite boggy conditions when he was stationed there, very politely informed me they were in the wrong place. In fact, though they love sun, most kniphofia require damp conditions for at least part of their growing season.

This was not the only exhibit where we tried to portray a hot, dry area. One stand we made had a large section separated from the beds beyond by a stone path and mulched with gravel and pebbles. Richard, who was helping, his dad and I worked right through the night feeding in gravel between the pots of artemisias, eryngiums and other iconic sunbathers. Although we had taken up most of the volume between the pots with packing, we used bag after bag of gravel; it was almost as though it was a bottomless pit we were trying to fill. Every time you thought you had successfully completed one piece, there would be a mini landslide and the gravel would disappear between the pots. Meanwhile it got lighter and lighter as the new day dawned. A blackbird began to sing.

There were always birds just outside the marquee and sometimes inside. One year blackbirds built a nest in the top of a pillar of foxgloves towering almost to the ceiling of the marquee.

Other wildlife visited too. Working late again on another display, we witnessed a fox sitting happily on the National Farmers' Union stand tucking in to some of the produce on display. It was a touch ironic, knowing how many farmers support the hunt.

When you build a stand like ours, most of the time plants are left in pots, though the pots must never be seen, since that would destroy the illusion. This way they are far more likely to be alive and kicking after a week or more in a hot tent. We used all manner of packing in between pots as a preliminary to finishing off with some sort of mulch, sometimes chipped bark, leaf mould, moss or old leaves depending on the kind of area. Packing could be almost anything – usually old pots, newspaper or if we were lucky the easy-to-use tissue paper that had been wrapped around tulips in transport. We would hang around the Bloms Bulbs stand like vultures as the girls started to unpack and arrange their perfect blooms. Scavenging was part of our schtick; people called me the bag lady – but this was recycling at its best.

The smallest member of our troupe was Veronica Borrett and on a few occasions we lowered her into some of the skips up and down Main Avenue to extract some choice paper or turf that had been jettisoned – we always got her out again. Our little team were rather different from the crews of some of the other exhibitors, with their matching polo shirts emblazoned with the firm's logo. We were a rather motley crew, although Edward Elfes, our main man who helped me with displays for years, might object to being referred to as motley. Edward was a florist in Harrogate, a Londoner by birth and an ex-Guardsman. Tall and slightly stooping with a splendid moustache, he had real artistic flair, a love of plants and a real understanding of how they grew, an important skill when it comes to making a display. After many years he decided he would no longer work with us. I am still not sure why, but he did go on to help Bleddyn and Sue from Crüg Farm Plants with a couple of their award-winning displays full of plants to make you drool, most of which they themselves have collected from far-flung places around the world, mainly in Asia though some from South America too.

Veronica helped us for years. I met her first at one of the Vincent Square shows when she bought something from our stand. We got chatting and at one stage she was kind enough to come and help us and went on to do so for years. She is very small, Edward very tall and they got on brilliantly well. Every so often they would disappear off together and return to the stand sometime later bearing plants they had bought. Without exception, Edward's plant was always something tiny whereas Veronica invariably returned with something enormous. Often all you could see of her was a pair of little feet whilst the rest of her was hidden behind huge leaves.

Jill Starnes was an absolute stalwart throughout so many shows, following a career as an air hostess with learning about plants and eventually selling special plants that she had raised. Many others helped us throughout the seventeen or so shows we attended each year. It was absolutely a team effort, and every person who took part got the opportunity to put a bit of themselves into each stand. We would often discuss one or other aspect of the stand and different solutions. I hope that everyone who took part got something from it as well as contributing significantly to our exhibits.

When we were setting up for Chelsea, we would have an array of tables alongside our stand. Most importantly and separate from the rest was a table devoted to labelling. Every plant included in the display had to bear its Latin name. Though I say it myself, for some shows ours were the best labels around – nothing to do with me. For our first Chelsea, my friend Polly, who was an ex-theatre sister but had recently taken up calligraphy, made us beautiful and distinctive labels in gold on green card. Later on Dick Thornton, a keen and accomplished gardener and a professional calligrapher, made our labels. Most were done in advance though he brought the tools of his trade to the show and completed extras on site.

Getting ready for a show, you do as much as possible to prepare your plants before they leave home, but it is not until you get to the show that the final primping and preening takes place. Every plant must be checked over, anything dead or disfigured or even vaguely dodgy removed so that as plants are passed over to whomever is arranging them in the display, they are at their very best.

Most of our shows had a vague theme, or I wanted them to feel a particular way. We were always guided by our plants rather than forcing them to perform for us. Although we knew where our paths and props might go, be it an old gate, a seat covered in lichen or a brick path, we would play around with the plants until they looked happy and in the place they wanted to be. We went to an infinite amount of trouble to make everything look real and relaxed. Once when we had an L-shaped brick path, we grew moss in between slabs on the nursery for months – yards and yards of it, in the shade round the back of our shed. It was all carefully lifted in long lengths, laid into bread trays and loaded into the lorry. Not for us grabbing handfuls of loose moss and pushing them between the bricks. When the beds and a sloping bank on either side of the path were planted, mulched and labelled, we worked backwards either side of a central point to feed our lines of moss gently between each brick and make them look as though they had been there for years.

Our first ever Chelsea display was part of a 'garden' with a dry stone wall running across part of it. It had to be built for real, from scratch. There could be no pre-planning, where everything is marked and slotted into place. It just had to be built then and there, adding plants as it ascended which had to look as though they had been growing there always. One of these plants was a ramonda, a plant from the high Pyrenees that grows in rock crevices with its rosette of leaves growing flat against the rock. Several friends were helping out including Bisi, who was giving out catalogues, perched on a shooting stick close by the ramonda, when a man in a mack approached, pulled the plant from the wall and ran off. Bisi gave chase still carrying her shooting stick, this time in a threatening manner. Out of the marquee they ran, she shouting 'Stop thief' as she gave pursuit. He dropped the plant and made off. Bisi picked up the plant, returned triumphantly to our stand and we reinstated the plant where it lived happily for the rest of the week and was much admired. On its return to Glebe Cottage it was planted between the stones on the shady side of our raised bed and I think it is still there though that was thirty-odd years ago.

Our stand generated quite a lot of interest amongst visitors, though nobody else helped themselves! We had several positive mentions in the press including one from Robin Lane Fox in the *Financial Times*. A few of my gardening heroes or heroines like Valerie Finnis visited the stand too.

On one of my rare exits from the marquee I spotted my all-time hero Roy Lancaster in the crowd and asked him please to come and have a look at our stand. I told him we had *Dracunculus vulgaris* on the display, in full flower (this was from the same plant I had liberated from a derelict garden years earlier in Ladbroke Grove). I started to tell him just where our stand was. He interrupted, 'Don't worry, I'm sure the smell will guide me right to it!'

The most important visitor we had that day was my mum. Unbeknown to me, my sister-in-law Helen had brought her to the show. She was so proud. We hugged and hugged and had a little dance all around the stand. It was only a couple of years before that I had taken my mum to Chelsea. We had spent most of our day visiting and revisiting Beth Chatto's stand. Little did we dream that my mum would be visiting my Chelsea exhibit just a couple of years later.

Over the years several royals visited our stands. The Queen and her eldest son came on several occasions. There was one year when we had more than our fair share, including both Queen Elizabeth II and the Queen Mother, who was being driven around in a buggy and called me over; we had spoken before. We saw Prince Charles and one of the other princes, I think it was Prince Edward. They would always be shown around by whoever was president of the RHS. One year the then-president Sir Robin Herbert was conducting Prince Edward along one of the main aisles between the stands, fast approaching us, when suddenly he steered the prince to the other side of the aisle, putting himself (he was very tall) between the prince and me. I was wearing a shocking pink culotte dress, a pair of Doc Martens, and had short punky red hair and big earrings. I am sure my appearance had nothing to do with this redirection.

In the year of the four royal visits, I showed the Queen around our stand – and made her laugh. We had dedicated our stand to the pioneering female gardener Gertrude Jekyll. There was a shady area with lots of woodland plants and a small pond, and beside it a pair of moss-covered boots from our garden. Miss Jekyll's boots were famous, immortalised by a painting of them by William Nicholson carried out in 1920 at Munstead Wood whilst he was waiting for her to sit for a portrait. Both works are in the Tate, donated by Sir Edwin Lutyens. Having inspected our stand and the boots, the Queen surmised that she could do with a new pair.

Those same boots, together with seven other pairs, were used in our 2023 Iconic Horticultural Hero garden at the Hampton Court Garden Festival, strategically placed. They are back in the garden here now. I have worn them all over the last forty-five years and put them outside when they came to the end of their working lives.

I have worked in all sorts of boots. There were army boots and Doc Martens, one pair of which lasted me for years. They were proper working boots, a rich chestnut colour, that I bought on eBay. They were very cheap considering they were practically new but it wasn't until they set off an alarm at Exeter airport that I realised they had steel toe-caps. I am used to setting off those alarms since I have two replacement hips made of titanium and often have to go through one of those body scans, especially since modern equipment is more sensitive. Eventually we realised it was the boots that were the culprits and I wasn't carrying anything forbidden.

Presently and on and off over the last few years I wear Blundstone boots, made in Tasmania. They are mainly pull-on boots although at one time they used to make lace-ups. In an unlikely coincidence, I once found two pairs of lace-up Blundstones in a fashion shop in Exeter, one black, one brown – and they were my size. I bought them both and they lasted for years. They're in the garden now.

* * *

We were awarded a silver medal for our first Chelsea Show and were thrilled to bits. The week passed by in a haze, talking plants from morning till night. But I will never forget the day we got our first gold.

On the Tuesday morning I came into the marquee, head down, almost running, dodging several well-meaning people who wanted to tell me how we had done. Somehow, probably by singing loudly,

'Please don't tell me what we've got' and looking at the ground, I made it to our stand, which was way over the other side of the marquee. Medal cards are about 8x5 inches and though they are not very big you can tell from a distance which medal you have been awarded. Although gold and silver gilt are both gold in colour, the gold medal depiction is much smaller as indeed is the medal itself. For once I was speechless – not for long though.

We won gold at Chelsea six times in all and were awarded gold at several other shows over the years including a Tudor Rose Award at Hampton Court.

I have many reservations about judging and awards. I was approached about becoming an RHS judge but said no. I suppose I feel the same way about judging floral displays as I do about judging children's art competitions. Perhaps this is hypocrisy, as I was only too delighted for the nursery to win our gold medal, but children make pictures the way they make them and are to be congratulated for making them, not for how well they succeed in conforming to some adult benchmark of what constitutes acceptability and merit.

Although nowadays there are clear criteria for judging and exhibitors are party to this, as they can read how marks are allotted, at one time judging was subjective and there were no explicit criteria laid down for assessment. The position now is:

'We have a different team of judges who assess the beautiful displays in the Great Pavilion. Among the elements they take into account is the endeavour of the display, how difficult it was to put together, how much of a challenge the planting has been, any new ideas or originality as well as overall impression.'

* * *

It was a big push to go to shows. The first ones were the hardest. Alice was eight and Annie ten when I started to go off to shows. When I was away at Vincent Square it was for four days each time, more than a week for Chelsea, Hampton Court, Malvern, Gardeners' World Live and Tatton. Each time I found it difficult to tear myself away. I missed the girls and Neil so much. Neil managed marvellously. He has always been the best dad but it was not until I had to go away to shows that we realised he could cook. Necessity is the mother of invention. He is a brilliant cook and has been responsible for most of the food we have consumed since then. He has real flair.

I missed my family and they missed me. On my first Chelsea trip Neil told me that before Alice went to bed she would go into our room and sniff my pillow.

Scent is the most evocative of all the senses. It travels straight to our memory without assessment or interpretation. When I sniff the pinky-purple flowers of *Daphne mezereum* thronged along its little branches I'm transported to my grandad's garden seventy years ago. Everything about it returns, the place, the people and of course the plants.

Sometimes scent is more abstract, not tied down to a specific place but creating a mood. In the garden here at Glebe Cottage we have a large viburnum; nobody is sure what it is. When it was planted it grew and grew and made copious leafage though it never seems quite sure whether or not it is evergreen or deciduous. Then, a few years ago, it flowered. Its flowers are pretty, small and in loose bunches held close to the branches. They're creamy-white with a touch of pink but you hardly notice what they look like, so overcome are you by its sweet fragrance. If I close my eyes I can recall it, the feeling of the air, a sense of the time of day, the temperature, how I felt.

As for the auriculas, was there ever a flower that looked more hand painted, or were they cut with dainty scissors by a skilled craftswoman from fragments of rich velvet? Such a tapestry of colours: rich ruby, faded taupe, such soft petals ... and the scent ... It is always difficult to describe perfume without comparing it to another scent. That of auriculas is like nothing else; there is a sweetness to it but it is spiced with nutmeg, pepper and cardamom. It is through our senses that we directly experience the world but of all of them it is our sense of smell that is the most evocative. If we have experienced a smell before, we are taken back to that moment, we are there again. Watch someone drink in the scent of jasmine; as they lift the flowers towards their nostrils, their eyes automatically close. In that instant all that exists is the moment and the memory.

Little wonder that the rich and affluent had theatres specially constructed where they could show off their wealth with their best auriculas displayed in pristine hand-thrown clay pots on painted shelves. At the other end of the social scale, miners and mill workers went out to tend their show auriculas after work, preparing them for fiercely fought competition. There were secret recipes for compost with extra magical ingredients, including dried blood – not a plant for vegetarians. The prize for supreme champions was a copper kettle. Standards were exacting.

Growing, especially showing, auriculas can become an obsession. It has never quite reached those proportions for me. Not quite, but nearly.

Plants can come to have so many different meanings. For the miners and weavers who grew auriculas for show, they were an opportunity to escape, to seek perfection through their own ability to understand and nurture in a world where hard work and grinding poverty dominated everyday existence. For the rich who displayed them in specially constructed auricula 'theatres', they were status symbols to get one over on aristocratic neighbours.

I confess to worshipping at the auricula altar. Our third flower show exhibit was in early April of 1990, and oh boy did we go to town. I have always set my sights high when it comes to exhibiting, some would say being totally unrealistic about what was possible with the resources available. It was auricula time and I had a wonderful collection of auriculas and was determined to show them to their best advantage. I was there to show off my wares and sell plants – our only income – but wanted this display to be an homage to all those who had poured their hearts and souls into growing these special flowers. The display had to relate to backyards and terraced houses. I took a ton (literally) of old bricks to form paths and separate three small beds full of perennial wallflowers including my favourite wallflower *Erysimum* 'John Codrington' whose colour someone described as being 'the colour of old bruises'. There were euphorbias, dicentras (we used to call them pink bells, one of the few plants that thrived in our tiny front garden at 87a Manchester Road), fritillaries, honesty and border auriculas.

More auriculas, striped, shows and fancies, all with mealy leaves – 'farina', after the Latin and Italian for flour – were displayed on a brick-paved area on a little set of cedar shelves that Neil constructed specially for the show. My farmer friend Molly took my collection of small clay pots – all of them hand thrown – and scrubbed them. Into each pot went one unique auricula to take its place on the shelf. We really could not have put more love into our little exhibit. The colours were exquisite, sharp acidic greens contrasting with fruity orange, subtle taupe and gamboge yellow next door to rich velvety crimson and midnight blue.

People loved our display. All of it was attainable, plausible for anyone to emulate.

That has been the unspoken premise with all our exhibits. Any display or garden at a show is necessarily a collection of fibs – after all it is constructed and dismantled within days. But Pierre Bonnard said, 'There is a formula that perfectly fits painting: lots of little lies for the sake of one big truth.'

Perhaps without being too grand, that is what we tried to do with our exhibits. These were plants that had been grown in pots, carried hundreds of miles in a van, arranged on a tabletop, packed with newspaper, mulch and moss all in order to attempt to envisage what could be done with them in a real garden.

How Do Plants Get Their Names?

I failed Latin three times; each time I retook it I got five marks less. Perhaps I couldn't see the relevance of translating stories about Trojan travellers or conjugating verbs that were no longer spoken. Before my results became even more ignominious I'd left school and ventured out into a world where nobody could have cared less about my lack of ability in Classics. Nowadays I recognise what a privilege it was to become acquainted with that language and most days now Latin and Greek names crop up several times at Glebe Cottage.

At first sight, giving plants Latin names and dividing up plants into families might seem an academic and perhaps rather a dull business. But both are essential in terms of identifying our plants and hugely interesting in finding out more about what plants are like, what they look like, where they want to grow – who they are.

'If you do not know the names of things, the knowledge of them is lost too.' So said Carl Linnaeus in 1751. He was responsible for the binomial system, giving plants two names to identify them accurately. His work was the basis of the system we use now, even though it was completed two and a half centuries ago. Before he stepped in plant nomenclature had become a fairly silly business with taxonomists, botanists, Uncle Tom Cobley and all inventing names and adding to others, sometimes resulting in names several lines long, impossible to remember and of no help to anyone. Often plants shared epithets, *molto confusione*.

Linnaeus gave plants a family name, the genus, and a second 'trivial' name, the specific epithet, the species. In addition plants often have a varietal name, a subspecies or a form.

This second name gave information either about the plant's use, its characteristics, where it grew or who discovered it or introduced it.

So *Pulmonaria officinalis* was supposed to resemble lungs, and *officinalis* means it was used as a medicine, after *opificina* – a store-room in a monastery. Anything including *sativum* means it was grown for food, hence *Pisum sativum*, our garden pea.

Naming plants helps protect biodiversity. It tells us where our plants come from, it celebrates the human love of plants and reminds us of our inextricable links with them.

But what's wrong with common names; do we really need all this complicated Latin? Common names are charming. They are useful too for ethnobotanists trying to discover the symbiosis between people and the plants that grow around them.

In the south-east, *Lychnis flos-cucullaria* is 'the flower of the cuckoo', and cuckoo-flower is otherwise known as ragged robin. In Lancashire, where I come from, the cuckoo arrives later. We call *Cardamine pratensis* 'the cuckoo flower', but we also call it 'May flower' and 'lady's smock'. *Pratensis* means 'of the meadow'. That is not to say that common names should be ignored – on the contrary they have huge value in telling us of the heritage, the history and the connection between these plants and humankind.

Having a common agreement and a scientific system for naming plants and every other living thing though is essential for accurate recognition. We can talk about them with the confidence that even if we are on the other side of the world we are all referring to the same thing.

A plant's family name is shared by all the other members of the group. Buttercups, clematis, hellebores, aquilegias, marsh marigolds all belong to the family ranunculaceae. *Ranunculus aconitifolius* 'Flore Pleno' is a buttercup with leaves like an aconite and double flowers. The *foetidus* of *Helleborus foetidus* tells us that the plants has an unpleasant smell (though I quite like it).

But it isn't just a question of identifying a plant and knowing who its relations are, nor of assuming that once you know to which family a plant belongs you can generalise about how to grow it or what it needs to thrive. Each family contains so many diverse members. What is it that makes it so interesting? It isn't a case of declaring a plant is from a particular family and thereby understanding everything about it. It's more a question of how fascinating it is to discover more and more about the relationships between plants, their similarities and their differences, noticing that the seed pods of a hellebore have the same construction as those of a buttercup and very like those of an aquilegia. When seed is ripe, the capsule containing them splits apart and is distributed simply by falling to the ground. Though it is different sizes, when it ripens the seed is black and shiny. On the other hand clematis, also belonging to ranunculaceae, have tiny seeds with fluffy tails attached; so too does the pulsatilla or pasqueflower. More than 1,800 species of plants belong to the buttercup family; there are so many because each species has evolved to fit into a particular niche.

In recent years, the names of a whole host of plants have changed. No sooner have we successfully reeled off a plant's Latin name than we're having to get our tongues around its new name.

Until relatively recently most plant names and the assigning of family names was mainly a result of educated guesswork. Botanists recognised the morphological similarities between plants and classified them accordingly.

There are three main reasons why a plant's name should be changed. Firstly, if it is discovered that a name was correctly published before the name that plant has since come to be known by, the first name registered is the valid name. This is a rule stipulated under the International Code of Botanical Nomenclature.

Secondly, sometimes plants are brought into cultivation, given a new incorrect name, and propagated and distributed with that name even though a valid name for the plant already existed. The original name has to be reinstated.

Thirdly, advances in botanical knowledge, specifically through DNA sequencing, have unlocked the true relationships between plants, sometimes leading to reclassification.

There are exceptions! Chrysanthemum, for instance, having been reclassified as dendranthemum, was reclassified as chrysanthemum due to pressure from many sources, particularly commercial interests. So a plant's renaming shouldn't be a source of annoyance, it's not those botanists and taxonomists short of something to do and making arbitrary decisions but an attempt on their part to clarify our understanding of the plants we know and love.

Chapter Thirteen

I suppose a lot of you are reading this book because you know me from television. Thanks for watching, as well as reading.

There are some TV presenters for whom it is the presenting that is important. I never thought of myself as a TV presenter. It has been neither a step nor a goal in my career path. But then I have never had a career path. Perhaps I should have had one.

Being a mum, teaching, growing plants, running a nursery, selling plants and going to shows were all things I needed to do. I have never felt that way about presenting, although I enjoy it hugely.

Some presenters, so I hear, get training in how to present. I have never had lessons. I have no desire to present for its own sake. The reason I love it so much is that it gives me the opportunity to talk about what I love – gardening and plants – and to share that love and passion with other people.

My presenting career began very accidentally. When we were exhibiting at the flower shows, particularly the Chelsea Flower Show, TV crews were often around. Whoever was presenting, often the lovely Geoff Hamilton in those days, would sometimes pass by our stand and occasionally stop. If we were engaged in talking to visitors when the crew paused, they would listen in. Invariably the conversation was about plants and I was doing most of the talking. One day as the rest of the crew moved on, one of their number, Amanda Lowe, stayed behind and chatted, asking if I had ever thought of presenting. I hadn't.

She took my details and months later I got a call asking if I could attend a 'screen test'. It was the late nineties, and the test was for a new Channel 4 programme called *Bloom*. I was to go up to Kew Gardens for the day so they could try me out! I had no experience at all apart from chatting to Geoff Hamilton at a couple of flower shows from my stand. This was a totally different scenario. Neil and I didn't have a camera to practise, so he used a shoe box instead whilst I took him on a tour of the garden.

Off I went to Kew in a coat I'd borrowed from one of my daughters and though I was nervous and still am to an extent before talking to a camera, I really enjoyed it, not least because the team were easy-going and the young man I was talking to was great – we got on like a house on fire. We talked about winter scent and edgeworthia, a Chinese shrub used in the production of bank notes. In the event I didn't get the gig. Anne Swithinbank was already going to lead the programme and they made Bill Chudziak her co-presenter. They were both really good. I was told they didn't want two women presenting together anyway. It was a useful experience and a while afterwards I was asked to attend another tryout, again for Channel 4, this time for a programme called *Garden Party*. A strange scenario, taking penstemon cuttings in a garden in December with snow forecast. Only on TV!

Somehow I got the job and for the next couple of years worked on the programme. It was a very different set-up from the one we work in now. The idea was that we visited a garden – always a grand one – alongside a lot of invited regular gardeners who wandered about and asked us questions using the garden as a vehicle. We had a splendid main presenter, a GP called Tom Barber, and I worked with two hugely knowledgeable chaps, lovely Paul Sturgess, a wonderful scientist and gardener, and David Jones, who was then in charge of parks and green spaces in the City of London. *Garden Party* was an outside broadcast with big vans and what seemed like miles of cabling. Those were the dying days of old telly, where director and crew would go off to the pub for a long liquid lunch and sometimes cooked food too. Nowadays we get a supermarket sandwich squeezed into a short break, sitting in the garden. Fine by me, we get plenty done.

We had some memorable moments. One of the best bits we did was a piece on water lilies on a moat surrounding a rambling Elizabethan mansion in Norfolk. Paul, who was hugely knowledgeable about aquatics, insisted on donning waders and fishing out entire roots to demonstrate how they grew and how to divide them. The water was deeper than he imagined and eventually he was in it up to his neck. The rest of us were rowing around doing something halfway between pleasure cruising and supporting the RNLI. I can also remember Paul splitting his sides when a sweet old lady asked him to identify what looked suspiciously like marijuana which had sprung up in her garden close to her bird feeder. It was probably hemp but it didn't really matter. It was C4.

After a couple of seasons the channel decided to end *Garden Party* but were keen to commission more gardening. The brilliant Mark Galloway became our commissioning editor. He asked me to come and talk about ideas. Neil and I had lots of them. Mark is such a nice man, far too principled to be involved with television. I didn't realise how unusual it was to be asked about the direction in which garden programming might go.

Neil and I had long discussions about what would make a really great gardening programme and soon afterwards I went up to London to talk to Mark. He took me out to lunch – I had never been taken out to lunch before. It must have been Tony Blair time because Alastair Campbell was eating in the same place and Mark told me he was a spin doctor. I had no idea what that meant. We discussed the ideas Neil and I had and a possible title for the series we had dreamed up. We wanted to call it *Real Gardens*. We all felt that what viewers would be interested in watching would be something down-to-earth and real, practical and inspirational. We wanted a programme that would involve our viewers and get them into their own gardens.

Mark also wanted to 'steal' John Percival, the series editor of the BBC's *Gardeners' World*, to produce the show. John formed his own company, Ark Productions, to make the programme. It ran for three years. I took part in every programme but sadly and inexplicably, even though the programme was popular and well-watched, Channel 4 and Mark parted ways.

Real Gardens was commissioned and ran for three series. It matched the hopes we had for a gardening programme that could inspire both newcomers and more experienced gardeners, and that promoted the best principles of gardening in the late twentieth century and now, come to that, in the twenty-first. Sustainability, recycling, organic growing plus creativity were at its heart.

I met several memorable contributors whilst filming *Real Gardens* and enjoyed making it tremendously. Two of our contributors, Gem and Drew, were such good value that since we had just about exhausted every practical aspect of their tiny Portsmouth garden, including installing a Derek Jarman-inspired beach, we persuaded them to take on a local allotment for the next season. It was a long drive to Portsmouth and back but they were so inspirational it never seemed too far.

The programme also paved the way for my first series, *Wild About the Garden*.

John Percival invited himself down to Devon to ask if I might be interested in taking part in the programme he was proposing to Channel 4. It was right up my street and the more we talked, the more we advanced the idea and agreed on the way the programme could go. The premise of the programme is a simple one: although our gardens are not nature, nonetheless if we study the natural habitat to which they are most akin, that can inform our understanding of our own patch, especially when it comes to plant choice. Each programme looked at one specific habitat – there were six in all: meadow, hedgerow, woodland, moor and mountain, seaside, wetland. Within each programme we first of all visited an outstanding example of that habitat, went on to visit gardeners who were already practising this ethos in their own plots and finally worked with gardeners, some of whom were newcomers and in every case were hoping to create a garden according to this ideology.

My director was a talented young woman called Caroline Hawkins who nowadays is the creative director of Oxford Scientific Films and a firm friend. Together with a brilliant researcher we travelled the length and breadth of the British Isles to find the most exciting venues and those that worked best for our story. We filmed way up in the Highlands of Scotland on precipitous mountain ledges with an alpine specialist, Ian Christie, who despite his deep knowledge of and love for plants from high altitudes is terrified of heights. The new gardeners we worked with for this moor and mountain episode were two very enthusiastic guys with a windy balcony high up in a Barbican apartment block. For our seaside scenario we visited a coastal Norfolk nature reserve complete with upturned boats, rusty chains and an oystercatcher's nest, went on to see a charming garden in Portsmouth which merged into the beach beyond and ended up in an opera singer's back garden on top of Telegraph Hill in south-east London. The latter might seem an unlikely venue for a beach scene but it had the lot, including fast draining soil full of pebbles and gravel – no doubt a glacier had long ago deposited stones, gravel debris and alluvial soil here. On top of this, Mary, in whose garden we were filming, was great value.

Humour and a light touch can often get the message home more effectively than a grave and serious script.

Each time you present, there are things to be learned. I gather that some people actually attend courses and classes to learn how to present. I love presenting because I love gardening and plants and love talking to people about them. To earn my living by communicating to other people on TV or through the written word is a privilege. It is not secure, though, and it is vital not to confuse it with real life.

* * *

Whilst I didn't present until much later, I first appeared on *Gardeners' World* in 1989, when the legendary Geoff Hamilton did a feature on Glebe Cottage. In a masochistic way, I had enjoyed the visit. He and his wife had turned up in the garden one day and had a good look round and a long chat. I was working in the small poly tunnel that we had erected towards the bottom of the garden with a small nursery beyond, a few benches with masses of plants. Geoff wrote about us in his 'Last Word' piece on the back page of *Garden News*. (I have written for this splendid weekly publication for the last twenty-five years and only dropped two weeks – I missed the deadline.)

Presumably Geoff thought we would make good TV and recommended us to *Gardeners' World*. I had come back from a show the night before filming, but adrenaline is a wonderful thing. We were lucky with the weather, and Geoff was encouraging and generous. His director Denis Gartside knew what he was doing but gave the impression that gardening was a bit beneath him, and I was lucid but humourless. Despite all Geoff's attempts to put me at my ease, not a single smile crossed my lips. Talk about taking yourself seriously! In the final shot I was working away on a small rock garden, kneeling forward and displaying to the world a twenty-pack of King Size Silk Cut in my top pocket. Accidental product placement, though thank goodness no lifetime supply was forthcoming or I might not be writing this now. My girls, especially Annie, were disgusted by smoking and relentlessly kept on at me to stop. It took me three attempts and two relapses to quit. I had shamelessly smoked in the house whilst they were little children. I apologise.

I was first asked to present on *Gardeners' World* in 2005 and to date have appeared in every series since, albeit in a much reduced role in the last few years. It is the BBC's flagship gardening show, and has been made since 1968, when it was originally filmed in the Oxford Botanic Garden. From 1969, it was filmed at the lead presenter Percy Thrower's own garden in Shrewsbury. Then came Arthur Billitt in his Worcestershire garden, from 1976. In 1979 came Geoff, who was a truly beloved presenter for almost two decades. The BBC *Gardeners' World* programme invited me initially to Berryfields, their then base in Stratford-upon-Avon, to film a piece. I drove there in a hired transit van with a load of plants from my nursery in the back. Eventually I was paid for the plants we used in the piece, but on leaving scraped the roof of the van on an overhanging cherry tree, having been guided out by one of the researchers. That shoot cost me quite a bit – I had hoped the hire firm would not check the top of the van, but of course they did.

My very first day filming there was terrifying but also humorous. There was a 'woodland' area at Berryfields, a couple of trees that made the area quite shady. Sarah Raven and I were to do a joint piece, she on one side, me on the other. Mark Scott was directing. Both Sarah and I were down on our knees and towering above us was a Jimmy Jib, like a small crane with a camera on the op end and its controls at the other end. I had never seen one before, let alone worked with one. Mark insisted on calling us by each other's names all day. Sarah was fine by me – if my mum had had her way I would have been christened Sarah Jane – but the prospect of Sarah Raven being called Carol was laughable. Mark persisted with our new names until later in the day we started calling him Graham.

I really enjoyed working on *Gardeners' World* and soon found my feet. The programme items and order were worked out but there was plenty of room for spontaneity and even a little humour, especially when I was sharing an item with Joe Swift. There should always be room for humour. On one occasion Joe, Monty and I were working in a couple of flower beds in one of which there were several plants looking decidedly chlorotic. Chlorosis, which makes leaves pale and yellow, is caused by the inability of the plant to produce adequate chlorophyll. This is especially so with acid-loving plants like camellias and rhododendrons and often occurs when soil is so alkaline that adequate supplies of trace elements and minerals such as iron and magnesium are inaccessible. Chalky and limey soils are always alkaline.

Pondering that, since this was such an old garden, perhaps lime mortar from old buildings previously occupying the site had contributed, we discussed lime and chalk and the way in which they can affect plants.

'Oh!' says Monty. 'I was brought up on chalk.'

'Well,' says I, 'I was brought up on chips!'

That discourse didn't make it into the edit.

With all the TV work I've done, it has always been important to me to be editorially involved. I love gardening and plants and though I enjoy presenting on TV, I am only interested in presenting my subject. It is rich and varied and there are so many aspects to it. Only on two occasions have I ever balked at what I've been asked to do, yet submitted to it. One was when I was required by my executive producer to use bright blue glass chippings to top dress a pot or collect my P45. On another occasion under extreme pressure of time – darkness was falling – I had to hastily shove herbs in pots whilst a distraught director tried to sort out childcare problems on their phone. It was pointless, arbitrary, ill-considered and uninspiring.

Generally, however, there has been harmony. In the twenty or more years I've been involved with TV, there has increasingly been real debate and positive co-operation, with everyone striving to produce first-rate pieces and series. I love working as part of a team where everyone contributes to making something that is worthwhile, edifying and, with a bit of luck, inspirational. What wonderful and talented people I've worked with, camera operators and sound men and women, directors and researchers, editors who through their talent and creativity have enabled me to sound as though I know what I am talking about and look a whole lot better than I really do.

We presenters are always referred to as 'the talent', but we are nothing without the people who really make our programmes. They are the real talent.

* * *

Early in 2008 Monty had a transient ischaemic attack, sometimes called a mini-stroke, and stood down from the programme. I was asked to step into the breach and did so from March to September. Meanwhile, to quote Anita Singh in *The Daily Telegraph*: 'The Corporation will now begin a search for a new presenter. Don followed in the footsteps of Percy Thrower, Geoff Hamilton and Alan Titchmarsh when he took over as main presenter in 2003.'

Over the next few months several likely candidates turned up at Berryfields to film short pieces. Matthew Wilson, Andy Sturgeon and Toby Buckland amongst others were duly 'auditioned' for the role. They were all men. Later that autumn, after a hard day's filming, I was taken out with my agent Jacquie to a very posh restaurant close to Stratford by my three immediate bosses. I was mucky but had brought a change of clothes and got the opportunity to clean up and patch up my make-up in the tiny bathroom at Berryfields. At that dinner, I discovered that Toby Buckland had been appointed the new host.

The next year *Gardeners' World* operations moved to a new venue on a sports pitch behind Birmingham Botanical Gardens. But at the beginning of Toby's reign we were still at Berryfields. I was due to do a piece about silverleaf, a fungal disease that attacks some trees, mainly in the prunus or cherry family but also sometimes laburnum and a few other genera. I was kneeling under a laburnum tree and was about to begin, but, it was decided, it might be nice if Toby was to stroll over, have a brief chat and then leave me to it. The strolling went well, but the 'chat' turned into a discourse on silverleaf. After several minutes, I gently reminded him this was supposed to be my item. That didn't go down too well ...

Television can be a cruel game. However proprietorial he felt about his role, two years later he had to step aside when Monty Don returned.

When I first filmed for the programme, my filming day would usually be Friday. I would drive up the night before and drive back on Friday after filming. Often departure would be quite late and on several occasions, especially on bank holiday weekends, the journey would take an age. Living in North Devon en route to many south-west holiday destinations, traffic was slow, occasionally stationary. Once I had to get out of the car and run round it several times in both directions to try and wake myself up. It was at such times I wished I had a better singing voice, since singing out loud was another means I employed to stay awake. Come to think of it, I was once banned from singing by Fred Moulton, my French teacher, who also took us for singing lessons – aka hymn practice – at secondary school. Although the school was co-educational, singing lessons were single sex. We were belting out one hymn when Fred tapped his baton sharply on his lectern. Silence fell. 'Where's that boy?' he asked, and proceeded to get each girl in turn to sing a short line until he got to me. After that I was banned from singing, though when it came to assembly I sang hymns as loudly as possible even though by that time I was a confirmed atheist.

* * *

Interviewing is an art and one where I still have a lot to learn.

When we were filming at Fast Rabbit Farm for *Wild About the Garden*, I was interviewing the woman responsible for this wonderful garden with ponds, streams and lakes. It was for the wetlands section. Although we didn't see much of him when we were filming, our producer, Laurence Vulliamy, was in attendance. Halfway through the interview, when we were sitting on a grassy mound, Laurence put up his hand and leapt across the intervening path. The camera was turned off. He took me to one side and started on a tirade in which, to summarise, he asked me what on earth I thought I was doing. I was supposed to be interviewing this woman because she had lots to tell our viewers about how to cope with wet soil, how to introduce water into their gardens and manage it successfully and generally enthusiastically impart what a joyous part of gardening water could be. That was why we were talking to her in that place. Instead of asking her questions that helped bring out not just her knowledge and expertise but also her enthusiasm, all of which she had in bucketfuls, I had launched forward with a long diatribe, hardly letting her get a word in edgeways. When you are conducting an interview you should enable the interviewee to put forward their ideas and if you don't want to hear what that person has to say or help them get it across, you shouldn't be doing it. I hope I have learned the lesson.

On another occasion, Laurence was present because I had to record an extremely important section of the broadcast. It was to be the introduction to the whole programme and would likely feature in the opening sequence of every episode. He enjoyed writing and was good at it. I was expected to learn verbatim what would have been two whole minutes of screen time delivered whilst walking (slowly, obviously) across our contributor's lawn alongside a busy A road. It was the end of the afternoon too – commuter time!

After twenty-seven takes I sort of managed it, but it was never used. Thank heavens for small mercies. Instead we filmed a short upbeat sequence in my own words. I have never been able to learn lines – it is a good job I mean what I say and try to say what I mean. To say that I don't always get it right would be an understatement. A few years ago we had a new senior executive in charge of the Chelsea Flower Show transmissions. He was enormously experienced and well respected. On my way back into the BBC compound at the end of the first day's filming he stopped me, a smile on his face. 'I just want to thank you, Carol, your editorial was spot on and your delivery was perfect. Just one little observation though … you do tend to say "wonderful" rather a lot. Don't worry,' he added as my face dropped, 'we managed to cut most of them out!'

Thank goodness for editors. Over the years some brilliantly talented editors and directors have not only helped me to sound like I know what I am talking about, but they have made me succinct. Mind you, I don't say 'wonderful' nearly as often as I used to!

In my favour, I often have so much to say, it is difficult to fit it all in, but then that is part of the skill, self-editing and concentrating on the most relevant, interesting and entertaining points. On the other hand it is always better to have too much to say than not enough, and it is always better to tell viewers *about* a plant rather than how you *feel* about a plant.

* * *

During these years Channel 4 won a three-year contract to produce the RHS Chelsea Flower Show coverage; before those three years and after them BBC Two has always covered Chelsea. I was asked to take part in that too, which I did, separate from but alongside exhibiting as Glebe Cottage Plants. They were busy times.

For many years after that I presented at most of the big RHS flower shows whilst exhibiting, and since closing my nursery have continued to do so.

Having exhibited for so long at all these venues I have first-hand experience of the hard graft and sometimes heartache involved in putting on a display, especially for those who run small specialist nurseries and grow their own plants. Thanks to the mass production of plants – or green products, as they are sometimes called, often imported from several continents – it is almost impossible to compete as a small grower. This also means the range of plants available shrinks. Commercial factors, the bottom line, as in every area of our lives, decides what is available. I was once told by someone working for a large and distinguished plant-centre chain that choices of what to grow were often determined by how many would fit on a Dutch trolley.

We should all cherish and support nursery people who grow interesting and desirable plants against all the odds. We are told diversity is vitally important; there are seedbanks that store seed from all over the world. We should recognise the role of our gardens in safeguarding this diversity and encourage small nurseries – and bigger ones too – to maintain and increase the availability of as many different plants as possible.

Gardening charities should recognise their role too. Unfortunately, the government is useless, and totally unimaginative when it comes to supporting the horticultural industry as they are in grasping the educational benefits of gardening. I've campaigned hard for gardening to be taught in schools. As I told the *Radio Times* in an interview, it would help restore our historic connection to the land, and would also teach children about the vital importance of plants for sustaining life on earth.

Bellflowers

We are lucky enough to have several campanulas, or bellflowers, amongst our native wildflowers. Perhaps the harebell is the most widely known and most dearly cherished of them all. It is a whisper of a flower, hardly there yet enormously tenacious. From tiny rosettes of neat rounded leaves, fine stems push up bearing dainty pleated buds. These are first erect but later hang down as the bells start to open, to protect the pollen secreted within from gale and tempest. Widespread throughout the British Isles, it is a flower of open exposed venues of moor and mountainside, of clifftop, as we filmed it near Bridlington glittering amongst fine, dense grass or, as my mum and I saw it running in ribbons across the limestone pavement of The Burren, growing in next to nothing. We met it on another occasion too in the Yorkshire Dales on a sunny day growing in springy turf. We had no choice other than to abandon socks and shoes and enjoy the feel of the grass between our toes, surrounded by these happy flowers.

Campanula rotundifolia needs little nutrient and often the poorer its soil, the more profusely it will flower. When I filmed a piece about campanulas, having seen harebells on the clifftop, we went to Burton Agnes Hall where, atop the big curved old brick walls that guide you in under an imposing arch to the drive up to the magnificent house, harebells have made themselves at home, seeding themselves generously in the lime mortar between the coping stones. Blue against blue with an azure sky above.

Surely bellflowers are one of the most enchanting of all plant families. Most herbaceous campanulas have soft leaves (*C. latifolia*, *C. lactiflora* and *C. glomerata* are examples) whereas evergreen campanulas, *C. persicifolia* and *C. latiloba*, and many of the lobelias have harder, shinier foliage. Bellflowers are versatile, gracious and easy to grow. June and July are their months. The season can be extended by cutting back flowered stems and feeding plants with a liquid feed – we use an organic seaweed extract. Their blue flowers create restful spaces in a sea of busy colour, lending distance and depth to plantings teetering on the brink of confusion. Those that make the boldest impact are big campanulas, some of them up to five or six feet tall. Some have symmetry, others rely on a wafty loftiness to command the scene.

If big bellflowers are to live happily and develop their true character, they need sustenance. Although the great majority are happy on alkaline soils, gardeners with thin chalky soils or light sandy soils need to give them preferential treatment and amend the conditions to give them as rich a diet as possible. Adding bulky organic matter helps and frequent feeding should be part of the regime.

Many of these resplendent flowers would have featured in the traditional herbaceous border; Miss Jekyll writes of them with affection and included them in many of her planting schemes. But there is nothing old-hat about them, their uses are legion. They can be employed as individual container plants repeated on a terrace or down steps or for maximum impact in naturalistic planting schemes. One plant could make the centre of a special cameo or bold clumps could be repeated along a border to give a feeling of integrity.

For the most part they are blue, often verging on purple, lilac or misty grey. Some are white. All of them are best viewed as the sun sets or comes up, or in shade or on a cloudy day when their colour is most telling.

Top of the list is *Campanula lactiflora*, aptly named the milky bellflower, one of the most appealing of all bellflowers. When it is blue there is white mixed in, and when it is white its flowers are tinged with blue, creating a 'milky' impression. This is emphasised when it is seen in shade where it grows just as happily as it does in full sun. On good ground it can make five feet easily, its large heads of small, clustered bells gracefully overlooking lesser plants. If you prefer more definite colour there is a deep blue selection, *C. lactiflora* 'Prichard's Variety'. Whilst you can raise a nice mixture from seed, *C. lactiflora* 'Prichard's Variety' must be propagated vegetatively, either from division or by taking short, basal cuttings in the spring. Stems must be solid – once they are hollow this method doesn't work.

One of the bellflowers that was once used extensively in pots, *Campanula pyramidalis*, is essentially a biennial and must be raised from seed year on year. Its vernacular name, the chimney bellflower, is apt – it makes a central stem from a rosette of basal leaves, which can reach he-man size, six foot, clustered round with separate bells. Its upright bearing makes it a perfect plant for a formal entrance where it can act as a sentry.

In the days when nursery labour was cheap, *Ostrowskia magnifica* could be found in many a nursery catalogue. It was propagated then from basal cuttings – a practice no longer considered commercially viable today though easy enough for the amateur gardener. 'Magnifica' is no exaggeration: substantial bells, white with a hint of grey and a darker centre, hang individually from tall elegant stems. It needs deep fertile soil and the protection of a warm wall.

Some of these campanulas make an impact not from their height but from the weight and volume of their bells and, in some cases, their colour. *Campanula* 'Sarastro' bears large purple-blue waxy bells opening from folded, slender buds of deepest purple. It is a recent cultivar and probably the progeny of a cross between our own *Campanula latifolia* and one of the long-belled Asiatic bellflowers, *C. takesimana* or *C. punctata*. A sterile hybrid, it flowers all summer long. Cut the flowering stems to ground level when they are finished. More will be forthcoming within a few weeks. Should you prefer deep blue to purple, *C.* 'Kent Belle', with a similar parentage, is the one to go for.

Some of our native bellflowers are as beautiful and useful in the garden as any. *Campanula latifolia*, the giant bellflower, is most commonly blue or white, but there is a variety with subtle pale lilac flowers which is particularly prevalent along the riverbanks of north-east England and Scotland. A cultivar, *C.l.* 'Gloaming', boasts flowers of the same hue and has the added attraction of dark purple centres, which can also be seen on the outside of the bell. It gradually builds year by year to form a statuesque clump up to three feet in height and two feet across.

Grey is a colour seldom seen in flowers and whilst it may sound unattractive, it is often a glorious addition to a humdrum scheme, bringing a touch of class to the proceedings. *Campanula* 'Burghaltii' has pale grey-lilac flowers. No one is quite sure of its origins but everyone agrees it is graceful and elegant. Despite its subtle demeanour, it is always noticed. Anyone would welcome it into their garden.

Summer borders are places where plants need to get on well, no room for prima donnas here, and bellflowers are great team players.

One of the most persistent in my garden is *Campanula persicifolia*. It is one of the most beautiful and poetic of summer garden flowers. It forms evergreen rosettes of narrow, pointed leaves giving it its common name, the peach-leaved bellflower. From midsummer onwards, straight stems shoot up vertically from the low, carpeting foliage until, at about 60cm, they stop to concentrate on opening their fat buds. The species plant has simple, single bells in blue or white. It seeds prolifically and seedlings may vary in flower colour and stature and occasionally in form. If double forms are to your liking, there are all sorts to choose from, some frilly, others cup and saucer and my favourite which is a blue cup in cup, with one flower held within another. We make more in early spring by dividing up the rosettes – we can't have too many!

In classic bellflowers, each bell has five points or tips and each seed capsule is divided into three chambers. Campanulaceae distribute their seed in an unusual way. Small apertures appear at the back of the capsule as it begins to brown and dry and eventually seed is scattered through these holes. It was whilst waiting to collect seed from an especially lovely *Campanula latifolia* that I realised this but by the time what was happening dawned on me, it had all gone. Campanula seed is very fine and there's lots of it but be sure to move in with paper bags and scissors before it disperses. On the whole growing campanulas from seed is straightforward and an exciting and cheap way to build up your stock.

Chapter Fourteen

In 1997, as a follow-up to *Wild About the Garden*, Channel 4 asked me to make a programme entitled *Wild About Chelsea*. It would be all about making a garden at Chelsea, which meant – making a garden at Chelsea! We went to Chelsea and filmed with various exhibitors and garden designers, and we nosed around behind the scenes investigating the little known corporate side of the RHS showcase show. Originally it was construed as six half-hours but the next year it was honed down to one hour. None of the previous year's footage was used but we filmed throughout the winter and spring of 1999.

The RHS needed all applications for gardens to be in by summer the previous year. Our application was comprehensive, to say the least. Computer-generated plans were in their infancy though even if I was applying this year, my application might take much the same form. We went to town with as many 'artist's impressions' of every part of the garden as possible, from compost bins to planting schemes. The folio we put together was all hand painted by Neil. It really is a work of art. I can never thank Neil enough for the huge part he has played in everything I have done, encouraging me always with humour and love.

It was not just our application that was different. Even nowadays the majority of Chelsea gardens are financed by sponsorship and from the designers' viewpoint are targeted at 'high-net-worth individuals', aspirational and exclusive.

We wanted to make a garden that was inspirational and inclusive. Unusually, perhaps uniquely, we grew all our own plants – indeed that was one of the themes of the garden, propagating your own plants. Side-by-side with that was an emphasis on recycling and sustainability. The bricks we used were recycled London Stock bricks, used to make a curvy retaining wall that doubled as a seat, beautifully built by Dave the Brickie, the best bricklayer ever. I was lucky enough to have met him when working on a garden in Hampstead for a Ferrari-driving entrepreneur who had fallen in love with the previous year's Chelsea display and wanted it installed in her garden, although when asking about our pink mallows, *Malva moschata*, said she would prefer them in beige!

Heat and carbon dioxide were produced by the compost bins underneath the benches to bring on our seedlings. Compost has always been dear to my heart, although not everyone appreciates it as much as me. Several years ago, our then new next-door neighbour and landlord of our nursery domain used the proximity of our compost heaps to his back door (they weren't all that close) as an excuse to hand us our notice. Relations had got steadily worse between us after I objected to his plans to cut down beech trees and to his burning enormous quantities of laurel and allowing it to smoulder.

Making and using compost has always been at the heart of our gardening regime. In our show garden at the RHS Hampton Court Palace Garden Festival 2023, the lovely folk from Waterperry Gardens knocked up a couple of compost heaps behind our propagating-made-easy Rhino greenhouse from recycled pallets, to show people how easy it was. We both brought compost from our respective gardens to fill one and gradually built the other one from all the detritus and plant trimmings that accumulated during the week. Visitors were as interested in the compost heaps as they were enthralled by the garden.

In 1999 the name for our show garden was '21 Century Street'. The name came from a chance discussion at a bus stop with a smashing girl who was a Drum'n'Bass record producer. She was interested in the idea of the garden, and I stressed it had to be attainable, sustainable, somewhere that anyone could create. She thought it should be an address, and since we were on the hinge of a new century we settled on 21 Century Street. Some of the most interesting and fruitful conversations I've ever had have been chance encounters at bus stops, on trains, waiting in queues.

We filmed on and off throughout the months leading up to the show. Programme makers love a bit of jeopardy and we had plenty of that. Once, we were coming back from visiting wildflower king Donald MacIntyre of Emorsgate Seeds to lift pieces of meadow and from visiting Chew Valley Trees to collect the bare-rooted trees that were going to make the native hedge boundary of our garden. My director and producer were just ahead of me in their hire car. We knew the lights of my beloved van, a long wheelbase Mercedes with no power steering, were dodgy, and as we continued they got dimmer and dimmer. I lost sight of their rear lights and had to continue at a snail's pace using the lights of overtaking cars to follow the road. By the time I crawled home I'm sure they had been tucked up in bed for hours, having wined and dined in their comfy country pub.

Never mind, we were all up bright and early the next morning to film me unloading the van, trees potted up and meadow turf laid out.

By the time Chelsea arrived, the van was very poorly but Graham, my then director, wanted a van-driving sequence for the programme. He persuaded another exhibitor to lend their similar vehicle for me to drive, camera crew behind the seat, down the King's Road at the height of Saturday morning's busiest time, heaving crowds and nose-to-tail traffic. To add insult to injury, when I got back to my garden, I was dragged off to a random King's Road hairdresser to film my blow-dry! All the while I was desperate to get back to the garden, my team of helpers awaiting instructions and three rival TV crews marching all over it.

Eventually we finished our display. There were a few hitches, the main one being that Neil was finishing the paintwork on the shed/greenhouse as we saw the judges, most in bowler hats, rounding the corner of Main Avenue. They were kind enough to judge us out of order but I had a haunting vision of their walking back up Main Avenue, having judged our stand, with green stripes down the back of their very dapper suits.

We were awarded a silver medal, not bad for a first go. Although it is nice to have your efforts at flower shows rewarded with a decent medal and I will never forget our first gold medal at Chelsea, what really counts is how your exhibit is received by the public. We could not have been more enthusiastically appreciated. Not only did visitors love our plants but they all seemed to 'get' the garden – it was friendly, inviting and above all doable. They welcomed its message about sustainability and recycling too. Our highest accolade was the presentation by the late, great Valerie Finnis of her top award, the Golden Banana, inscribed in her fair hand with a biro: 'Awarded to Glebe Cottage Plants by Valerie Finnis – Gold Medal'. Although we have photos to prove it, we ate the banana later.

For the last few years the RHS has made it compulsory for all show gardens to have an afterlife. 21 Century Street was the first garden ever to do this after we lobbied Channel 4, who sponsored the garden, to pay for the move. Our garden went to the NSPCC to their headquarters in Penge. We didn't take the garden to pieces and immediately re-erect it. At the end of the show we took everything home and then in September of the same year we moved many of the plants plus a whole load more plus hard-landscaping materials back to Penge and built a garden. The headquarters there employed several people and was used in part to prepare children before court hearings. Hopefully the garden had a positive effect on all involved.

When interviewing Toby Buckland in 2008 about his 'ethical garden' at Gardeners' World Live for which he was awarded an RHS Gold Medal and Best in Show, I mentioned the sustainable ethos of 21 Century Street. 'Oh yes,' says he, 'but it wasn't an issue back then, was it?'

21 Century Street was also deemed a success by Monty Don, who wrote: 'I loved Carol Klein's garden, 21 Century Street, for its exuberant planting and lack of pretension. Plants-people can often be snooty and intellectual about their obsession, whereas Carol's garden made one smile with visceral joy.' He went on to describe another garden that shared my ethos: 'I loved the planting in James Alexander-Sinclair's Horti-couture, which made what he called a "tameflower meadow" using grasses planted thickly between verbascums, irises, foxgloves and other tall border plants. This was genuinely inspired, and the decision of the judges to award him a bronze medal was an inexplicable injustice.'

* * *

Channel 4 pulled the plug on *Real Gardens* in 2000. We had three years and an IMDb rating of 8.9. It was a very positive development in gardening programmes.

Although it was quiet on the TV front for a while, my life was as hectic as ever. Running the nursery and exhibiting at shows was always more than a full-time job. Over the years, we exhibited at almost 300 shows, opened the nursery four days a week, opened the garden for the National Garden Scheme on about 500 occasions, gardened and wrote.

My first book, *Plant Personalities*, was published in 2005 in collaboration with the lovely and incredibly talented Jonathan Buckley and edited by the superb Erica Hunningher, she who called me 'the mistress of digression'.

I enjoy writing, though I still have a lot to learn. I had written odd articles for gardening publications but my first regular contribution to magazines and newspapers was a weekly column for *Garden News*. I am still enjoying writing it and have done so for more than twenty-five years.

I was the *Guardian*'s gardening correspondent for five years, taking over from Christopher Lloyd, I wrote regularly for *The Telegraph*, for *Gardeners' World* magazine, I was the *Sunday Mirror*'s gardening writer for several years, wrote for *The English Garden*, *Gardens Illustrated* and weekly for *The Lady* until Rachel Johnson took over as editor, and my services were no longer required.

I love writing for papers and magazines. I especially enjoy writing my weekly double-page spread in *Garden News*. It is challenging, but because it is based on what is happening in my garden week by week, it is real, and because no two years are ever the same, it is always fresh and new although I've been doing it for twenty-five years.

Writing books is a totally different proposition. I find the most difficult part of it – precisely because it is not a part – is seeing the whole thing. It's so easy to get lost in the detail.

This will be my eleventh book, and the garden at Glebe Cottage remains the hub of my gardening writing, and to a greater or lesser extent my presenting.

* * *

From the early 2000s until the last few years, I part-presented just about every episode of *Gardeners' World*. At first it would be from Berryfields, then later I was allowed to help devise and feature in numerous strands, from wildflowers and their cultivated cousins to plant families. Some of them were filmed all over the country, some in my garden. I was involved in coverage of most of the main flower shows.

In addition to these I was asked to make several specials, an adjunct of the *Gardeners' World* programmes where all the main presenters (there were fewer of us in those days) were asked to make one-hour pieces on a specific theme. I thoroughly enjoyed these. Here was an opportunity to delve far more deeply into a subject than was possible on the short items that made up the main programme.

We got six days of filming per programme. I made 'Scent', 'Women in Gardening' and 'Botany' all with Patty Kraus, an intelligent and creative director. As I write I relive the experience of making these programmes, dressing up in knickerbockers and waistcoat as the first Kew women gardeners had to do to hide their sex from passengers on the buses that passed by the walls of Kew Gardens, pollinating tomatoes with an electric toothbrush to emulate the buzzing of a bee and enable pollen to fly about, getting close and personal with an orchid and a French parfumier on a sunny slope in Kent.

Part of our 'Scent' programme was to be filmed in Egypt. I went straight from filming at Gardeners' World Live to Birmingham Airport, right next door, took a flight to Cairo via Milano, arriving at four in the morning, lying down for half an hour, getting up and being thrust in the back of a van to travel many miles to film young girls picking jasmine and scented pelargoniums in huge fields when they should have been in school and boys wading in deep water to harvest mint. I was introduced to YSL Touche Éclat sitting in a little room next to a perfume distillery in the midst of fields of scented-leaf pelargoniums.

Back in Cairo, we wanted to find the blue water lily famed for its perfume and trace its history back to the time of the Pharaohs. We visited a thronging park in the middle of the city and discovered them growing underneath a bridge, had hilarious times with walkie-talkies, visited a tomb with the most exquisite bas-relief where we could imagine the funeral procession entering the chamber, including slaves with water lilies draped over their arms, and see them portrayed on the walls of the tomb.

We smelled frangipane in the hotel garden floating across a pool where we swam in sight of pyramids.

I got to meet some of my gardening heroes and drive a Sunbeam Alpine. My dad would have been proud of that part – except when the only way I could get back up an almost vertical slope close to the coast in North Devon was to put it in reverse and back up to the road I should have followed. Unbeknown to viewers, crouched in the passenger seat well was our smashing researcher Gareth, who shared the driving and stayed in touch with our crew. We criss-crossed the country, and on one memorable occasion my friend Helen and I found ourselves in a high Yorkshire meadow, which had me recalling the time when my mum and I danced barefoot on Yorkshire turf sprinkled with harebells. I gave Helen a little plant of harebells as a keepsake. Thanks to her loving care it or its progeny survive to this day.

* * *

In 2006 I had a phone call from Nick Patten, then head of features at BBC Bristol, to ask if I would be interested in making a six-part series about growing vegetables. He thought that growing your own was becoming more popular and the time was right for such a programme. Although I have grown vegetables since we came here, I wasn't keen at first. Perhaps I was just so closely associated with my beloved perennials that it seemed a bit of a comedown. How snotty can you get? Surely when one of my ambitions on moving us to Devon was to make us as self-sufficient as possible, this was a great opportunity to extol the practice. Eventually I was persuaded. My director was the lovely and talented Juliet Glaves, ex-ballet dancer and nowadays florist extraordinaire, a creative floral stylist and set designer. She and her husband Neil grow all their own flowers. It is so good that she has followed her own dream. She is a brilliant and innovative director; she even shot a few sequences herself on Super 8 and we had a prog rock soundtrack. We had a wonderful researcher, a veteran of gardening programmes galore with the perfect name, though it might have been even more apt had we been a Scottish gardening programme: Phil McCann.

The programme was very well received and viewer numbers were good. It was the right programme at the right time. I was even asked to write a book together with the RHS to accompany the programme. It proved to be the most popular gardening book in the year of its publication and the next year too. Sadly as far as the Klein coffers went, I didn't strike a very profitable deal. I think my royalties worked out at about a penny a copy.

* * *

Throughout my association with television, I have always wanted to put forward my own ideas. Presenting gardening TV for me is all about the gardening. I couldn't 'present' for the sake of it and do a property programme for instance. There are many presenters who are just that, professional presenters, and can turn their hands to anything. For me it is the gardening that is important. Contributing to content or especially creating it is vital – that is what gives anything, from a short piece on *Gardeners' World* to an eight-part series, credibility and authenticity.

I had always thought that television lent itself to gardening since gardening is about process not product, and here is a medium that can show you how things grow and develop, from seed sown to plants put out in the garden, from plunging hands into paper bags full of conker-brown tulip bulbs to celebrating their flamboyant flowers the following spring. It's a medium that can wonder at beech buds bursting and take you through the seasons to their autumnal array.

From time to time I have approached directors, producers, executive producers, series editors, commissioners and even controllers with my ideas. Here are a couple of ideas I put forward to a couple of those people dating back to 2007 and 2005. The same ideas have informed the three recent series I have made for Ben Frow at Channel 5, and in 2024 I am to be allowed to make a short strand, probably entitled *Plants for Free*, which when it was first mooted more than a year ago I had wanted to call *Grow Your Own Garden*. This title was not approved because I have already published a book with that title. This is the concept I pitched to a senior executive at the BBC:

Grow Your Own Garden
An inspirational insight into how to achieve beautiful beds and borders through growing your own. How to get the look – propagating your own plants and putting them together.

Carol has created the garden at Glebe Cottage from scratch. She's done it and she can show other people how to do it themselves, however far they want to go.

Most viewers don't have thousands of pounds to buy the plants to stock their gardens. Carol Klein shows you how to 'Grow Your Own Garden', propagating all the plants you need for next to nothing, *and* she shows you how to put them together to create beautiful planting schemes – even if you've never done it before.

Using the garden at Glebe Cottage we dive into the exciting arena of growing your own plants. Carol shows you how to grow plants from seed, whether they're collected from the garden, bought from the garden centre or free from the covers of your gardening magazine.

We see how to take cuttings from plants, from their shoots and their roots, and how to divide them to make more. Carol takes us through the whole process, enabling the viewer to make barrowloads of beautiful, healthy plants. We watch them growing step by step from tiny seeds to chunky thriving beauties, ready to face the outside world. Then we see how to plant them together with perfect partners in the right place.

Because it is such an established garden, Glebe Cottage offers a wealth of wonderful planting schemes and the scope to make new ones in a variety of different situations reflecting other gardeners' challenges!

It has all the ingredients essential for success, from a wide range of the best plants from which to source propagating material to all the facilities to carry it out.

Whatever the viewer's level of expertise or confidence, the programme relates to where they are at and where they want to go. It's only when you grow your own plants that you get to know them intimately, you learn what they like and how to treat them and help them thrive. The whole process is creative, choosing what you want to grow, seeing it develop and putting together your very own planting schemes. The programme enables you to 'Grow Your Own Garden'!

And there are other ideas I've pitched that haven't yet made it to screen:

Earthed

Surely the most magical part of gardening is making new plants from thin air. Carol Klein initiates viewers into the compelling world of propagation, passing on the power to everybody watching to create their own plants.

The series is full of wonderment and magic – and it dispels the mystique created by so many experts that growing from seed or cuttings is too difficult. There are no rules to remember. Carol reveals what mother nature does and empowers viewers to do the same, instilling them with her passion.

Watch what happens at ground level, understand it and emulate it, and smile.

This is the most intimate gardening programme there has ever been. It's just you, me and the plants.

At each moment it will be clear exactly what time of year it is; the sense, taste, smell of the season will always prevail. This is no clinical operation carried out in a sterile environment with pristine pots and rubber gloves.

Instead it celebrates the earthiness of the process and revels in the cycle as equinox follows solstice and spring gives way to summer.

Within each of the six programmes, the whole process of each propagation method is intimately tracked from seed or cutting, division or tuber to the magical moment when the new plant reaches adolescence and is gently lowered into the ground to start an independent existence.

Propagation is the subject that gardening TV has been waiting for. TV can reach places other media can't when it comes to telling the story of how plants grow.

Because the series would be filmed at one place, Glebe Cottage, there will be a wonderful sense of continuity as we trace individual stories. The process – from a seed germinating to the appearance of roots and shoots, or the transformation from a snippet of a mother plant to a self-contained viable individual – can be revealed in all its intimate detail at every stage of its development.

Meanwhile the beech trees at the edge of the field become a measure of where the year has reached, at one time stark silhouettes against a snow-laden sky, at another burgeoning with the freshest of pale green leaves.

This six-part series investigates how to make new plants and use them. Sometimes pacey, often contemplative, the programmes will luxuriate in breathtaking imagery. There will be no rush and hurry, nature dictates the pace – a complete antidote to the forced drama of artificial deadlines. This is television to enjoy and indulge in.

There is practical, dirty-fingernail information, awe-inspiring intimate detail seen through the bee's-eye view of a borescope, and simultaneously a sense of the poetry of growth and regeneration.

The viewer sees the knife severing the shoot, hears the seed vibrating in its capsule, smells the roots in the humusy soil, feels the softness of the leaf as it is sliced into sections to make new plants ...

Unfortunately, that was as far as it went.

* * *

Both showing and presenting require a great deal of travel, and so I was reliant on my trusty van. My youngest brother Pip found me my lovely van, green and white, a long wheelbase Mercedes 307D with no power steering, from a scrap metal merchant contact who agreed to throw in two large stainless steel tables, probably made for ammunition, the best potting-up benches ever; they are still going strong. It was amusing to see people's faces when I came around the corner in my van, having told them I was just going to bring round the Merc.

The van finally gave up the ghost on a trip to Gardeners' World Live. There were only a few miles to go on the M42. It was a very hot day but the cab seemed exceptionally hot; I glanced at the temperature gauge and realised that something was very wrong. I pulled onto the hard shoulder, lifted the bonnet and very gingerly, with my hand covered, attempted to undo the radiator cap. There was a lot of hissing and steam. The radiator was empty. For some of the previous breakdowns I had been involved in there was no mobile phone. This time, I called the AA. There was a tiny hole in the radiator. The engine was done for. There were two options, the nice AA man told me, both involving further transportation on a breakdown truck. Either they could take me home or to my destination. There was no choice. These shows, financially, were everything. Packed into that truck was my display, my sales plants but also our mortgage repayment, our food, our electricity bill, our tax payments. I asked to be taken on to the NEC.

In those days the immense RHS marquee was erected on a tarmac car park by the lake. Fortunately our allocated stand was close to one end which meant it was possible for the breakdown truck to roll me and my van close to my allotted space without inconveniencing my fellow exhibitors. For the couple of days setting up, it was extremely handy to have my van and all my plants so close, but, as the show's opening became imminent, panic set in – how was I to remove my van, where was it supposed to go and who could take it there? The AA had done their bit, but what now? In the end the official Mercedes garage in Birmingham came to collect it and eventually it made its way back to Devon. Profits from the show had almost disappeared before it had even started. Thanks to the generosity of several of my fellow exhibitors though, my precious display plants and the residue of our sales plants survived. They took them back to their respective nurseries until I could collect them and bring them home. There is always a camaraderie that tempers a healthy competitive element amongst exhibitors.

Perhaps more than any other flower show Gardeners' World Live has indicated the change in attitude amongst gardeners over the last thirty years. Glebe Cottage Plants exhibited at the first show in June 1992, always in the second week of June, which means since then I have been away for all our youngest daughter Alice's birthdays.

In its infancy, a gardening show was a new phenomenon for Birmingham; the great majority of visitors had never attended such an event. People were attracted to anything in flower and I got few questions about what a plant needed or where was the best place to grow it or how to make more of it. Things changed. Over the years often the same customers would return (I still bump into some of them at the show), and every year, the great majority became increasingly discriminating. Nowadays across the board, gardeners are more and more interested in the provenance of plants and how to make more for themselves!

In the early days of selling plants at shows I was told on more than one occasion, always by old nurserymen, though I hasten to add this was not the attitude of most old nurserymen, that it was a mistake to tell folk how to propagate plants – the argument being that if they grew their own plants, we (the nursery trade) would all be out of a job. In fact the truth of the matter is that the more gardeners get into propagation, the more deeply they become immersed in horticulture, the more they want to expand their knowledge and their plant vocabulary and the more new plants they want to try. A few years ago I was stopped by a lady at Gardeners' World Live, who wanted to tell me how much she was enjoying my *Grow Your Own Garden* book and my bits on *Gardeners' World*. She was already laden with plant purchases. Another lady came along, similarly laden, and concurred with the first lady. Then began a chat about propagation – they discovered they had both successfully tried root cuttings after reading my book. Having to go to my next event, I left them having a very animated conversation, delving into each other's bags to inspect purchases and having lots of giggles. I don't even think they realised I had left.

In many ways Gardeners' World Live was Geoff Hamilton's show, set up in association with the TV programme and the RHS. He was always there and often used to put on his own display. He loved talking to people; there was no pretension about him either in real life or on our screens. Little wonder he was the most popular presenter ever of *Gardeners' World*. His ideas led the way, always at the vanguard. Until he came on the scene, if you extolled the virtues of organic growing, you might be expected to wear sandals, a djellaba and a hippie headband. Wearing jeans and a Viyella shirt, he opened our eyes to the malpractice of using chemicals on our plots. As well as sharing his gardening, he brought important issues such as peat depletion and the demise of wildflowers and their habitats into the realm of public debate. On one occasion, having heard about the wholesale theft of rocks, especially limestone, he showed us how to make our own limestone pavements by digging into the soil, filling holes with concrete then upending them to make our own rock gardens.

He was politically correct before it was politically correct to be politically correct. He was a personable, lovely man who did more for gardening and gardeners than anyone I can think of.

He was such a force for good and so encouraging. He would always come to our stand and have a quick chat and when I was given that chance on Channel 4's *Garden Party*, he gave a quick critique of the programme and told me I was doing well. (He asked me about possible contributors for his cottage gardening programme too, which turned out to be a great success.)

His untimely death shocked and saddened us all. It is heartening to see one of his sons, Nick, picking up the baton and running with it at Barnsdale.

* * *

For a long time I had nurtured the idea of writing a book and making a programme that took you right through the gardening year, not in a dry, listy sort of way but celebrating each season and watching plants change and develop. BBC Books, in the shape of the creative and far-seeing Lorna Russell, were up for the idea, and the book was commissioned. It was to be a collaboration with my favourite photographer and friend, Jonathan Buckley. We set to work, Jonathan taking his pictures, me writing and all of it revolving around the garden at Glebe Cottage. I wanted to call it *Life in a Cottage Garden* and thought it would make a good TV series. I talked to a few senior people involved with *Gardeners' World* at the BBC, but nobody seemed inclined to push the idea. Since there was nothing to lose, it seemed daft not to go straight to the commissioning editor. She agreed to see me and we got a presentation together using some of the photographs that Jonathan had already taken together with some of my writing and ideas for different episodes. Normally for an 'in-house' pitch, someone senior within the BBC would take the idea to a commissioning editor, but no one was interested so I cold-called the commissioner, got an appointment, presented our wares and after a few weeks got the green light.

Television is essentially a visual medium, and instead of the one-page written pitch that is the usual submission to a commissioning editor, we presented pictures, giving a real flavour of what the series could look like. At first they wanted to sex up the title a bit and call it *Life and Death in a Cottage Garden*, which I thought was a bit counter-productive. It wasn't a crime drama, it was six feel-good, informative, relaxed episodes with loads of take-home, attainable ideas and inspiring, beautiful segments taking you gently through a year in my garden.

As soon as it was commissioned the BBC hierarchy took over. Another producer wrote a one-page pitch for it, complete with stills lifted from our daytime programme *Open Gardens*, which I read with interest and a certain amount of disbelief, or was it amusement? What did it matter.

We made the programme over a whole year. Mark Scott, supremely talented, was our director and David Henderson was our researcher, simply the best and a knowledgeable, practical gardener too. Mark encouraged him to swap roles for two of the episodes, which meant, amongst other things, that for those two episodes Mark was responsible for lunch. Heinz Tomato soup always featured and became so iconic that in tribute I even named one of my dahlia seedlings 'Mark Scott's Heinz Tomato Soup'. It is still doing well and so is Mark. I have been lucky enough to work with him on several occasions since. Not enough, but beggars cannot be choosers.

Life in a Cottage Garden was well received. People enjoyed it and got lots of ideas and inspiration from it. Viewing figures were good, 3 million plus, and the programme must have done the BBC some good; they have repeated it over and over again.

Because it is so beautifully shot and researched, directed and edited so artistically, and the music and the sound are so good, it does not seem to age. It helps of course that gardening itself is timeless, and it is cyclical. There is always a spring followed by a summer then an autumn succeeded by a winter and that succession itself is part of everyone's experience. The animals and I are older now, in fact we can no longer stroke Fleur, but in our hearts she is still sitting with us and frequenting the garden. As for my clothes, they are pretty timeless; when I glimpse old photos I sometimes realise I am wearing that jumper today.

One of the best things about *Life in a Cottage Garden* was that it was a one-off, free-standing, independent of *Gardeners' World* or any other programme and totally original, unlike any other gardening programme. Together Mark, David and I worked out what we would do when and because we followed the garden's lead rather than following an arbitrary timetable, the programmes became organic; the garden told the stories. Recognising this process in no way undervalues the craft and artistry of the post-production team, who turn what we have shot into a programme. Special recognition also goes to Tim Green, who manned an extra camera to give us some of the most enjoyable effects, seeing specific parts of the garden change from season to season.

Everyone went above and beyond. There were such special moments: leaving my shed after dark on a cold winter's night, treading in a puddle, making the reflection of the moon quiver then calm. A cloud of midges made golden, dancing in a sultry summer sunset. A furry caterpillar humping up its body then stretching out as it crosses our screens.

* * *

Another of the most exciting series I have presented was *Plant Odysseys*, where we looked at four of our most popular and influential flowers – the rose, the tulip, the iris and the water lily – and considered their evolution, their history and geography and their botany. We told their story and travelled to see some of them in their original homes and in some of the places, including gardens, where mankind has interacted with them. We saw tulips on the mountain slopes above Lake Van, Turkey, collected *Iris florentina*, grown for its roots for perfumery, baking on an Umbrian hillside, and found our native dog rose sprawling over the hedges of an English country lane bedecked in its perfect single pale pink flowers.

Our water lily episode was exciting and unusual, a real case of immersive journalism! A Korean TV company loved the idea so they came in as co-producers and invited me out to Korea to film water lilies there with a local crew. They were wonderful. Our diminutive camerawoman Son was a star and tireless, capturing everything from tea ceremonies in a tranquil Buddhist temple (she was a Buddhist herself) to an explosive lantern lighting festival, to the boat I was in being punted across a vast expanse of water through prehistoric blue water lilies. There I donned waders with a little help from the boatman, a bit like being two again, and interviewed a Korean botanist standing in waist-deep water, who told me about the evolution of the water lily and explained their ancient origins, being one of the first true flowers on the earth. Apart from our presence the scene had not changed for millions of years.

Back home at Ventnor Botanic Garden we awaited the first ever flowering of a brand new giant water lily. This flower would open in the dark under a high roof in a giant pond so we had to film in the middle of the night and I had to wear a wetsuit to wade, then swim, into the murky depths to see its emergence. I had never worn a wetsuit before; it was borrowed from one of the staff there and it took such an age to get into that when I discovered I had it on inside out just before I was about to plunge into the water, it had to stay that way. I just hoped nobody would notice since all eyes would be on the grand opening of the water lily. Although we had guidelines, nobody could accurately predict when the event would take place. We had to make an educated guess. If we were wrong the tight budget would not allow us to return – we would have to forego this astonishing event. Serendipity and the goddess were on our side. What a privilege and how wonderful to see it happen, and share the excitement and the magic moment with our viewers.

* * *

In 2016, *Gardeners' World* was revamped, with each episode becoming an hour in length (an earlier experiment with this format, in 2009, had not been successful). By this time, the show had 2.5 million loyal viewers and along with refreshing the format, the BBC brought in some new presenters, including Nick Bailey, Frances Tophill, Adam Frost, Flo Headlam and Nick Macer. I continued to appear on *Gardeners' World* and at the flower shows.

In 2019, Gary Broadhurst took over producing the show. I had already worked with Gary on two series of *The Great British Garden Revival*, which he produced with Outline Productions for BBC Two and which was transmitted in late 2013 and January 2015, and respected him.

These were glorious programmes where two presenters shared a one-hour slot, half an hour each to address the demise of styles of gardening and groups of plants and, by showing us how wonderful they were, ignite a passion to return their popularity.

I took part in four of these, covering rock gardens, conifers, daffodils and cottage gardens. Each of them presented opportunities to meet engaging, knowledgeable people and to view beautiful gardens and extraordinary plants. What a treat to share this with viewers.

Gardeners' World managed to keep going during the Covid lockdown, albeit under huge constraints. We filmed a few pieces in the garden, at first on two mobile phones with two tripods. Neil was on the 'camera one' phone, set up for us to video-call our long-distance director, Simon Brant, at home in Somerset, whilst he did the actual filming on the second phone. Later on, a real camera was delivered to and collected from Glebe Cottage in full observance of lockdown rules.

More significant were two one-hour programmes for Channel 5 entitled very succinctly *Gardening with Carol Klein*. These were shot in our garden with a socially distanced crew of two, Tom Weston and Adam Scott, who innovatively in this completely new and unknown territory (I mean Covid, not my garden) managed to produce, with the help of Keith Brown editing in his garage in the Midlands and other brilliant personnel playing their part, two superb one-hour programmes. People loved them. I have worked with Tom on and off over the last twenty years. He is a most creative and original director and filming with him is always a pleasure, rewarding and hugely enjoyable.

They were followed up with two five-part series in 2021 and two six-part series in 2022. Previous to and then overlapping with these were two series of *Great British Gardens Season by Season* for Channel 5, hour-long programmes visiting prestigious British gardens in all four seasons. As well as glorying in their beauty we got to see what made each garden tick, talking to those who gardened there and delving behind the scenes to understand what it was that made each garden unique.

I have to thank Ben Frow at Channel 5 for commissioning all these programmes, and for inviting me to present them. A brave and a bold step but one that I am sure he will agree did the channel's image some good.

Where to next? Well, as I said I have never had a life plan …

How to Make Your Garden

Gardening needn't be about maintaining the status quo and keeping everything ticking over in the same old way. At its best it's a much more dynamic process, and to get the most out of it sometimes it's essential to close your eyes and give your imagination free rein.

Do you ever garden in your head? It's an interesting exercise, digging up plants that are past their prime, rejuvenating them and putting them back refreshed and reinvigorated or taking everything out of a bed or border and starting from scratch – and all without ever touching a spade. Imagining what could be instead of accepting what is constitutes an important part of any gardener's activity, and if it's tempered by practicality, then it can play a central role in the progress and vitality of all our gardens.

Dreaming is the first step, but it's putting the dreams into practice that is the real joy of gardening. The materialisation of what we have envisaged is at the crux of gardening. The process involves all the elements of our gardening passion: design, choosing plants, their colour, form and personality, fitting plants to the conditions in our plots as well as to our own aesthetic and marrying all this to the craft of gardening, propagating, planting and maintenance.

As winter approaches most of us are less obsessed with the day-to-day business of gardening, where we are dealing with the routine. There is more scope at this point in the year to envisage new scenarios and to put them into practice. It's the perfect time to think and act on such ideas. Because so much in our gardens is dormant at this time of year, there are better opportunities to undertake major upheavals, to move plants, to dig and prepare the soil and to replant.

We have lived at Glebe Cottage for more than thirty years and the garden has grown and changed gradually during that time, but there have been occasions when new ideas have surfaced and been put into practice, where different areas have been given not just a complete overhaul but a completely different emphasis.

Gardening and fashion have little in common. It isn't a question of giving the plot a make-over, it has much more to do with developing our own ideas within the framework we have built or inherited. Very few of us are starting from scratch – even new gardeners usually inherit hard landscaping and planting from their antecedents. It can be expensive, time-consuming and therefore frustrating to tackle the lot but if you fit your plans to what you can afford both in time and money and think hard about what changes will make the most impact, your efforts will have best effect.

Whether you're tackling the whole garden or a small bed, the strategy is the same. During the last few years I've taken on a few new schemes here at Glebe Cottage. During *Life in a Cottage Garden* we set to work to revitalise 'Annie's Garden', a 13x4 metre terrace where planting had become very samey and confused with a preponderance of bumptious plants riding roughshod over gentler individuals – a common story in many gardens and a good reason to start again. There is such richness and diversity in plant choice that when things have reached such a sad state of affairs it seems complacent to just put up with it.

In a more recent new project, a result of changed circum-stances, we've used materials, sleepers, soil and compost from our old nursery next door, which we were forced to vacate, to make a series of new raised beds. Although it has involved some pretty back-breaking work, in some ways this has been an easier project without the difficult choices of what should stay and what must go.

In both these and many other scenarios the emphasis has been on experiment and innovation, though in every case what we have come to know of our garden, its soil and situation, has had a big influence on the solutions we've chosen.

Neither of these projects has been planned to the letter, though in both cases we had a clear idea of where we wanted to go and the sort of effect we wanted to achieve. Although there was originally a rough impression, a painted colour guide for Annie's garden, there were no detailed drawings or notes. Do you need a plan when you are undertaking a revamp? It depends on how good you are at visualising, how happy you are to improvise and how confident you are in allowing spontaneity into the frame. Everyone is different and nothing is ever cut and dried, but because every planting is a fluctuating sum of different relationships varying very often year by year, it's surely better to imagine the scheme in broad brush strokes without becoming hamstrung about minute details.

Work out what you want from your new bed. Are you happy with its shape and how it is viewed? Perhaps it has always been looked at from one side and arranged in tiers, tallest at the back, shortest at the front. Maybe that's not the only way to see it. Perhaps even in a small bed there could be a path or even just a couple of stepping stones into it so you can be involved with the plants, not just a dispassionate viewer. Maybe you could try wave planting with numbers of the same plant (easy to produce adequate numbers if you're prepared to divide existing clumps) and get the plants to create movement within the bed so as you walk along the path you are treated to an ever-changing picture with some tall plants making you hesitate and other low plants creating recesses that lead your eye into the planting. As you walk along the path, new pictures are created. As well as height and bulk, try to think about contrasting leaf shape, about colour and form and about the impression you want to create.

To paraphrase Christopher Lloyd, 'All good ideas are worth copying,' so look to other gardens for inspiration – not just Chelsea show gardens but perhaps a garden in your street with a particularly lovely, possibly accidental plant combination, a park planting or a picture or photograph, a paint-chart or a favourite painting.

The dimension in gardening that is most difficult to fathom is the fourth dimension – time. But you will be looking at your new planting for many months of the year. Do you want it to peak, or would you prefer it to offer interest throughout the year?

Which plants do you want to keep and how much of them do you intend to replant? Do they need to be divided? If plants are completely tired out and producing no new growth, chop them up and confine them to the compost heap. New divisions from plants you want to salvage can be lined out in a nursery bed (just a strip of another bed or the veg garden will do) where they will make weight before they are returned to their new home.

Put in more plants than you need – you can always take some of them out later. A simple drawing on graph paper with each plant represented by a circle (that's how most plants grow) will help when working out numbers.

Remove existing plants from the area and keep them in or on old compost bags until you are ready to deal with them. Especially if your soil is compacted, dig it over and incorporate as much good organic matter as you can – your new plants may be in there for some time, so make them feel welcome. Always work from a board if you can, especially during wet winter months. Don't dig frozen ground, though if it's already turned over, frost will help break it down. If you're a weekend gardener, cover the ground with plastic if rain is forecast midweek.

Most importantly, keep returning to your plan even if it's only in your mind's eye, and as you're working, supplement it with fresh ideas for stretching the interest across the whole year.

Five ways to keep down cost

1) Recycle as much plant material as you can, but give it a different role when you replant; perhaps a geranium that has always been an unwieldy clump can become a sinuous line of colour next to a tall grass which overtakes it later in the year.

2) Introduce new plants from other parts of your own garden. Perhaps they won't divide easily or you don't want to disturb them, but you may be able to collect seed from them and/or take basal cuttings from them.

3) If it's too late in the year to sow annuals directly, you can sow seeds of hardy annuals such as pot marigolds (calendula), love-in-a-mist (*Nigella damascena*) or poached egg plant (*Limnanthes douglasii*). Sown thinly in seed trays, pricked out individually into modules and given the protection of a cold frame, they can be planted out in March to swell the ranks of perennials.

4) Buy young versions of woody plants, shrubs and trees rather than going for mature (and expensive) specimens. They will establish fast and grow rapidly, soon catching up with older plants. With perennials look for pots full of growth and multiple crowns so you can split them straight away and make several for the price of one.

5) Before the advent of garden centres, friends, family and neighbours would frequently swap plants. We still do and many of our gardens get going with gifts; my mum gave me all sorts of bits from her own garden, many of which she started from seed or cuttings. Thirty years later many of these and their progeny are still in our gardens. Look out for bargains at car boot sales and bring-and-buys.

Planting the bones

If your new or restyled bed or border is to include woody plants to form its structure, now is a great time to plant them. Nowadays most of us buy our trees and shrubs as containerised plants but in the past such subjects were often planted as bare-root trees and they are becoming more popular once again. Providing the weather is mild and the ground is well prepared, there should be no problems. Water pots well and allow them to drain before planting, and in the case of bare-root trees, immerse their roots in water until the last moment. Trim any damaged roots, and tease out roots gently. Firm soil around roots gently, shaking the tree to make sure it is well settled and there are no air-pockets between the roots. Always ensure that the final planting depth is the same as it was in the pot or on the nursery. Water in well. Frost can lift plants so after very cold nights check newly planted shrubs, trees and perennials and gently firm them in if necessary.

My new raised beds have no woody plants in them. Their permanent inhabitants will be perennials, grasses and bulbs. During mild spells through the winter, more plants will be added, mainly divisions, cuttings and seedlings that are now well established in pots. Big clumps of *Miscanthus sinensis* 'Flamingo' run in a sinuous wave from top to bottom of the beds, forming an undulating backbone.

If the soil is still warm enough and workable, perennials can be planted throughout the winter. Most will have lost their leaves and will concentrate on putting down roots. Planted now they should be well established by next spring and should flower well during the summer.

I've always deplored the idea of colouring books, of painting by numbers; it ignores human artistic creativity and sentences it to impotence. Such blinkered practices instil a feeling of dependence and rob us of belief in our own abilities to invent and create. It's the same with formulaic gardening: the idea that people can adopt a blueprint that they can impose on their garden regardless of the site or soil flies in the face of what gardening is all about.

Putting plants together in what quantities, in what formations and using what varieties has everything to do with what will grow in the prevailing conditions. It's only when the individual, the gardener themselves, recognises this reality that they are able to create the sort of effect they want.

A cultivated garden is not the same as nature, but if our choice of plants and the way we put them together are guided by what we see in wild places, then our plots are liable to have an uncontrived and happy feel. This is not an exhortation to plant nettles and brambles and watch our plots turn to wilderness, but to observe the way in which nature creates communities of plants and to emulate it.

Some of you must have had the same thing happen in your plots as frequently happens in mine. Plants will put themselves together, seeding into the gravel where feet seldom tread and creating miniature gardens without any input from me. There is one such 'happening' on the track between the sunny and shady sides of my garden at the moment: a tall *Geranium pratense* with flowers of softest blue intermingles with a self-seeded bronze fennel, both rising up from a mat of *Geranium oxonianum* and *Alchemilla mollis*. The icing on the cake is the appearance, with a flourish, of three 'walking' onions, each with its small spherical head and a tail, like three comets only prevented from flying into orbit by their strong, straight stems.

On other occasions a plant will seed itself through a border, creating a series of satellites that link the whole planting together. You see the same in nature, clouds of dog-daisies interspersed with other flowers, perhaps buttercups, in great vivid crowds.

In other situations, different flowers predominate and the patterns and arrangements they create can be hugely instructive in our own plantings.

Corn meadows used to be full of annual wildflowers and though sadly, overuse of pesticides has meant a decline in such sights, with organic farming on the increase we are treated more often to a reprise of this inspiring vision. There would have been all those things beginning with corn – corn cockle, cornflowers, corn marigolds and corn chamomile, plus the ubiquitous corn poppies. Red, blue, yellow, pink and white sparkling amongst the ripening gold. We could use such ideas in patches of our own gardens, not necessarily using the same ingredients but in the same spirit, with annuals and perhaps annual grasses rather than cereals. Keith Wiley's South African-veldt-inspired plantings before he left The Garden House were a tour de force when it came to interpreting the spirit of a planting.

To move the idea in another direction, I once saw an Andrew Lawson image that personified the spirit of adventure that we can all adopt when using an idea from nature and reinterpreting it. A whole bed of *Dahlia* 'Gaiety' was planted amongst *Hordeum jubatum*, a grass closely allied to barley. You could just imagine the breeze swishing around, giving the whole planting an almost filmic quality.

No matter what your garden is like, there are always opportunities to emulate wild landscapes and natural habitats.

Herbaceous beds, for instance, can draw inspiration from perennial meadows by recurring plants in mounds and swathes. In fact, the whole idea of repeating plants in the border is akin to the sort of colonies of plants we see in the wild (although our wildflowers and their spread are often curbed, controlled by cultivation, ploughing, grazing and the use of pesticides). Though random patterns of plants, both flowers and grasses, vary from vicinity to vicinity, different plants predominate according to soil type and situation and therefore different patterns emerge. These patterns are further reflective of whether or not plants spread by self-seeding or creeping rootstock or other vegetative means.

A creeping buttercup, *Ranunculus repens*, will constantly creep out in ever-increasing circles, eventually dying out in its centre and allowing an opportunity for other plants to move in. The exploding seedpods of geraniums will set up random satellite colonies all around the original plant. In our brick garden and beyond, these cranesbills constantly surprise by appearing almost out of the blue amongst more sedentary members of the troupe.

In other places *Alchemilla mollis* makes itself perfectly at home, though it tends to scatter its seed close by and loves edges and cracks in pavement. Verbascums throw their seeds around, shaking, rattling and rolling them into any suitably well-drained spot. On shingly beaches the round seeds of *Crambe maritima* will roll around until they meet some obstacle, a big pebble perhaps, and then provided there are adequate resources of fresh water and some semblance of soil will germinate and add to the colony. By the same token seeds of the horned poppy, *Glaucium flavum*, are thrown into the air as the foot-long pods coil up on a hot day. You can hear the pods of euphorbias exploding in the heat of a summer's afternoon.

I remember once seeing a crowd of *Lilium svotzianum* in a small wooded area in my friend Joan's garden. She explained that she hadn't planted a single one though she'd put in a few bulbs in the main garden and had come out on a hot windy day to see the air thick with the lily's seeds, depositing them on the fertile leafy soil of the wood. In the garden here at Glebe we have mats of bugle, *Ajuga reptans*, that have spread themselves around, neatening obtrusive corners, perfect when their vertical flower spikes erupt and as a foil for foxgloves, self-seeded or craftily planted amongst the carpet. We use woodruff in the same way.

Very few of us are in the position where we're starting from scratch, where we have the proverbial 'blank canvas' to paint or embroider, but there are always opportunities to change, modify and exalt our plantings to emulate the scenes we so admire from the wild. The plants that lend themselves to these ideas are simple, unsophisticated plants not far removed from their wild cousins. Informality is all important and overbred hybrids with stiff bearing and disciplined demeanour don't lend themselves to this sort of treatment. Though it is difficult to set out distinctly the different ways in which native plants disport themselves, it helps to understand the sort of effects we might achieve in our own beds and borders by understanding the wild arrangements that initially inspire such ideas.

None of these is set in stone and there are no rules or formulae to follow or apply. Looking at the ways in which different forms, flowers and foliage are juxtaposed is helpful. Learning lessons from nature about colonies of plants and how emphasis between them changes during the year is vital. Is it multi-layered? Are bulbs an important factor?

Block planting

For those to whom straight lines and geometric blocks appeal, this 'style' utilises plants that lend themselves to regimentation.

This sort of idea can almost be planned on a matrix. It is the least 'natural' of any method of using perennials. The intransigence of straight lines, or any lines come to that, means that every so often plants are bound to step out of line and spoil the master plan.

Drift planting

Much favoured in recent years, especially in show gardens at Chelsea and Hampton Court flower shows, are arrangements where irregular swathes or drifts of plants are encouraged to embrace each other, mixing and mingling at their boundaries so that the effect is softened and drifts overlap and intermingle.

Fluidity is everything. The juxtaposition of colour, both of flower and foliage, is one of the most important ways to integrate the planting. Colour should highlight rhythm rather than interrupt it. Subtle colouring – the soft shades of achilleas with grasses, for instance, so that colours blend together rather than jar, epitomises this sort of planting.

Wave planting

This has its inspiration in nature but seeks to simplify and adapt these ideas to a modern garden setting where frequently beds are rectangular and viewed from one side.

In the garden at Glebe Cottage we recently planted a series of new raised beds in gradual steps that descend the slope. Though there are paths between them I wanted to create a feeling of continuum by arranging plants in a series of undulating waves, using the same plants flowing through from bed to bed to establish a rhythm that constantly supplies movement from spring to winter.

In wave planting there are no arbitrary drifts arranged like interlocking crazy paving. Instead ribbons of plants sweep backwards and forwards so that wave upon wave laps against the next in continuous succession.

Such an arrangement creates dynamism, movement, sound. There is a feeling of mobility – a sense of excitement – and though there is nothing directly analogous in nature, the whole idea is inspired by the wild.

Epilogue: A final reflection

Just before Christmas 2022, Clare Matterson, director general of the RHS, wrote to ask if I would accept the RHS Iconic Horticultural Hero award, which was both shocking and flattering in equal measure. Because of that, I was able to design a big 'show garden' for the Hampton Court Palace Garden Festival the following summer.

What a privilege, but since I hadn't designed a show garden since 1999 (and that had been my first one), it was somewhat daunting – a complete change of direction – and promised to be very hard work.

It would be true to say that for more than six months it completely took over my life. It was a huge space, 375 square metres, and when I walked it out for the first time I was astonished. It was big. When we paced it out on camera at home on a large area of gravel where we usually park cars, I had to walk through the greenhouse, which shares that site, to assess the actual length. It wasn't the size of a football pitch but bigger than a tennis court.

It was a huge honour to be asked, but this was matched by a feeling of enormous responsibility to create something that was just as competent as expected but also as beautiful and meaningful as it could possibly be. This was a garden that was to sum up, in physical form, my gardening ethos and to demonstrate my gardening principles.

One of the best parts of making this garden was working with other people in a wonderful collaboration to produce something which expressed a joint perspective. Everyone was different, though of course the factor we all had in common was our love of plants and gardening, and in some cases, people came in pairs already knowing each other and to a greater or lesser extent having worked together before. There was a trio from Beth Chatto's Garden and the lone 'Scottish John', although he had worked alongside Alan and Catherine from Landform, the contractors for the garden.

When you're creating a show garden, it's a very different proposition to making a real garden: it has to be at its peak at a specific time. Making a real garden is an ongoing process, whereas making a show garden is a performance. Nonetheless, the show garden has to be plausible, it has to represent a reality that is possible, and although it is put together, built and planted over two or three weeks, each part of it must feasibly have been planted in a real garden.

The garden I designed was themed around the loose idea of going with the flow and working with nature and the kinds of conditions you've got, being attuned to the plants that thrive in them. I have always felt that we should be guided by natural habitats when choosing plants, looking to the species that grow in the same environment we're working with – in other words, 'right plant, right place'. The garden was to be divided into six habitats – wetland, woodland, hedgerow, meadow, seaside, and moor and mountain – and include a vegetable patch. Quite a challenge, and almost impossible to marry all those different habitats in one space, though with a bit of ingenuity and everyone contributing ideas, I think we pulled it off.

The habitats had to flow together with no physical divisions. It was quite a test when on one side there was a boggy garden and then on the opposite side a dry, well-drained area. The garden was not meant to replicate wild areas exactly, but to take its lead from nature. As such, each area had physical features representative of the habitat – for instance, trees, mossy logs and mysterious paths in the woodland glade. A lovely young Irish man, Luke, from Great Dixter, who was helping with the garden, came around the corner and, seeing our woodland mound, declared it 'a fairy fort' that evoked the magical places of Irish folklore. I cannot tell you how encouraging that was!

We had huge chunks of Scottish granite in the moor and mountain bed, which had first seen service at the Chelsea Flower Show several weeks earlier in Jihae Hwang's thought-provoking garden based on Jirisan, a magical South Korean mountain. They were turned into a splendid alpine garden by Josh Tranter, a trainee of the Alpine Garden Society, and his friend Chris Howell, then working at the Birmingham Botanic Garden and now at John Massey's superb garden at Allbrighton.

Also helping us were two brilliant lads from Rosemoor, Lawrence and Jay, and three lasses from Beth Chatto's Plants and Gardens, Âsa, Malin and Emily. It was Emily who not only grew all the plants for the seaside habitat, an area of particular interest for anyone with poor, dry soil, but also stocked the greenhouse that formed part of the display with tray after tray of seedlings she had raised specially, then set-dressed the venue and gave talks on propagation to our visitors once the show was underway. Behind the greenhouse was a double compost heap, swiftly but adroitly constructed by a three-person team from Waterperry led by Pat Havers; they also brought compost from their own heap and the second bay was filled during the build and the week of the show. We planted up loads of containers and pots to inspire visitors who are not lucky enough to have a garden.

Once the show began, there was a constant flow of people all week from first thing until closing. In our naiveté, we had imagined that folk would just stroll around. In the event, there were swarms of people everywhere, and the RHS (in the shape of the festival manager, Natalie Gearing, and her wonderful team) stepped in and implemented a one-way system. The problem was resolved and rather than limiting people's access it ensured everyone got a chance to see everything, take pictures and notes and ask questions.

On the first day, Press Day, several of my favourite people, including my heart-throb Roy Lancaster and his wife, came to see the garden and me. My two husbands, Neil and John Massey, arrived at the same time. I am not a bigamist, honest, but for years *Hello!* magazine had John and I as happily married with an equally fictitious net worth. Although John and I are not man and wife, he has been one of my best friends for many years. As well as being the most generous and kindest person there is, he is modest and diffident, yet his horticultural knowledge knows no bounds. He adores plants and loves people.

Without doubt it was the interactivity within the garden, between those helping to make it and those visiting, that made it so special and so unique. The sun shone and the visitors loved it. What they liked best was the opportunity to walk into the garden, to become immersed in the plants and experience the garden as opposed to looking at it from the outside. Gardens should not be places you do things to and then stand back from. I hoped visitors would be able to take something from it (though I don't mean surreptitious cuttings and flowerheads), whatever their own gardens were like. It was intended to be inspirational rather than aspirational, somewhere that excited you and prompted you to go home and get gardening.

The other philosophy inspiring the garden was 'grow your own'. The design emphasised the plants people could grow and propagate themselves, and to that end the greenhouse on the edge of the garden was used to teach visitors practical skills. One side of it had no glass and visitors could sit outside and hear lovely Emily Allard, chief propagator from Beth Chatto's, and me dispense some helpful information. There's nothing more rewarding than growing your own plants.

I didn't use rare or difficult plants. I ran Glebe Cottage Plants for thirty years and we went to Hampton Court seventeen times, so I was well versed in which plants thrive during the summer months! My garden at Glebe Cottage is bursting with herbaceous perennials and grasses, and many of them featured prominently in the meadow area of the show garden.

There were three beds separated by paths, but they didn't feel separate because the same plants were used throughout. I've already defined the concept of wave planting, with plants in great swathes. As you walked up and down each of the paths, your view of the border constantly changed, and when you turned around and walked back, there was a beautifully different view again.

The ethos of this garden has informed all the garden consultations I have made over the years and will continue to do so. Creating this exhibit gave me the chance to express those ideas in physical form to the widest gardening public.

* * *

Many of you reading this book will already know that early in 2024, I was referred to the Breast Care Clinic at the North Devon

District Hospital and after a few tests was diagnosed with breast cancer. Fortunately this was caught at an early stage: there was a small malignant tumour in my right breast and in my left breast there was pre-cancer but in, to describe it in laywoman's terms, 'a scattered formation'. Because of this distribution, my oncologist, Dr Anna Conway, advised that I have a mastectomy on the left side, and since I was going to need surgery on the right side anyway, I opted for a double mastectomy – I am a stickler for symmetry and this seemed the best solution. My sentinel lymph nodes on the right side were removed at the same time. For those of you who do not know, the first place breast cancer may spread to is the sentinel nodes. Unfortunately, when the post-operative results came through, it was discovered that in fact I also had cancer in my left breast. We decided that I should have the sentinel nodes on my left side taken out too, for investigation and hopefully reassurance that the cancer had not spread and was gone.

All this happened just before another of the year's important shows, the RHS Chelsea Flower Show, but, having recovered well from surgery, I was able to present there. Not only that, I met up with masses of old friends and later had the time of my life strolling around the Great Pavillion in the exhilarating company of Tom Allen, his boyfriend Alfie and his lovely mum, Irene. Both Tom and Irene are keen gardeners. Tom's gardening posts on Instagram are entertaining, instructive and hilariously funny.

On Thursday, just after recording podcasts for *Gardeners' World* magazine, my surgeon telephoned me to tell me my results were back and I was cancer free. May 23rd has definitely joined my list of memorable dates!

Perhaps it is not until a diagnosis like this that you begin to appreciate what others go through and just how many people this disease affects. One in eight women develop breast cancer. Instead of asking myself 'Why me?' it really was more a question of 'Why not me?' You know exactly how old I am, because I told you at the beginning of this book. The older you are, the more likely you are to get breast cancer. It seems idiotic then that invitations to routine mammogram screenings cease for women over seventy. We are told that women over that age may request a mammogram, but how many of us over-seventies know that we are more likely to get breast cancer at our age? How many of us assume that since we are no longer automatically called for breast screening, perhaps that is because we are less likely to suffer from it? The opposite is the case. We oldies are more likely to get it and less likely to be on the lookout. This has to change.

Although I thought immediately about myself and women in my age group when I was diagnosed, I have since discovered how many young women with breast cancer go undiagnosed. It is in fact only between the ages of fifty and seventy that women are automatically called every three years for a mammogram. Because of this lack of routine screening, it is vital that young women know the importance of checking their breasts regularly. It should become part of every girl's education. When breast cancer is diagnosed early, the chances of treatment being effective are so much higher than when it is discovered at a more advanced stage.

There are so many brave women out there with this disease, some of whom, despite undergoing difficult treatment themselves, are campaigning on both these fronts (no pun intended). It is yet another instance of women helping one another. We should all do whatever we can to promote breast awareness. The more breast aware women are from an early age right the way through to when they die, the better the chances of detecting breast cancer and therefore the better the chances of treating it and living longer.

I am one of the increasing numbers of lucky ones whose breast cancer was diagnosed early. I am incredibly lucky too in having my family's total support and unconditional love throughout this. The news of such a diagnosis must have been as big a shock for them as it was for me.

Having now informed the outside world in a little post on Instagram, I have received so much support and encouragement from so many people all over the world that I feel uplifted. A spell of fine weather helped too, enabling me to get outside and look after some of my plants – even though it was a distraction from putting the finishing touches to this book.

We have all heard so much recently about how gardening and nurturing plants is good for both our physical and mental well-being. The pandemic brought this home to millions of people. It also reminded us of the millions of people who have no access to gardens and no way of directly communing with the earth. Surely everyone should have that opportunity. To live without any contact with nature is true deprivation.

* * *

On the front wall of our cottage is a Banksian rose. Its full title is *Rosa banksiae* 'Lutea'. It is a Chinese rose and was first brought into cultivation here early in the nineteenth century. Its flowers are a pale and pretty yellow. They are small and dainty, semi-double and borne in bunches all along the stems. It is a vast rose suitable for a huge wall, perhaps in a stately home or at any rate in an expansive space, not at all a rose to grow on the walls of a humble cottage. Yet I am so glad I planted it, and though it needs pruning attention every year (which I was unable to perform this year, though hope to continue next), I have been able to enjoy its blossoming bounty from the time of my diagnosis and throughout my recuperation. There are several of its branches just below and right in front of the lower pane of our bedroom window, and on even the dullest day, they seem to cast a warm glow into the whole room. Covered in raindrops or basking in the sun it is equally beautiful, but its presence here at this moment is serendipitous and makes me smile even more. Researching when this rose first arrived on our shores, I learned about its medicinal properties: it can be used as a treatment for wounds and to help formation of tissue.

Rather than worrying about dying, which after all is going to happen, I realised what a lot of living I still have to do. There is so much to live for and nothing more important than my lovely family. I must make more of them, I must talk more to them and above all I must tell them how much I love them.

There have been so many happy times that must be remembered. The world is a sadder place without our loved ones in it. I was thinking first of my brother Bill, and then of Neil's brother Peter, both of them uncles to our girls, and Peter's wife, Penelope's mum, Jo, but then of my mum and dad and Neil's parents and all the friends who are no longer here in body but always present in mind. The memories are still there, sometimes just as bright, though some of them fade almost to the stage of disappearing. That doesn't mean they are less important, far from it. Every so often, though, a memory will flash back and remind us. It is not necessarily of a hugely significant or momentous occasion; it might be a snapshot, a memory of a certain turn of the face, a smile, maybe a skirt caught on a rose or a hand receiving a flower. On a recent visit, our grandson gave me a tiny bunch of flowers on his arrival, a fragment of cow parsley, a red campion, a buttercup and two bluebells. I will always remember that. Perhaps he will too.

* * *

Fifi and I have just come in from a walk. It is May, early evening. I'll leave for the Chelsea Flower Show in a couple of days.

Just over a week ago I had another minor operation, the one to remove the sentinel nodes on my left side after the result came back from my first operation suggesting this might be a sensible course of action. This has held me up a bit and limited gardening activity slightly – but not for long.

It is exhilarating to leave my desk and my good old computer and step outside into the fresh air. I have been dimly aware of what is happening outside whilst I have been inside, getting distracted every so often when a bird, usually a blue tit, lands on the stems of that Banksian rose outside my window, looking for greenfly but also inspecting the window frames for possible insect activity.

Collar on, lead on, we're off, but held up for a moment by the freshness of everything. We walk past the small greenhouse, along the big slate path (these were once the beds of billiard tables), out onto the gravel. Fifi is raring to go, but much to her consternation I swerve into the big greenhouse where all the action is. For the last quarter of a century with the exception of 2020, I have had to leave whoever is at home and my garden at this most burgeoning time of year and head to London and the show. There are so many crucial jobs yet to be done. Trays of seedlings at the perfect stage to be pricked out: tagetes, rudbeckia, antirrhinums. *Those tomatoes are coming on well*, I think, *but will they be tall and etiolated when I come back from the show if they are not potted on before I leave?* A tray of rainbow chard catches my eye, lush dark leaves with crimson, pink and chrome yellow stems. *Will there be time to plant them out before I go? Should I abandon the walk and do it now?* You shouldn't go back on your word, especially to a dog, even though you know you would be forgiven. In any case I want to be outside, I need to catch up with where the real world has reached. At this time of year, nature moves so fast. You can almost hear its heartbeat getting faster, its breathing deeper as every day, hour, minute, new shoots appear, new fronds unfurl. And yet there is a gentleness about these changes, perhaps in part because all the movement is forwards, on the increase, positive; it is all about being alive.

We walk past our four huge vegetable troughs. Well, that is what they are supposed to be, though as usual over winter they were pressed into service to accommodate all manner of perennials needing a home, to gather heft until they could join the garden this spring. Many of them are still in situ although we have managed to transfer some to their permanent homes. I have potted lots of them up and they are looking strong and robust. Planting them out after Chelsea will be my first priority, joining a long list of equally pressing jobs vying for my attention on my return. To occupy their present position in these troughs, they should be edible. Not much evidence of that being the case. The bees, though, are feasting on cerinthe and its relative borage, self-seeded nearby. They are tucking into the sea holly flowers too. At a pinch perhaps these could qualify as edible – you float borage flowers in your Pimm's, and in Elizabethan times (the first one), eryngium roots were candied and consumed as an aphrodisiac, though neither usage really constitutes high nutritional value. Nothing more to be done for a while; at least the pollinating insects are happy and well fed.

Down the track go the dog and I, up the track on the other side, but before we do, we pause to admire the hawthorn growing where the two tracks meet, overhanging the stream. It is in full flower, so it should be. Where I come from we call it may. Travel anywhere in the British Isles during May, look out through the windows of train, car or charabanc, and the edges of fields everywhere are illuminated in glowing white from its blooms. For me it is the unsung heroine of British trees.

As we walk up the track, the hair-fine grass that skirts the field to our left sparkles here and there with the tiny brilliant blue flowers of Germander speedwell. Such an intense blue – oh to have eyes of that colour! It is said to 'speed travellers on their way'. It always does that for us and welcomes us on our return.

Between the fields and the road is a little lane, 'Pixie Lane'. That is what it has always been known as locally and there is something magical about it. Another hawthorn greets you as you enter and there are hedges either side with a wealth of native trees. It is said that every species in a thirty-metre length of hedge (though you feel you should measure it in chains or links or perches or yards at any rate) represents a hundred years. There are at least ten species here so this is probably an ancient hedge. The trees play host to brambles, ivy, honeysuckle, bryony and dog roses. The latter are in bud now and their simple five-petalled flowers in porcelain pink will soon adorn the green tapestry. When you read this, those of you who have bought the book hot off the press in September, those flowers will have become hips. The hedge is rich in food and shelter for birds and small mammals and there are passageways through it, doubtless the work of the strong shoulders and sharp claws of badgers.

Shockingly, some vandal in a tractor with a blunt flail attacked the hedge in the most brutal fashion a few weeks ago, hacking it back to half its height and leaving the lane thick with debris and twisted and contorted branches. As well as access to Glebe Cottage, Pixie Lane is part of a public footpath. We try to keep its hedges, especially the one on the right, trimmed sympathetically so that plants can grow well yet people and vehicles are not impeded. Quite apart from not having permission, there was no reason for this savage attack to have taken place. This was just before birds were starting to nest and as primroses were making seed. Most of them were ripped out and, to use a Devon word, 'drashed'. Very onomatopoeic.

Nature usually heals itself. No doubt one day the earth will get over what we have done to it.

Already new shoots and leaves are emerging from the ghastly wounded branches. Birds are dashing around too, trying to find safe spaces amongst the debris to build their nests. Most of the lanes around here and many of the lower branches of some of the older trees are thick with one of my favourite ferns, the polypody. All ferns are survivors – they were some of the first plants on the planet and are still going strong – and the polypody is one of the toughest. Though it was severed and its stoloniferous roots torn up during the recent rampage, it has already reasserted itself and fresh fronds are springing into life. Mankind has only been around for a minute of ferns' lifetime.

As Fifi and I reach the lane's end, we emerge onto the road (not a very big road, more of a lane). We turn right and walk towards the crossroad. All our crossroads have names. This one is Swing Gate Cross. The cow parsley is out at last, effervescent, wave after wave of it rolling along the hedgerows in a spumy celebration. There are so many names for our wildflowers; the more there are, the more we recognise how much a plant is loved. Queen Anne's lace is another name and describes precisely the delicacy of each head of flower, composed as it is of scores of tiny flowers, each one perfectly poised. Our flowers can be appreciated on so many levels.

Who could help but smile? When we first came here and for at least twenty years afterwards, the hedge that forms a backdrop to the cow parsley was laid each year, vertical growth skilfully half-severed and brought down to the horizontal so that lateral growth headed upwards, resulting in a thick, strong barrier. It was labour-intensive but a beautiful vernacular way to stop livestock disappearing and to encourage wildlife galore. Nowadays the tractor and the flail have taken over and the plant that is most encouraged by this process is bracken, the least desirable of all our ferns.

On the other side of the road things are different, thankfully. The hedge is thick and deep and full of trees. There is hawthorn and spindle here too, and rowan, that most magical of trees. It is often found close to habitation, planted to keep away evil spirits and bring good fortune.

Most exciting, though, are the oak trees, planted not so long ago as saplings far enough back from the road to be safe from council 'tidying'. As we walk along I notice that each one already has its own personality, its own shape, and that the leaves of each individual tree, whilst clearly oak leaves, are all different from one another. The gentleman who planted these trees was looking far into the future but also acknowledging the past and continuing a tradition. As we approach the crossroads, there are mature oaks on both sides of the road, wizened and wind-blasted, fissured and full of ferns. Some are on their way out, with bare branches, yet you know they will go on for a long time, and even after they pass the point of no return they will continue to give succour and shelter to a host of creatures. This is the haunt of tawny owls, tree creepers and woodpeckers.

The trees on the left are standing within the field. Sheep shelter in their shade in the summer's heat and huddle there together when the snow comes. Then we walk faster. We make footprints and our warm breath is visible in the cold, crisp air. But now the air is soft, spires of foxgloves rise from the hedges, the grass is green and growing apace as is everything, rushing towards its glorious zenith.

We walk on down the lane past the most majestic oaks of all

until an abandoned combine-harvester comes into view. This is our full stop or at least our comma. We turn around and head for home. Back along the road, right at the crossroads then left down Pixie Lane. As we walk through to the field, we stop and look across to our little cottage, snuggled into the hillside, and below it, in a long triangle, the garden. All those patches of different greens and silvers and bronze, merging together, are trees that I have planted since we came here so long ago. Yet it feels like yesterday. How can they have grown so tall?

I have been immensely fortunate to have chosen the life I have lived. Few people in the world can say that they are lucky enough to do that, to follow their dreams, engage in the work that they choose to do and live in a beautiful place with the people they love, surrounded by nature.

Life is not idyllic, for that somehow implies that everything is at a standstill and that nothing ever goes wrong. In fact there is constant movement, development, change.

Have I always wanted to garden? What if I didn't have one? It would make life difficult – I was going to say unbearable, but perhaps that is unfair to the millions of people throughout the world who cannot garden. Nonetheless, I feel gardening for me is a necessity rather than a luxury. It is part of me; it is what I do and who I am. No doubt I could survive without gardening, but it would be so hard. My family are all I could not live without, but gardening is my next raison d'être.

* * *

A final note. There is no sex in my book. That is not because I haven't engaged in any but the book is already too long.

Acknowledgements

There have been lots of ups and downs with this book, not so much a difficult birth as a prolonged one. Thanks to all those who have helped with its final successful delivery.

Midwives all. Robyn Drury and her indefatigable team, Jess Anderson, Miranda Ward and Phil Spencer, who have somehow melded this into a readable book. Thanks to everyone at Ebury.

To my agent Gordon Wise for his persistence and patience even when he was poorly, and to Jacquie, Emma and Bella of Curtis Brown. Here's to lots more gigs.

There have been a few hitches, crashing computers – prompting security alerts and assorted warnings galore: 'Someone in Russia is downloading files.' And 'Someone is downloading Files from You … Is it you?' No it bloody well isn't! 'Critical Virus Alert. Click Here To Turn On Antivirus.' No I won't.

I have been unable to access the first twenty years of my written work from my Finder – why is it called that? – but, thanks to various search engines I have been able to find some of it – so can you and my other books are still in print come to that, no hints!

Although I am a matter-of-fact sort of a person, delving back over almost eighty years, every so often I have burst into tears whilst writing this. Memories of people foremost, and places and plants too, bring tears to my eyes but also make me smile and sometimes laugh out loud.

Thank you to all those people, many of you who I have written about in these pages but even more of whom I would have mentioned if only there was a bit more room and time. You know who you are. Thank you for making my life worthwhile. Thank you for making my life.

Work has played an important part. Thanks to all those who taught me and to those I have taught and from whom I have learned so much. Thanks to all those who have worked alongside me and put up with me, in the garden, on the nursery and at shows and have made it a joy.

Thanks to editors and sub-editors for nurturing my words and helping them make sense.

Thanks to all the film crews and production teams with whom I have been lucky enough to work over the last twenty-five years.

Thanks to all those who have organised my tours and speaking engagements both here, in Canada and in the USA. Special thanks for the hospitality, food and drink, never too little nor too much!

Thanks to lovely Tom Allen for his kind words and gardening advice.

Thanks to all our pets, who have been an integral and important, probably vital, part of our lives. Our dogs Shinky, Fleur and her daughter Fifi who was born here, the only survivor of her litter, who is now going on fifteen years old despite a shaky start involving mouth-to-mouth resuscitation and CPR. Our cats Thomas the first, Cobweb (so named as a tribute to my housekeeping) and her four litters of four, one of which was born in a wardrobe drawer on Annie's birthday (see photos of girls cuddling them), and to our present-day pair Sylvie, dainty, silvery grey, naughty and bright, and Sylvester, big, black and white, reserved but affectionate, from the same litter but clearly fathered by different dads. They are getting on and their stage of arthritis is about the same as mine.

There have been rabbits too, Speedy and her progeny, and guinea pigs and goldfish and the escapee hamster.

Biggest thanks of all to our inspirational daughters and their dad, Neil. He has been immensely helpful in the writing of this book, keeping me a prisoner in my writing room when I just wanted to go out into the garden but also feeding me regularly (sometimes lavishly), like the Mekon, nemesis of Dan Dare of the Eagle (funnily enough Gordon Wise is Dan Dare's agent too).

Neil is the kindest, gentlest, most empathetic person in the world, hugely creative and imaginative and funny, really funny. He has been the best dad anyone could wish for and my love of fifty-three years and counting.

He is a Cancerian and was born in the Chinese Year of the Snake, who it is said are intelligent, charming and wise. They see the world in aeons. Although I am also a Cancerian, I was born in the Chinese Year of the Rooster, which epitomises me and this book, lots of crowing and scratching around in the dirt—

And I see everything in minutes. Good-bye and thanks for reading.

Previously published works

'Poppies' first published in *Gardeners' World*, 2014

'Foxgloves' first published in *Gardeners' World*

'Sweet Peas' first published in the *Sunday Mail*, 2014

'Trees' first published in *Making a Garden* (Mitchell Beazley 2015)

'Lupins' first published in the *Telegraph*, 2014

'Morning Glory' first published in *Gardeners' World*, March 2013

'Lilies' first published in *Gardeners' World*, 2015

'Cyclamen' first published in *Gardeners' World*, February 2014

'Ferns' first published in *Gardeners' News*, 24 March 2015

'Primrose' first published in *Wild Flowers* (BBC Books, 2013)

'A tribute to Alan Street' was written by Chris Ireland-Jones and published in the Avon Bulbs catalogue and on its website, October 2022

'Taking Root Cuttings' first published in *Grow Your Own Garden* (BBC Books, 2010)

'How Do Plants Get Their Names?' first published in *Gardeners' World*, December 2017

'Bellflowers' first published in *Wild Flowers* (BBC Books, 2013)